100 THINGS
WISCONSIN FANS
SHOULD KNOW & DO
BEFORE THEY DIE

100 THINGS
WISCONSIN FANS
SHOULD KNOW & DO
BEFORE THEY DIE

Jesse Temple

TRIUMPH
BOOKS

Library of Congress Cataloging-in-Publication Data

Names: Temple, Jesse, 1984- author.
Title: 100 things Wisconsin fans should know & do before they die / Jesse Temple.
Other titles: One hundred things Wisconsin fans should know and do before they die
Description: Chicago, Illinois : Triumph Books LLC, [2016]
Identifiers: LCCN 2016015551 | ISBN 9781629372358
Subjects: LCSH: University of Wisconsin—Football—History. | Wisconsin Badgers (Football team)—Miscellanea. | University of Wisconsin—Basketball—History. | Wisconsin Badgers (Basketball team)—Miscellanea.
Classification: LCC GV958.U5867 T43 2016 | DDC 796.043/63097758— dc23 LC record available at https://lccn.loc.gov/2016015551

This book is available in quantity at special discounts for your group or organization. For further information, contact:

Triumph Books LLC
814 North Franklin Street
Chicago, Illinois 60610
(312) 337-0747
www.triumphbooks.com

Printed in U.S.A.
ISBN: 978-1-62937-235-8
Design by Patricia Frey
Page Production by Nord Compo
Photos courtesy of AP Images unless otherwise indicated

To my wife, Jamie, and my family.
Thank you for your love and support.

Contents

Foreword

The story of the turnaround of the Wisconsin football program, and subsequently the entire athletic department, is by now well known not only to Badgers sports fans but most who follow college athletics as well. Yes, it was a difficult process. It took a lot of hard work by a great many people on and off the fields of play.

There was, however, one element in the whole rebuilding process that helped to make it all just a bit easier and that was the passion and loyalty of the alumni and fans who bring such energy and commitment to Wisconsin sports. When I came here in 1990, it was obvious that people were hungry for a winner. They wanted to wear the "W" proudly. They wanted to compete for championships and go to bowl games and NCAA tournaments. And they wanted it done the right way. The Wisconsin Way.

I had a plan for how I felt the football program could be resurrected. It was important to keep our best in-state student-athletes at Wisconsin. We had to hit the recruiting trail hard and we had to sell our vision not only to potential student-athletes, but to the fan base. The same was true for our athletic administration at the time. Tough decisions had to be made and goals had to be set. Eventually, though, it all worked out. The Rose Bowl win over UCLA on New Year's Day of 1994 was one of the highlights of my career and it turned out to be a jumping-off point for Wisconsin athletics.

I'm not always one to dwell on the past. I prefer to focus on today and the future. There is always more to be done and we want to keep Wisconsin athletics healthy and competitive. But when I do reflect back on the past quarter century, I'm filled with a great sense of pride and satisfaction in what has been accomplished. The bowl games, the Final Fours, the national titles, the legendary student-athletes and coaches, along with a million memorable moments have made this a magical ride for so many people.

As I said, however, I like to focus on what's ahead. College athletics faces a great many challenges, but also a great many opportunities. Sports in our country have never been more popular and, with all the great technology available now, there have never been so many avenues to connect with and follow our favorite teams. Sporting venues are tailoring everything toward creating an exhilarating experience for fans. It's a great time to be a sports fan.

At the same time, legal issues, health and safety concerns, and changing attendance patterns are just a few of the challenges we face in the sports world. We have to tackle those issues head on so that we continue to provide a great experience for our student-athletes and for the fans who follow them in person, online, or on television or radio.

College athletics and Wisconsin athletics in particular are steeped in tradition. We want to maintain those great traditions while also remaining current and competitive as the landscape continues to change. In the pages that follow, you will read about our traditions and many of our memorable moments. Enjoy it, and know that we'll keep trying to create more of them.

On Wisconsin!

—Barry Alvarez
January 2016

Introduction

Success is not measured by what a man accomplishes, but by the opposition he has encountered and the courage with which he has maintained the struggle against overwhelming odds.

—*Charles Lindbergh*

Kickoff for the inaugural Big Ten football championship was fast approaching, and most sportswriters sat in the press box above Lucas Oil Stadium, engrossed in their own Twitter dialogues, stressing over late-night deadlines, worrying about themselves and nothing else.

Tom Mulhern never was like most sportswriters.

I had known Tom all of eight weeks when Wisconsin and Michigan State were to meet in the 2011 title game, which is to say we didn't know each other well at all. Just before kickoff, Tom stopped what he was doing and turned to me. He wanted to let me know he'd appreciated the questions I had been asking on the Badgers football beat, to tell me he thought I'd done a good job in my first two months and to keep it up. He didn't have to do that, of course. But knowing a well-respected veteran on the beat was paying attention and taking an interest in my growth meant everything.

That was Tom in a nutshell—someone who was more concerned about other people, who was always there to offer encouragement, even to those younger sportswriters he hardly knew.

Tom died October 3, 2014, at age 56 from complications of Creutzfeldt-Jakob disease, a rare, degenerative brain disorder that affects one in a million people. The Madison community, and by extension Badgers fans everywhere, lost a thoughtful, caring man whose prose as a sportswriter was second to none.

As this book is published, Tom remains at the forefront of my mind. He was the one, you see, who was supposed to write this book. He began working on it but was unable to complete the project because of his diagnosis. Later, family members and colleagues searched for remnants of chapters he'd written to no avail. It is an honor and a privilege, then, to try and carry on the work that Tom started.

Tom grew up in Madison and achieved his dream of covering the Badgers football program for his hometown paper, the *Wisconsin State Journal*, in 1999—a job he performed better than anybody for the next 15 years. Three times he was named the National Sportscasters and Sportswriters Association state sportswriter of the year, in 2005, 2010, and 2014. But the accolades and recognition never mattered to Tom. It was always about the people—both on and off the field.

I always admired the way in which Tom found unique and interesting angles of covering the football team. He asked intelligent, pointed questions of players and coaches with a level of research and refreshing positivity that was infectious to people around him. And even when his writing sometimes offered criticism, it came from a place of fairness, which earned him the respect of those he covered.

In addition to the effort he put into covering the beat, Tom demonstrated a genuine interest in the work of others. He once emailed words of encouragement out of the blue after reading a feature story I wrote on a Badgers basketball player. "Nice way to start my day, reading that," he wrote.

We began to forge a stronger bond just as his time on the beat was coming to an unexpected close. One July night at the Big Ten preseason media days in Chicago, we talked about football and about life. I had recently gotten married, and he had served as an officiant in one of his son's weddings. Talking to him was easy because he was so relatable, someone with whom I could swap journalism stories, hear about Badgers games from yesteryear, or simply share how our days were going.

During Tom's final weeks, a gathering was held for him so family members, friends, and colleagues could celebrate his life and let him know how much he was loved. The turnout showed just how many people Tom had impacted. And through the hours of greeters, Tom's zest never faded.

I told him how much he'd meant to me, how he'd shown me what it was like to handle oneself with passion, humility, and grace in a profession that does not always encourage writers to do so. He responded by offering me one last bit of encouragement. He told me I was a bright, young talent on the beat. He told me to keep it up.

Even in his last days, Tom never made the story about him. He made others feel good when he had every reason to be down. The true measure of a man is the people whose lives he touched in a positive way, and Tom did so until the very end.

Tom Mulhern is gone, but he won't be soon forgotten.

1 Barry Alvarez

Recent history suggested Barry Alvarez's bold statement was preposterous on the day he was hired to coach Wisconsin's crumbling football program. Call it bravado. Call it cockiness. Call it confidence. But whatever it was, even those closest to the team wondered whether his viewpoint aligned with reality.

Alvarez stood at a podium in Madison on January 2, 1990, and unleashed the kind of belief-building rhetoric that would rally Badgers supporters and become a staple of his tenure as coach. "Let me just say this," he began, addressing the fans in a moment of spontaneity. "They better get season tickets right now because before long, they probably won't be able to."

The line has become etched into lore over the years, played on the Camp Randall Stadium video board as part of pre-game montages thanks to the Badgers' remarkable turnaround since then. Yet to understand how outrageous Alvarez's comment appeared at the time was to know how far the football program had actually fallen.

The year before Alvarez arrived, in 1989, Wisconsin's home attendance plummeted to 41,734 fans per game—the lowest mark since 1945. During a three-year descent into the Big Ten basement from 1987 to '89 under previous coach Don Morton, UW won only six of 33 games overall. The lack of football success contributed significantly to the athletics department's $2.1 million debt. In other words, the Badgers were considered a national laughingstock.

In order for Alvarez's prediction to come true, Wisconsin would have to rebuild its entire team and lure in another 35,000 fans on Saturdays in the fall. The task required a broad uprooting of ingrained program beliefs that few coaches likely could have achieved.

University of Wisconsin legend Barry Alvarez stepped out of retirement to coach the Badgers to victory in the Outback Bowl on New Year's Day, 2015.

"I thought, 'I wonder if he knows what he's getting into,' because it was a mess," longtime Badgers radio announcer Matt Lepay said.

Alvarez, of course, was ready for the challenge. And then some.

"That question was asked to me, about what do you tell your fans who are tired of losing and not coming," Alvarez said. "There were less than 20,000 people here for that last game of the season the year before we showed up. I had coaches going out, driving around the state, going to high school coaches in towns where we had players. We went to the Wisconsin ticket office and said, 'Give me some specials on tickets.' Then we told high school coaches, 'Bring a bus. Bring your players down, bring people down, we'll give you discounts on tickets.'

"We were doing anything. I'd buy 50 tickets a game myself and give them to Boys and Girls Clubs. I'd give them to youth groups just to put somebody in the stadium. We were working. We just weren't sitting around waiting for it to happen. I knew as soon as we were competitive that people would come back."

Come back they did, as Alvarez orchestrated one of the single greatest rebuilding projects in college football history. His offseason-conditioning program was notoriously difficult in 1990, which helped change the culture and run off more than 50 players from the previous team. Alvarez used his gift as a master motivator to maximize players' talent, galvanize the fan base, and raise expectations. His no-nonsense approach established a program based on toughness and an unrelenting desire to win. He did so by recruiting blue-collar players often overlooked at other programs and building a so-called fence around Wisconsin to secure in-state commitments.

The method gradually worked. Though Alvarez's first Wisconsin team finished an underwhelming 1–10 with mostly overmatched young players, home attendance increased by an average of nearly 10,000 people per game over the previous year. Following consecutive 5–6 seasons that saw Wisconsin just miss out on bowl game opportunities, Alvarez attained the breakthrough he recognized was possible from the start.

With a team stocked full of in-state products such as receiver J.C. Dawkins, outside linebacker Chris Hein, defensive back Jeff Messenger, running back Brent Moss, free safety Scott Nelson, right tackle Joe Panos, right guard Steve Stark, defensive tackle Mike Thompson, and left tackle Mike Verstegen, Wisconsin finished the regular season 9–1–1 to reach the 1994 Rose Bowl—the school's first appearance in the game in 31 years. Wisconsin ultimately defeated UCLA 21–16 for the Badgers' first-ever Rose Bowl victory.

Alvarez, ever the advantage seeker, pulled out every trick he could that season to motivate players. He famously convinced the team to wear sunglasses during the day and keep lights on at night to adjust body clocks to the time difference in the weeks before the team's regular season finale in Tokyo, Japan, against Michigan State. Multiple players said that, before another game that season, Alvarez told the team he would beat up an opposing coach who had spoken badly of his Badgers to prove Wisconsin would not back down from anyone.

"We all went crazy," Panos said. "Coach was one of us, man. We really, really thought that we truly, deeply knew that he believed in us and loved us very much. If you get a guy that does that, a guy that bleeds for you, has got your back, you'll do just about anything for him. I always said we would follow Coach through the gates of hell. That was the kind of guy he was."

That Alvarez constantly came armed with a plan to restore confidence was nothing new. He had developed his reputation as a team builder well before rising up the college coaching ranks. As a 29-year-old head coach at Mason City High School in Iowa in 1976, he renovated the school's training facilities, knocking out walls with a sledgehammer, rebuilding it by hand with the aid of assistant coaches and adding workout equipment. In 1978, he rallied the team by offering to shave his head as part of a fundraiser if his players avenged their only regular season loss—a 26-24 triple-overtime defeat to Fort Dodge—in the playoffs. Mason City won that semifinal rematch, he shaved his head, and the Mohawks went on to win the Class 4A state championship.

Those qualities carried forth when Alvarez joined Hayden Fry as a linebackers coach at Iowa in 1979 and steadily built his career. He eventually coached alongside Lou Holtz as defensive coordinator at Notre Dame in the late 1980s, where the pair helped the Fighting Irish win a national championship.

Dan McCarney, who worked with Alvarez at Iowa and served as his defensive coordinator at Wisconsin from 1990 to '94, said he recalled a conversation the two shared on Alvarez's first day at Wisconsin. Alvarez, a former linebacker at Nebraska under coach Bob Devaney, said he wanted the Badgers to mirror the

Cornhuskers' success. He hoped to fill the football stadium, to have all of his senior classes experience a bowl game, and to someday become the school's athletics director.

"All those things happened, and it sure as hell didn't come easy," McCarney said. "You talk about a guy that had a vision and knew what he wanted and then went and got it."

At every step, Alvarez found ways to win, which proved no different at Wisconsin despite tremendous initial obstacles. He coached Wisconsin from 1990 to 2005 and left as the winningest coach in program history. Alvarez's teams won three Rose Bowls, in 1994, 1999, and 2000, and he possesses a career record at Wisconsin of 119–74–4. Camp Randall Stadium, meanwhile, has averaged at least 75,000 fans per game every year since 1993, and Wisconsin has become a perennial top-25 program.

Season tickets, as Alvarez once suggested, are hard to come by these days. And Alvarez, undeniably, is among the most significant reasons for the sustained success.

"I just have a strong belief [that] when you compete, I always want to give my guys the advantage," said Alvarez, who has served as Wisconsin's athletics director since 2004. "When I'm confident, they're confident. If you've got a little swagger, they get a little swagger."

2 Bob Johnson

The most remarkable collapse Wisconsin hockey fans had ever seen was only a few minutes old, and 8,662 people shuffled out of the Dane County Coliseum in disbelief. Just one day earlier, Wisconsin had blitzed Colorado College 8–2 in a Western Collegiate Hockey Association playoff game. All the Badgers had to do 24 hours later was not lose by seven goals, and the two-game, total-goal series belonged to them, keeping their NCAA tournament hopes alive.

Then it happened. Colorado College buzzed up the ice, swarmed the puck, scored in the first minute, and kept on coming. Three goals in the first six minutes of the second period narrowed the total margin further. Until, finally, Colorado College left with a stunning 11–4 victory to take the total-goal series 13–12. Wisconsin, at 23–14–1, was eliminated from the league tournament on March 8, 1981, and the season seemed doomed.

"It was like a nightmare out there," Wisconsin coach Bob Johnson said afterward.

But this is not a story about surrender. Johnson would never allow it. What made him one of the most effective coaches in Badgers sports history was his enthusiasm, determination to succeed, intensity, and attention to detail, and all those traits would be on display in the coming weeks.

Johnson already had two national titles under his belt at Wisconsin, and he was known for having plenty of influence and political clout in college hockey. The NCAA tournament had expanded to eight teams for the first time for the 1981 postseason, and Johnson lobbied hard to the NCAA selection committee for an at-large berth. Before there were computer rankings, decisions often were made based on financial considerations or fan support, and Johnson knew the Badgers could be in good position.

Still, nothing was guaranteed. Players weren't sure if they would ever play a game together as a team again. Johnson, however, kept the Badgers practicing for a full week despite the uncertainty, keeping them sharp just in case.

"There was a question in players' minds: Was this all worth it?" former UW winger Ron Vincent told the *Milwaukee Journal*.

Tournament bids were announced more than a week later over the phone to Johnson with 25 of his players looking on. There was good news: Wisconsin had secured an at-large berth. And 20 days after losing in the WCHA playoffs, Wisconsin captured its third national championship by crushing Minnesota 6–3. The game completed a magical run for a team that became known as the "Backdoor Badgers" for the manner in which they sneaked into the postseason.

"It was classic, vintage Bob Johnson," Thomas Osenton, a former administrative assistant, told the *Journal*. "It was almost as if he willed it to happen. We became a team of destiny. A lot of coaches would have collected the jerseys and called it a season."

Johnson embodied the spirit of Wisconsin hockey. His favorite expression was, "It's a great day for hockey," and with Johnson at the helm of the Badgers program, it usually was.

The son of a Swedish immigrant who changed his surname from Olars, Johnson played hockey at North Dakota and Minnesota and was good enough in baseball to sign professionally with the Chicago White Sox. His baseball career was interrupted by the Korean War and, married with two children, he accepted a high school coaching job in 1956. He moved to Colorado College in 1963, and three years later he came to Wisconsin, where he was 367–175–23 in 15 seasons.

"My early years there were more fun than the later years," he said in July 1991. "It was fun developing that program, getting into the WCHA, getting into the Dane County Coliseum, and seeing the people of Madison getting excited.

"The first year, we drew about 2,000 [per game], then 3,000, then 4,000, and all of a sudden the rink was sold out, and now it has been all these years. The timing was just right, and a lot of the fans were Badger fans, not hockey fans. They had just dropped boxing as a sport at Wisconsin, and the football team didn't win a game my first two years there. The fans were thirsting for something to latch onto, and hockey became it."

Wisconsin's hockey program was only three years old as an intercollegiate sport when Johnson arrived, and he turned the

Badgers into a national power using his optimism and discipline. Jeff Sauer, a friend of Johnson's and his successor as Badgers hockey coach, once said Johnson's enthusiasm was contagious.

"He could lose a 12–2 game and after talking to him, you had the funny feeling the score was actually 13–12 and he won," Sauer said.

Johnson coached Wisconsin to national titles in 1973, 1977, and 1981 and was named NCAA coach of the year in 1977. He gained the enduring nickname "Badger Bob." He also coached the 1976 Winter Olympic hockey team and U.S. National teams from 1973 to '75 and in 1981.

During his time as a coach, he had a low tolerance for gloom. If a player didn't get caught up in his upbeat attitude, his relationship with Johnson was usually short and tense, the *New York Times* noted. The coach always encouraged players, prodding them to reach for a higher level.

"There are a lot of ways to coach," Johnson told the *New York Times* about his philosophy. "You can coach from fear, when it's, 'You do it this way or you're gone tomorrow,' or you can develop pride in performance."

Johnson left Wisconsin to coach the Calgary Flames from 1982 to '87 and led the team to its first Campbell Conference championship and the Stanley Cup finals. After supervising USA Hockey for three years, he returned to coaching and led the Pittsburgh Penguins to their first Stanley Cup championship in 1991, in what proved to be his only season in charge there.

"It's sort of like the frosting on the cake," Johnson said after the season. "When I returned to coaching last year, I never dreamed we'd win the Stanley Cup."

In August 1991, following hospitalization due to a brain aneurysm, Johnson was diagnosed with brain cancer. He died November 26, 1991, at age 60.

"He taught us how to win," Pittsburgh Penguins captain Mario Lemieux said. "We're a very tough team to coach, a team that was known for offense, but he taught us how to play defense. He was the main reason why we won the Stanley Cup."

The Penguins wore a memorial patch in honor of Johnson the following season that read 1931–1991 with the word BADGER underneath. Players at Wisconsin wore initials on their helmets. Pittsburgh paid tribute to Johnson in a 10-minute ceremony before a game against the New Jersey Devils one night after his passing.

Fans were given miniature battery-operated candles as they entered the Civic Arena. After the Pittsburgh players took the ice, the house lights were turned off and the building illuminated with candles held by the 16,164 fans. A soloist sang the Lord's Prayer, which was followed by Linda Ronstadt's "Goodbye, My Friend." During the second song, the Penguins revealed another tribute.

Painted outside each blue line was Johnson's favorite phrase: "It's a Great Day for Hockey—Badger Bob."

Johnson was inducted into the Wisconsin Hockey Hall of Fame in 1987, the United States Hockey Hall of Fame in 1991, and the Hockey Hall of Fame in 1992. He was elected to the Wisconsin Athletics Hall of Fame in 1993. In 2012, Wisconsin's hockey playing surface in the Kohl Center was named Bob Johnson Rink.

"I don't think anyone has contributed more to national, international and professional hockey as a player, a coach and an administrator than he has," said John Mayasich, chairman of the U.S. Hockey Hall of Fame's selection committee.

Johnson remains the only coach to win NCAA and NHL championships.

3 Pat Richter

If Pat Richter had followed through on his initial college commitment, Wisconsin Badgers supporters would have lost the opportunity to cheer on a hometown hero—and perhaps later witness a remarkable turnaround of an entire athletics department. That's because Richter, a Madison native, originally picked the University of Kansas on a basketball scholarship.

Yes, Richter, one of the greatest all-around athletes in Wisconsin history, was nearly a Jayhawk. He committed on a visit to Lawrence, Kansas, even though he never even saw the famed Allen Fieldhouse gymnasium. He recalled watching a Kansas City Athletics baseball game and being awestruck on his only recruiting visit in the spring of 1959 that a program was so interested in his talents.

"It was just probably one of those youthful reactions and kind of quick judgments type of thing," Richter said.

Richter viewed his college choice, in part, through the prism of what school might help him play professional athletics. He thought that sport would be baseball and had not considered what a future in football might look like. When he returned home, however, a close friend and advisor named Gene Calhoun told him he'd be better off playing baseball in the Big Ten and that Kansas was not a very good baseball school. It was enough to convince Richter to switch allegiances, and a month later, he was a Badger. Opting out of a letter of intent those days, Richter said, was not nearly as difficult as in today's college landscape.

"I would say that's probably the wisest decision I ever made, for sure," Richter said. "No question about it."

Richter would earn nine letters in football, basketball, and baseball at Wisconsin and be involved in some of the most well-known athletics contests in school history. He does not list a singular favorite but rather one for each sport he played. In football, he cited Wisconsin's 23–21 victory at third-ranked Minnesota during his junior year in the 1961 regular season finale, before the Gophers went on to win the Rose Bowl. In basketball, he was a part of Wisconsin's thrilling 86–67 victory against No. 1 Ohio State, which featured Jerry Lucas and John Havlicek. That March 3, 1962, game marked the first victory against a top-ranked team in the basketball program's history.

Richter's favorite baseball memory involved a doubleheader sweep against Michigan. Before the games, he received several phone calls from friends on the University of Illinois baseball team, which needed the Wolverines to lose both games for the Illini to capture the Big Ten championship. Richter had played with Illinois players in a baseball league the previous summer in South Dakota, and they promised to buy him a watch if Wisconsin won.

With Wisconsin trailing 5–4 in the bottom of the seventh inning of the second game, Richter belted a line-drive home run to center field off Wolverines left-handed ace Fritz Fisher to give the Badgers a 6–5 victory and complete the sweep. The win prevented Michigan from sharing first place in the Big Ten with Illinois. Richter had fulfilled his end of the bargain, though he never did receive his promised gift.

"I still talk to them once in a while," he recalled. "I said, 'I'm still waiting for that watch.'"

Richter's most famous athletic feat at Wisconsin came during the 1963 Rose Bowl, when he caught 11 passes for 163 yards in the Badgers' wild 42–37 loss against USC. He earned All-America honors in 1961 and 1962 as a tight end, led the Big Ten in receiving twice, and topped the nation in receiving yardage as a junior. Richter held or shared every receiving mark in the Wisconsin record books when he left. He caught 121 passes for 1,873 yards and 15 touchdowns. He was inducted into the National Football Foundation College Hall of Fame in 1997.

Football proved to be the sport that helped Richter elevate to the professional ranks quickest. The 6'5", 229½-pounder signed with the Washington Redskins as their top draft choice in 1963. To sign Richter, Washington had to outbid the Denver Broncos of the American Football League and at least five major league baseball teams. He signed for what was said to be the highest salary a Washington rookie ever received, an estimated $21,000.

"He's the best pass catcher I've seen in college football since I've been in the coaching business, and that goes back seven or eight years," Washington coach Bill McPeak said at the time.

Richter went on to play eight seasons with Washington and then worked as Vice President of Personnel at Oscar Mayer from 1972 to '88. Wisconsin's athletics programs had taken a significant tumble, and then-chancellor Donna Shalala ultimately convinced Richter to become the school's athletics director in 1989. Richter was reluctant to take such a high-profile position within the university. But he noted he could sense his job at Oscar Mayer might require him to move to Chicago, and he and his family hoped to remain in Madison.

Richter's tenure as athletics director lasted from 1989 to 2004 and was a smashing success. He eliminated a $2.1 million athletics department debt and was responsible for hiring football coach Barry Alvarez and basketball coaches Stu Jackson, Dick Bennett, and Bo Ryan, among other coaches. Three teams won national championships, and UW sports teams won 50 Big Ten titles during his tenure.

Richter, after all his years at Wisconsin, remained most proud of helping to rekindle the tradition, spirit, and pride in Badgers athletics.

"When we started here, the players, a lot of people were just getting beat up in the press," Richter said. "They weren't wearing their letter jackets. They were embarrassed. Bringing back that respectability would probably be the biggest thing.

"No matter what game or where it might be, you run into people and they'll come up and stick out their hand and say thank you. That's all they need to say. That's what's really kind of neat because I know what they're talking about. They're just saying, 'I'm proud to be a Badger now, and thank you for being part of that.'"

Life in Bronze

Two of the most significant figures in Wisconsin football history are featured prominently and permanently at Gate 1 in front of Camp Randall Stadium. Life-size bronze sculptures of former head coach and current athletics director Barry Alvarez, as well as former player and athletics director Pat Richter, remind Badgers fans of their successes in helping to turn around the athletics program in the 1990s.

The sculpture of Alvarez, which stands 6'1" and weighs approximately 300 pounds, was unveiled on October 13, 2006. The sculptor was Lou Cella of Timeless Creations, Inc., who created the piece at The Fine Art Studio of Rotblatt-Amrany in Highwood, Illinois. One month later, on November 17, Richter's sculpture was unveiled. The designer was Sean M. Bell, also of The Fine Art Studio of Rotblatt-Amrany.

4 Ron Dayne

The first time Barry Alvarez saw Ron Dayne play football, he was sitting in an office with assistant coach Bernie Wyatt staring at a grainy VHS high school game tape of the burly fullback from South New Jersey. What he witnessed that day made his mouth salivate and his jaw drop.

Alvarez estimated Dayne was probably 255 or 260 pounds then. On film, he'd line up right behind the quarterback, take the handoff, disappear into the pile, and move everyone with him at least a few yards.

"When he got in the secondary, the defensive backs took funny angles to avoid him, and he had sprinter's speed," Alvarez recalled during Dayne's Rose Bowl Hall of Fame induction ceremony in 2012. "I said, 'You know what? He could be a great tailback.'"

Dayne was a natural high school athlete who starred in track and field at Overbrook High in Pine Hill, New Jersey. As a senior in 1996, he won state titles in the shot put and discus. That same year, he set a New Jersey record by throwing a discus 216 feet, 11 inches at a national track competition in California—the fifth-best distance ever thrown by an American high school athlete.

And boy, could he run a football.

He earned consensus first-team All-America honors and was considered the No. 1 fullback prospect in the nation after amassing 1,785 yards rushing and 24 touchdowns his senior year. Dayne could have pursued college football just about anywhere. But his affinity for Wisconsin grew while sitting in the Overbrook football office listening to former Badgers receiver Lee DeRamus, a fellow South Jersey product from the same school district, talk about his Wisconsin experience.

Two things then sold Dayne on Wisconsin during his visit to Madison: Alvarez's charisma and his promise that Dayne could be a tailback.

"The first time I met Coach, we came out on a big hug," Dayne said. "My last game was a big hug. Every time I see Coach now is a big hug. He treats me like a son. I look up to him like a father.

"Coach Alvy told me I could be a running back. Other schools were looking at me at fullback and linebacker. I just wanted to be able to get the opportunity to play and be a running back."

Alvarez and Dayne bonded immediately. But neither could have foreseen just how good Dayne would be at Wisconsin, where he still owns dozens of rushing records, both at the university and nationally. Among his most notable achievements:

- He is the FBS career rushing leader, including bowl games, with 7,125 yards, and is the only player with more than 7,000 rushing yards.

- He was the first three-time Big Ten rushing champion.
- He outrushed opposing teams 29 times in his 43 career starts.
- He was named the MVP in three bowl games (1996 Copper Bowl, 1999 Rose Bowl, and 2000 Rose Bowl).
- He left Wisconsin with 48 school records.
- He won the Heisman Trophy in 1999, becoming only the second Wisconsin player in program history to earn the honor.
- A consummate workhorse, he carried the ball an astounding 1,220 times in his Wisconsin career—296 more carries than Montee Ball, who holds second place on the school list. "He didn't know what he was getting into," Alvarez said. "Because I liked to give him the ball. As I always say, I liked to get Ronnie lathered up."
- Dayne also owns the school record for rushing attempts in a game (50 against Minnesota on November 9, 1996). He held the single-game school rushing record of 339 yards, set against Hawaii as a freshman, for 18 years until Melvin Gordon broke the mark with 408 yards against Nebraska in 2014.

"To this day when we go back to Hawaii, the media still thanks me for having pity and taking him out of the game," Alvarez said. "Their defensive coordinator said tackling Ron Dayne was like trying to stop a Mack Truck with pea shooters."

Dayne made his name known in college football circles immediately by rushing for a then-FBS freshman record 1,863 yards during the 1996 regular season, a mark later broken by Oklahoma's Adrian Peterson. Dayne added 246 yards and Copper Bowl MVP honors to finish with 2,109 yards despite not starting the first four games of the season.

As a sophomore, Dayne was a finalist for the Doak Walker Award and a first-team All-American from College Football News. He missed two full games and parts of two others and still ranked fifth nationally with an average of 142.0 rushing yards per game.

During his junior season, Dayne again was a Doak Walker Award finalist, leading the Big Ten in rushing and earning Walter Camp first-team All-America honors. He led the Badgers' upset of No. 6 UCLA in the 1999 Rose Bowl, rushing for 246 yards and earning MVP honors. That game also set the stage for his Heisman Trophy campaign the following season.

In Dayne's senior year, he rushed for 2,034 yards and lived up to all preseason hype. He capped his career with 200 yards rushing in the Rose Bowl, helping the Badgers win in back-to-back years in Pasadena. For his efforts, he earned a second straight MVP award to become just the third player in Rose Bowl history to earn that distinction. In addition to winning the Heisman as a senior, he won the Maxwell Award, Walter Camp Player of the Year Award, Doak Walker Award, Chicago Tribune Silver Football and was a unanimous, consensus first-team All-American.

Dayne's No. 33 was officially retired by Wisconsin in 2007, and he was elected to the UW Athletics Hall of Fame in 2009. Four years later in 2013, Dayne was inducted into the College Football Hall of Fame, becoming the 13th former Badgers player or coach to earn the honor.

"There are a lot of guys that played this game, and no one did what he did," Alvarez said. "He was durable. I think anyone today that follows college football, when you mention Wisconsin, I think they picture Ron carrying the ball and us running the ball. That describes the brand of football that we established here, and that's how everybody pictures it… He goes down as one of the greats that ever played college football to this day."

Bo Ryan

Deep in the recesses of the Kohl Center, Bo Ryan approached a podium in a good mood. That is to say, as good a mood as you were likely to find Ryan during the heart of basketball season.

It was a half-hour after Wisconsin had shellacked No. 12-ranked Illinois 74–51 midway through the 2013 season, and Ryan had every reason to crack a smile as wide as the Wisconsin River. The Badgers had secured their biggest victory of the early season, tying them for first place in the Big Ten.

But the smile on Ryan's face never materialized. The man who had devoted his entire life to basketball was pleased but not satisfied. Never satisfied.

"That's probably as good as we've played this year," Ryan told reporters. "What you have to do is know that tomorrow we're practicing for [what's] next. And that's how short-lived a victory like this can be."

Three days later, Wisconsin collected one of its most monumental regular season victories, defeating No. 2 Indiana 64–59 inside a boisterous Assembly Hall. It was the highest-ranked opponent Wisconsin had ever beaten on the road, and the win marked the first time the Badgers had defeated any top-five opponent on the road since 1980.

Back in the locker room, Ryan told his players he was proud of them. This time, he instructed them to celebrate the victory… for 24 hours.

What made Ryan such a force as a basketball coach over the years was his complete and utter consistency. Ryan focused on the process of improving every day, of utilizing his team's strengths and taking advantage of the opponent's weaknesses. He didn't revel too

Bo Ryan had a celebrated career at Wisconsin, punctuated by leading his team to consecutive Final Fours and the national championship game in 2015.

long in victory or mope about a bad loss—save for watching game tape to improve down the road.

"Winning and losing was never talked about," said Greg Gard, who began coaching as an assistant alongside Ryan in 1993 and spent time with him at three different schools. "[He] talked about doing things the right way all the time and then the end result will be being successful in whatever contest you're in. That's how he took it continually."

Ryan, who was named Wisconsin's coach before the 2001–02 season, became the winningest coach in school history by sticking to his fundamental beliefs about passing, cutting, and team defense. He preached toughness and discipline and demanded that every player be held accountable. Often, he guided teams full of less-heralded players and melded them into such a cohesive unit that they could compete with any team in the country. There is a reason Ryan won everywhere he coached, and it had nothing to do with luck.

He began his college coaching career in 1973 at Dominican College of Racine in Wisconsin under Bill Cofield. One year later, Ryan, a Chester, Pennsylvania, native, moved back to the Philadelphia area as the head coach at Sun Valley High School. He earned Delaware County Coach of the Year honors for leading the school to a second-place finish in the Philadelphia Suburban League. The next year, he guided the high school to its first state tournament appearance.

In 1976, Ryan reunited with Cofield, who had become the head coach at Wisconsin by then. Ryan worked under Cofield and later Steve Yoder until 1984 when he landed the head coaching job at UW–Platteville.

Outsiders tended to think of Ryan as cantankerous because of his fiery on-court demeanor. But what made Ryan so successful, according to former players, was his combination of determination, honesty, fairness, consistency, and loyalty.

"He's a competitor. He's ferocious," said T.J. Van Wie, a two-time All-American at Platteville who played for Ryan from 1991 to '95. "He expects his players to be like him. He wants you to compete and give it your all. Then after the game, he'll point out some of the good and point out some of the bad and you get ready for the next game."

At Platteville, Ryan developed a reputation for squeezing the maximum ability out of his players, and no detail was too small— while there, he once wrote a book titled *Passing and Catching: The Lost Art*. He also understood his personnel and inserted a hard-and-fast rule that no player would ever leave his feet on defense.

"We will lead the nation in the least amount of blocked shots," Ryan would say.

Platteville won 82.2 percent of its games and four national championships during Ryan's tenure (1991, 1995, 1998, and

1999). And during the 1996–97 season, the Pioneers set the all-time Division III scoring defense record, allowing 47.5 points per game.

When Ryan accomplished all he could at the Division III level, he accepted the head coaching position at Division I University of Wisconsin–Milwaukee. He led the Panthers to back-to-back winning seasons for the first time in eight years and finally earned his dream job as head coach of Wisconsin in 2001. All Ryan did was lead the Badgers to at least a share of four Big Ten regular season championships and three conference tournament titles, earn conference coach of the year honors four times, and help Wisconsin reach 14 consecutive NCAA tournaments. In 14-plus seasons at Wisconsin, Ryan's record was 364–130 (.737 winning percentage). In his entire college coaching career, he went 747–233 (.762).

The signature moment of Ryan's Badgers coaching career came when Wisconsin downed previously unbeaten Kentucky in the 2015 Final Four to reach the program's first national championship game in 74 years. It marked Ryan's second straight Final Four appearance and seemed to validate the idea that his old-school methods could work in the modern game.

Ryan, at age 67, wanted to retire that offseason and hand the coaching reins to Gard, his assistant of 23 years. Instead, he announced a plan to retire following one more season, ultimately doing so for two reasons. First, he noted Gard had been busy that summer with family, as his father's health declined. Second, Ryan did not have assurances from athletics director Barry Alvarez that Gard would be named the head coach without a national search being conducted.

But on December 15, 2015, after Wisconsin's victory against Texas A&M–Corpus Christi, Ryan unexpectedly announced his retirement, effective immediately, just 12 games into the season. Ryan provided Gard, who was named the interim coach, with an opportunity to earn the head coaching job.

Ryan had prepared a speech but couldn't bring himself to read from it, instead opting to speak from the heart in an emotional postgame news conference.

"I knew it would come," he said. "It's just we can't always do it the way we like. But Greg's ready. The staff is ready. All the way through, top-flight people. And I feel really good about that."

Ryan had done all he could at Wisconsin, approaching heights many didn't think were possible for the program. Even in retirement, however, he were concerned about what came next, leaving the team with a trusted confidant and a dear friend.

John J. Walsh and a Boxing Powerhouse

Fans wedged in by the thousands, pressed side by side, necks craning toward the ring in the center of the UW Field House for a glimpse of the greatest spectacle in town. At the height of its popularity in the 1930s and '40s, college boxing in Madison was rivaled only by football. And when Badgers devotees came to see a show, their pugilist heroes rarely disappointed.

Consider the scene one night on March 29, 1940, when a record crowd of 15,200 people witnessed a dual meet between Wisconsin and Washington State. As Doug Moe noted in his definitive book on the history of Badgers boxing, *Lords of the Ring*, Joe Louis defended his professional heavyweight title in New York's Madison Square Garden against Johnny Paycheck the same night. Louis knocked out Paycheck in the second round. Announced attendance: 11,620.

The Madison crowd that night was no anomaly, either. In E.C. Wallenfeldt's book *The Six-Minute Fraternity*, on the rise and fall of NCAA tournament boxing, he wrote that from 1939 to '43, the smallest audience to watch a Wisconsin home dual meet numbered 8,500. The average dual meet attendance in Madison for that time period was 12,888.

"They'd march you down the aisle with 10,000 people cheering you on, and when you got into the ring, you were so pumped up to go you'd be embarrassed to lose," Dick Greendale, a member of UW's 1956 championship team, later told the *Milwaukee Journal Sentinel*.

But it wasn't only the pageantry of it all that drew in fans. Wisconsin's boxing program, quite simply, was as dominant a force in college athletics as perhaps anybody had ever seen, before or since. During Wisconsin's run from 1933 to '60, no other college program came close to matching the Badgers' success under coach John J. Walsh and later Vern Woodward.

Walsh's teams won eight national titles, and he coached 29 boxers that won 35 individual titles in NCAA tournaments. For perspective, San Jose State held the second-highest team championship mark with three. According to Wallenfeldt, the second-most individual NCAA championships belonged to Idaho State with 18—20 fewer than the Badgers' 38 total under two coaches during that era.

"I liken boxing at Wisconsin to football at Notre Dame," said Cal Vernon, who won the 175-pound national championship for the Badgers in the 1948 NCAA tournament at the UW Field House.

The two men who deserve the most credit for the program's success are Walsh and George F. Downer, athletic publicity director for Wisconsin until his death in 1941. Downer organized the first university team in 1933. Walsh was coach for 23 years and a member of the team when UW fought its first match in 1933 against St. Thomas, a 4–4 draw.

As an amateur boxer, Walsh won 98 out of 100 bouts, 95 of which were by knockout. He was Minnesota's state champion, Northwest Golden Gloves champion, and also won his weight division when the Midwest Intercollegiate ratings for 1932 were created. Walsh was a 1932 U.S. Olympic trials participant and beat Wisconsin's Fausto Rubini so impressively at the Field House that UW athletics department officials asked him to stay and coach the team.

According to Pete Ehrmann of the *Journal Sentinel*, Walsh was about to begin law school as a student at St. Thomas and initially said no to Wisconsin's offer. The next day, he found out the St. Thomas law school was being eliminated at the end of the semester, so he called Wisconsin back and took the job. He was 20 years old, and his first-year boxing coach salary was $600, but he also had to pay $100 tuition for attending law school.

During Walsh's tenure, he coached the Badgers to an astounding 116–22–1 record (.838 winning percentage) in dual meets. In nine different seasons, Wisconsin went unbeaten and untied (1935, 1938, 1939, 1941, 1942, 1943, 1946, 1947, and 1948) and in three other seasons only a single draw marred an otherwise unblemished record. Wisconsin's record in its first 82 home matches was 77–2–3.

The 1943 and 1956 seasons represented high points for Wisconsin's program, when five boxers took home individual NCAA titles and the Badgers set scoring-margin records at the championships. Wisconsin also won four individual championships in 1939 and 1942.

Wallenfeldt wrote of Walsh, "No other coach in the history of intercollegiate boxing even approached that kind of success," and Walsh was nicknamed by one sportswriter the "Producer of Champions." His featured boxers at Wisconsin included three-time national champions Gene Rankin and Cliff Lutz, as well as stars Omar Crocker and Woody Swancutt.

The UW Field House remained the center of the college boxing world, routinely hosting the NCAA championships, until an infamous final bout in 1960 involving San Jose State's Stu Bartell and Wisconsin's Charlie Mohr in the 165-pound final of the NCAA tournament. Bartell won a second-round technical knockout in front of 10,322 fans. But Mohr rested in his corner for several minutes following the loss and collapsed in the dressing room 10 minutes after he left the ring.

"When we got to the dressing room, Charles complained of a headache and we told him to take some aspirin," recalled Woodward, who had taken over as coach for Walsh in 1958. "We didn't think it was anything serious. A doctor checked him and said he would be all right."

Mohr, a 22-year-old senior from Merrick, New York, underwent three hours of surgery for a brain hemorrhage and died eight days later. Wisconsin's entire faculty voted to drop boxing from the university. The NCAA also discontinued boxing following that 1960 season.

Woodward later noted the surgeon who operated on Mohr said he'd had "a weak artery in his brain" and "just about anything could have caused it—even sneezing." Boxing, however, already was under attack at the time as overly violent, with college programs dropping the sport by the dozens, and Mohr's death was the spark that ignited the cause to end it.

"Charles' parents came out and said boxing wasn't to blame for his death," Woodward said. "But there's no doubt that when Charles died, college boxing died with him."

Prize Fighters

Wisconsin boxers won 38 individual NCAA boxing titles from 1936 to '60, more than twice as many as any other school. The individual champions:

1936: Bobby Fadner, 125 pounds
1939: Gene Rankin, 135; Omar Crocker, 145; Woodrow P. Swancutt, 155; Truman Torgerson, 175
1940: Woodrow P. Swancutt, 155; Nick Lee, heavyweight
1941: Gene Rankin, 135
1942: Gene Rankin, 135; Warren Jollymore, 145; Cliff Lutz, 155; George Makris, 175
1943: Cliff Lutz, 145; F. Don Miller, 155; Myron Miller, 165; George Makris, 175; Verdayne John, heavyweight
1947: Cliff Lutz, 147; John Lendenski, 165
1948: Steve Gremban, 119; Don Dickinson, 147; Cal Vernon, 176; Vito Parisi, heavyweight
1951: Dick Murphy, 155; Bob Ranck, heavyweight
1952: Bob Morgan, 147; Bob Ranck, heavyweight
1953: Pat Sreenan, 147; Ray Zale, 178
1954: Bob Meath, 156
1956: Dean Plemmons, 112; Dick Bartman, 139; Vince Ferguson, 156; Orville Pitts, 178; Truman Sturdevant, heavyweight
1959: Charles Mohr, 165
1960: Brown McGhee, 132; Jerry Turner, 156

7 Alan Ameche

The story of Alan Ameche's college football recruitment is said to have involved a notoriously famous underhanded tactic that backfired on Notre Dame. It also spoke to Ameche's character and humility, traits that Wisconsin fans would come to know and love during an incredible football career and beyond.

In Dan Manoyan's biography, *Alan Ameche: The Story of "The Horse,"* he wrote that every major college program in the Midwest, and others such as Kentucky and North Carolina, offered Ameche scholarships after he starred at Kenosha Bradford High School. But his decision came down to Wisconsin and Notre Dame.

Wisconsin was less than two hours northwest of Ameche's hometown of Kenosha, Wisconsin. It also was the school where his brother, Lynn, had attended. Plus, six of his high school teammates were going to play football there. Notre Dame, meanwhile, was a school with considerable and obvious college football tradition. It also possessed "very rich, important, and persistent alumni who had made it their mission in life to adorn Ameche's head with a golden helmet," Manoyan wrote.

One such alum was Fred Miller, owner of the Miller Brewing Company. Miller had been an All-American offensive tackle under Knute Rockne at Notre Dame, and he was not used to taking no for an answer. Ameche's childhood friend, Bobby Hinds, recalled Miller sitting in Ameche's home writing a check out for $1,500 to his mother in exchange for convincing her son to verbally commit to Notre Dame. The amount was nearly as much as what Ameche's father made for a year's worth of work. It also was illegal under NCAA rules.

"Just to show you how sophisticated Alan was, he walks over to Fred Miller and said, 'Don't you ever do that again,'" Hinds recalled. "He was genuinely pissed that Fred Miller had used that sort of bribery on his mother."

The Ameches did not accept Miller's check. Alan chose Wisconsin and he became a statewide hero. He earned the nickname "The Horse," from Wisconsin's freshman coach, George Lanphear, and even then was seen as a special player. The rationale behind the name is said to have involved either Ameche's high, horse-like gait or the fact that Ameche's work ethic mirrored that of a horse. Either way, the name stuck with Ameche for the rest of his life.

In four seasons at Wisconsin, from 1951 to '54, Ameche rushed for 3,212 yards, a school record later broken by Billy Marek. In 1952, he became the first Badgers running back to exceed 1,000 yards, gaining 1,079. During the 1953 Rose Bowl, he gained 133 yards rushing despite Wisconsin being shut out 7–0 against USC. He led the Badgers all four years, was an All-American in his junior and senior years, and was elected in 1975 to the National Football Foundation Hall of Fame.

But the season that truly stands out took place during his senior campaign in 1954, for both his on-field performance and the gracious manner in which he handled his success and fame. Though Ameche gained only 641 yards that season, he scored a career-best nine touchdowns and ran away with Wisconsin's first Heisman Trophy award.

During that time, the Heisman committee awarded just one trophy, and it went to the player. Ameche and 1949 Heisman winner Leon Hart from Notre Dame ultimately spoke to the Heisman committee and asked that two trophies be given each year, one to the player and one to the school.

It was this gesture, among many others, that prompted *Milwaukee Sentinel* sports editor Lloyd Larson to wax poetic to his readers. He noted what made Ameche's recognition more meaningful was that he never allowed it to change who he was as a person.

"That's the real test for an outstanding athlete," Larson wrote. "Does the hat size increase with increasing fame or does he stay level, modest, and humble? Everybody who has come in contact with Ameche will tell you that he falls into the latter class. In my mind, that's more important than all his thrilling runs, his blocks and tackles, his breath-taking exhibitions of lowering the boom."

After the 1954 season ended, Ameche was honored in his hometown of Kenosha. He came home to a banquet in his honor perched on a fire engine at the head of a motorcade with his oldest son, Brian, and his wife, Yvonne. According to an Associated Press article at the time, the Ameches netted close to $6,000 in cash and assorted gifts, including a palomino horse and the title to a brand new Hudson Hornet car. He also received a scroll officially recognizing his selection on the Associated Press All-American team, as part of "Ameche Day" festivities. The event was held at the Eagles Club, across the street from Lake Front Stadium, where he earned his football fame as a high school star.

The attention followed Ameche during an NFL career that saw him drafted in the first round with the third overall pick to the Baltimore Colts in 1955. He scored the game-winning touchdown in the 1958 NFL championship from one yard out to lift Baltimore to a 23–17 victory against the New York Giants in sudden-death overtime. The game has often been called the "Greatest Game Ever Played." He was a two-time NFL champion and a four-time Pro Bowl selection.

"There was no Super Bowl then, but that game was like the Super Bowl to all of us," Ameche said. "I was in it for every [offensive] play, and I was relieved when the game was over."

In his later years, Ameche found particular joy in music, citing Beethoven symphonies as his favorite. He even served as a trustee of the Philadelphia Orchestra and took great pride in defying the football-as-jock stereotypes. He also remained unimpressed with football glory. He held a Heisman Trophy vote as a former winner, and in 1982, he was asked what the winner should do with the bronze statue.

"He should put it on his shelf and forget about it," Ameche said. "That's where mine is now."

Ameche died in 1988 of a heart attack at age 55, and he was remembered as selfless, warm, and caring, the superstar athlete whose modesty shined brightest.

"The awards and honors never had any effect on him," Baltimore Colts Hall of Fame quarterback Johnny Unitas said. "He was a great athlete, a super football player, and a regular guy."

Wisconsin and the Heisman Trophy

The Badgers have produced two Heisman Trophy winners with Alan Ameche and Ron Dayne. But on nine other occasions, a Wisconsin player has finished in the top 10 for college football's highest honor. In 1962 and 2011, the Badgers placed two players in the top 10.

Year	Player	Place	Points	Winner
1938	Howard Weiss	6th	60	Davey O'Brien (TCU)
1942	Dave Schreiner	10th	60	Frank Sinkwich (Georgia)
1953	Alan Ameche	6th	211	John Lattner (Notre Dame)
1954	Alan Ameche	1st	1,068	Alan Ameche (Wisconsin)
1959	Dale Hackbart	7th	134	Billy Cannon (LSU)
1962	Pat Richter	6th	276	Terry Baker (Oregon State)
1962	Ron Vander Kelen	9th	139	Terry Baker (Oregon State)
1999	Ron Dayne	1st	2,042	Ron Dayne (Wisconsin)
2011	Montee Ball	4th	348	Robert Griffin III (Baylor)
2011	Russell Wilson	9th	52	Robert Griffin III (Baylor)
2014	Melvin Gordon	2nd	1,250	Marcus Mariota (Oregon)

Frank Kaminsky

Those privileged enough to watch Frank Kaminsky the basketball player saw a specially skilled big man, a devastatingly versatile killer on the court who could destroy opponents in the paint or stretch them to the perimeter and bury three-pointers for days.

Those who saw Kaminsky the person during his four years at Wisconsin were equally privileged. In an era of me-first, spotlight-grabbing college athletes, Kaminsky represented something of an enigma: a shy, soft-spoken, 7'0" goofball who generally didn't seem to care just how big of a deal he was on campus. In college, his preferred transportation was a $1,000 moped he purchased off Craigslist, which helped him avoid the mobs of people who surely would have stopped him for a picture or an autograph.

All of it made him one of the most refreshingly candid characters in the sport, a reluctant star who never felt comfortable handling attention off the court but demanded it with his stellar play on the court. His bashfulness revealed itself at the Big Ten's preseason media day in October 2014, after Kaminsky had been selected as the conference's unanimous preseason player of the year. While tape recorders and bright camera lights surrounded an open seat at a table reserved for Kaminsky, he veered off to lean his frame against a wall next to the table and said rather stoically, "I see you guys enough already."

"I don't necessarily like talking and having people surround me," Kaminsky said then. "But at the end of the day, I don't hate it as much as I used to."

He then clarified: "I hate it less than I did. I still hate it, though."

His persona endeared him to coaches, fans, teammates, and reporters, because he was a down-to-earth college athlete who seemed to only take something seriously when he stepped between the lines of the basketball court. Following a freshman season in which he averaged only 7.7 minutes and 1.8 points per game and grew out of shape thanks to an unhealthy affinity for Qdoba burritos, Kaminsky transformed his body—and quickly transformed himself as a player. He spent his sophomore season in a backup role once again to teammate Jared Berggren, but when the starting spot opened up during Kaminsky's junior campaign, he took full advantage.

Kaminsky thrived as a full-time starter for the first time in his college career in 2013–14, using the skills he honed while battling Berggren in practice. Four games into the season, Kaminsky drilled all six of his three-point attempts and scored a single-game program record 43 points against North Dakota in only 28 minutes. But the run that transformed Kaminsky into a campus-wide celebrity and beyond began in March, when Wisconsin put together a magical push to the Final Four.

His 28-point, 11-rebound effort during Wisconsin's 64–63 overtime victory against Arizona in the Elite Eight propelled him

Frank Kaminsky was named the consensus national player of the year in 2015 and helped Wisconsin reach the NCAA championship game. The Charlotte Hornets selected him that summer in the first round of the NBA draft.

to national stardom. For his performance, he earned the West Region's most outstanding player award and became a viable early NBA draft candidate before he opted to return for his senior season.

Few players in the country entered the 2014–15 season with as much hype and promise as Kaminsky. Yet he managed to exceed all of those expectations. Kaminsky was the only player in Division I to average at least 17 points, eight rebounds, two assists, and 1.5 blocks per game. He led the Badgers in points (18.8), rebounds (8.2), assists (103), blocks (57), field-goal percentage (.547), and three-point field-goal percentage (.416).

He became the first Wisconsin basketball player to be named the consensus national player of the year, winning the Wooden Award, the Naismith Trophy, and the Oscar Robertson Trophy. He also earned national player of the year honors from the Associated Press, Sporting News, and *USA Today*, while garnering consensus first-team All-America honors.

Wisconsin, meanwhile, finished the season 36-4, returned to the Final Four, and toppled previously undefeated Kentucky in the national semifinal before losing 68–63 in the championship game to Duke. And Kaminsky was at the center of it all, averaging 22.0 points and 9.3 rebounds during the team's six NCAA tournament games. He became the first player to average a double-double at the Final Four since Carmelo Anthony did it for Syracuse in 2003.

"We were getting a player who we knew was hungry and wanted to prove that he could get to be pretty good," Badgers coach Bo Ryan said during the 2015 Final Four. "We tend to enjoy having those kinds of guys around. But for somebody to go to the level he has, from start to finish—no, I've never had a player like that."

Kaminsky ultimately was drafted ninth overall in the 2015 NBA draft by the Charlotte Hornets—the highest Badgers player taken since Devin Harris went fifth to the Washington Wizards in 2004.

Despite all the attention Kaminsky received for his play, he acted like the same person he was before reaching stardom, when he played high school basketball at Benet Academy in Lisle, Illinois. There, he received few high-major Division I scholarship offers—the others came from Northwestern, DePaul, Northern Illinois, Southern Illinois, and Bradley—and never developed a big head about his talents.

Kaminsky's most memorable off-the-court stories from his senior season at Wisconsin would be better suited for a television sitcom. Some examples:

- He performed a dance battle to the Taylor Swift song "Shake It Off" as part of a sketch comedy video with a student a cappella group, which drew more than 300,000 YouTube views.

- He bought a dog in the final month of his college basketball career and named her Khaleesi after his favorite *Game of Thrones* character.
- He routinely wore a GoPro vest strapped to his chest to chronicle his memorable final year of college. When asked on his senior day why, he simply said, "For the archives." Except he pronounced the word Ar-Chi-Ves, which drew laughter from his teammates seated next to him after the game—part of an inside joke among Badgers players in which they purposely tried to mispronounce easy-sounding words.

Yes, Kaminsky certainly was a one-of-a-kind person. And a once-in-a-generation talent.

"He's a different type of guy," former Wisconsin forward Sam Dekker said. "You've got to take that with a grain of salt. Hopefully it doesn't offend anybody. He's a good guy. He's just a goofball, and he's different than everybody else, and I think that's what makes him good. He's different on the court, different off the court."

Record-Breaker

Badgers center Frank Kaminsky put together a game for the ages on November 19, 2013, at the Kohl Center. He set the team's single-game scoring mark with 43 points against North Dakota, eclipsing the record of 42 points previously shared by Michael Finley (1994 against Eastern Michigan) and Ken Barnes (1965 against Indiana). But the final bucket, a driving shot in the lane with 1:14 remaining, almost didn't happen.

Wisconsin coach Bo Ryan said he had no idea Kaminsky was on the verge of history late in the game. Instead, it was his players on the bench who pleaded with Ryan to allow Kaminsky to re-enter the game while stuck on 41 points as the student section chanted, "We want Frank." Kaminsky exited the contest with 2:03 remaining when Evan Anderson subbed in for him, drawing a chorus of boos. But he returned with 1:27 left and got one more chance to make history.

Ryan said he thought back to his days as a player at Wilkes University in Pennsylvania in 1969 during a game in which he had 43 points and was pulled with four minutes remaining, just shy of the school's single-game scoring record.

"My dad held a grudge against my college coach since 1969," Ryan said of his father, Butch, who passed away at age 89 in 2013. "So I thought about Frank's folks. I'm serious. I thought about his folks. I thought about his friends. And it wasn't like it was a 40-point game. So, one more possession. That's all I said. If the team didn't get him the ball, that was it. And guess what? They got him the ball."

Kaminsky came out of the game for a final time after his basket. With 1:04 remaining, his record night was announced over the public address system, drawing one more standing ovation from the crowd of 16,653 people, who watched a 103–85 Badgers victory.

In the locker room afterward, Ryan—ever the stickler for team play—still found time to razz Kaminsky for not recording a single assist.

"I said sorry," Kaminsky said, "but I didn't mean it."

9 Why Not Wisconsin?

The question had been posed hypothetically in small circles of the media for a few weeks, but no one possessed the audacity to ask players on a Barry Alvarez–coached Wisconsin football team for a response.

The Badgers had been so inept for so long that it seemed almost absurd to contemplate the idea they could actually win a Big Ten championship in 1993. Wisconsin hadn't even produced a winning season since 1984, let alone contended for a conference title. And when Alvarez took over the program in 1990, it stood in complete shambles, a perennial bottom-feeder considered an afterthought in the college football world. During his first season, the Badgers finished 1–10.

"They were a bad program," Alvarez recalled. "It was one of the worst programs in the country at the time. They weren't being run the right way. The athletic department was $2 million in debt. It was bad. It was pathetic. Basketball was bad. Football was terrible. The people running the ship didn't know how to operate at a Big Ten level."

To suggest, then, that Wisconsin could be crowned king of the Big Ten three seasons removed from that mess appeared far-fetched. Although the Badgers began the 1993 campaign undefeated through the month of September and were nationally ranked, they had yet to play Big Ten powerhouses Michigan and Ohio State, which loomed in the coming weeks.

But after Wisconsin's 27–15 victory against Indiana on September 25, a reporter dared broach the subject, finally mustering the courage to ask Badgers right tackle Joe Panos the question on everyone else's mind: "Can Wisconsin win the Big Ten and compete with Michigan and Ohio State?"

Panos provided a short but stern answer that demonstrated the players' beliefs in their talents.

"Why not Wisconsin?"

"Someone has to win the Big Ten Conference title," Panos continued. "It might as well be us."

The rallying cry stands among the most important ever uttered by a Wisconsin football player. In an instant, Panos had let the outside world understand that expectations inside the program already had changed. Settling for mediocrity wasn't enough. And since the Badgers had reached 4–0, they might as well shoot for the moon, win the Big Ten, and reach the Rose Bowl.

"That was the attitude that we had," Panos said. "We were like, 'Why not Wisconsin?' I was just echoing what everyone felt. Like why not us? Who's better than us on paper after the first four games? Who's worked harder than we have? Why can't we win the Big Ten? Now in saying that, I put our neck out on the line. But that's okay. We loved challenges. We weren't being cocky or any-thing. I was just being very truthful. Why not us?"

Wisconsin would go on to defeat Northwestern and Purdue to reach 6–0 before a loss at Minnesota set the Badgers back. But UW churned on, upsetting Michigan at home, tying Ohio State, and then beating Illinois and Michigan State to reach the Rose Bowl. Even today, Alvarez credits Panos for having the fortitude to speak his mind.

"I think that sent a strong message to all the other guys," Alvarez said. "We're not [messing] around. We're pretty good. That was a burden lifted off everyone."

Panos' story typified so much of what made Wisconsin's football program special in those early years. He began his college football career as a defensive tackle at Division III UW-Whitewater before transferring to Wisconsin, a dream spurred on after watching the Badgers play their spring game. He arrived as a non-scholarship player with much to prove and ultimately became an all–Big Ten offensive lineman and a captain on the 1993 Big Ten champion-ship team that defeated UCLA in the Rose Bowl. He was inducted into the school's athletics hall of fame in 2009 and remains one of Alvarez's favorite players because of his blue-collar approach and effectiveness in leading teammates.

"I'm a product of Greek immigrants who didn't have high school educations," said Panos, now a sports agent. "They were self-made people in the restaurant industry. I grew up peeling potatoes and washing pans in the restaurant. So yeah, I fit that mold just fine."

Alvarez trusted Panos enough to police his own teammates that senior year. When Panos learned a teammate burglarized his shared apartment with three other players, he told Alvarez he would take care of it himself so it wouldn't become a team-wide distraction.

"Joe was one of those guys that wasn't afraid to throw somebody up against the wall if they didn't buy into what we were preaching back then," former Wisconsin assistant coach John Palermo said.

His famous words helped galvanize a once-dormant program. And the Badgers carried that can-do mind-set the entire season, all the way to a memorable Rose Bowl victory.

10 1994 Rose Bowl: Darrell Bevell's Run

The most unlikely scamper in Wisconsin football history came from a man whose 40-yard dash time could be clocked with a sundial. But the unexpected nature of the play, coupled with the high stakes, also makes Darrell Bevell's biggest moment as a player a run to remember.

Wisconsin clung to a 14–10 lead against UCLA in the fourth quarter of the 1994 Rose Bowl in a game that already had seen its share of bad blood. Players from both sides were ejected in the third quarter when a fight broke out near the Bruins' sideline. UW lost fullback Mark Montgomery and receiver Lee DeRamus, while UCLA lost defensive backs Donovan Gallatin and Marvin Goodwin. Down two offensive starters, and with the outcome hanging in the balance, Bevell looked to make a play at quarterback.

On a second-and-8 from UCLA's 21-yard line, he dropped back to pass out of a four vertical set after the fullback had been motioned out wide. But he noticed all his receivers were covered on the right side as the pocket collapsed around him.

"As I dropped back, Mike Verstegen on the left side, I don't know if the guy made an inside move on him or what, but I just felt the whole left side cave in," Bevell said. "He kind of pushed him in. It just gave me this lane outside, so I took off.

"As I turned up, I caught J.C. Dawkins coming out of the corner of my eye. I just kind of moved to go behind him. It looked like he was coming to set up a block. Next thing you know, I was in the end zone."

Bevell juked UCLA defensive back Teddy Lawrence and scooted in for the score, prompting radio announcer Brian Manthey to sarcastically remark, "That blazing speed takes him into the end zone!" The play gave Wisconsin a 21–10 edge and caught players from both sides completely off guard.

"The Darrell run in and of itself, I think a lot of us did a double take at each other like, 'Who the heck was that?'" Badgers safety Scott Nelson said. "Then you realize it was Bev, running for his life, running scared, or just running for a dream. Who knew?"

Added former Badgers offensive coordinator Brad Childress, "What an unlikely candidate to take off and run anywhere for any yardage, let alone a 21-yard touchdown run. I've kidded him more than once on that. That's when you knew things were happening the right way, that's for sure."

The play helped validate a Badgers team that felt it had been disrespected in the lead-up to Wisconsin's first Rose Bowl appearance since 1963. Defensive tackle Mike Thompson and nose guard Lamark Shackerford said Bruins players engaged in smack talk, even during joint team events at Disneyland, and the general sentiment was UCLA thought it would walk all over Wisconsin.

Badgers coach Barry Alvarez had other plans and found every advantage he could. He made sure Wisconsin, which was the home team on the scoreboard and therefore picked locker rooms, took UCLA's usual locker room at its own stadium and forced the Bruins to change in the visitor's area. He did not allow UCLA to frighten his team, which had won only a single game three seasons earlier and hadn't played in a bowl of any kind since 1984.

"I'm going to tell you one thing: you're not going to intimidate my guys," Alvarez said. "They'll go to a back alley with anybody. They were not going to be intimidated by guys wearing powder blue uniforms. Are you kidding me?"

Wisconsin defeated UCLA 21–16 to capture the program's first Rose Bowl victory when Bruins quarterback Wayne Cook ran past the line of scrimmage on an inexplicable scramble as time expired. The victory, in front of a tremendously pro-Badgers crowd hungry for a winner, established the start of a two-decade run for the Badgers as a perennial top-25 program. And Bevell's run—the longest of his career—will go down as the most unforgettable play in the program's most important game.

"Being able to run it, it's great to this day because everyone gives me a hard time, talking about how slow I was and all those kinds of things," Bevell said. "But it's great to have a play like that and to be able to get in the end zone.

"Even I knew that it was kind of a special play at that moment, thinking, *Jeez, how in the world did I pull that one off?*"

11 1941 National Champs

On the day Wisconsin's 1940–41 men's basketball team returned home after absorbing a 44–27 drubbing at Minnesota, there was little reason to suspect anything about the Badgers' campaign would be magical. It was January 6, 1941, Wisconsin stood at 5–3, and the Badgers were simply trying to finish with a winning record for the first time in five years.

In what could only be described as a dream season, however, Wisconsin would reel off 15 consecutive wins to capture the program's only basketball national championship—a feat as stunning now as it was then.

Behind the strength of standout players Gene Englund and John Kotz, the Badgers won 12 straight games to win their first undisputed Big Ten championship since 1918. The game that truly showed Wisconsin's strength came when UW secured a 38–30 victory against an Indiana team that featured virtually the same lineup that won the 1940 NCAA championship.

Wisconsin's record was good enough for the Badgers to host the NCAA tournament's Eastern Regional at the UW Field House. In those opening two rounds, Wisconsin defeated Dartmouth 51–50 on March 21 in front of 12,500 fans and then topped Pittsburgh 36–30 the next day in front of 14,000 people. Those victories set the stage for Wisconsin's national championship game appearance against Washington State on March 29, 1941, in Kansas City, Missouri, at Municipal Auditorium.

Washington State was considered a six-point favorite, and a column in the *Kansas City Star* the morning of the title game indicated Wisconsin had little chance to win. The headline read, DON'T GO COUGAR-HUNTING WITH A BADGER.

"Reading the newspapers, it was as though we were only going to Kansas City for the train ride," Englund said. "That riled me up."

The Associated Press game preview noted, "The clubs haven't met a common foe this season but experts name Washington State a slight favorite because of its accomplishments in collecting 1,445 points in 31 games and an average of almost 47.

"Wisconsin has its backers, too, who argue that any team capable of holding 22 assorted opponents to an average of 36.4 points is capable of the best the Pacific Coast conference can offer."

The game provided a duel between two of the nation's best centers: Paul Lindeman of Washington State and Englund of Wisconsin. Lindeman, 6'7" and 230 pounds, had averaged 20 points against Creighton and Arkansas in the Western semifinals the previous week. Englund, a 6'4", 195-pound All-American team captain, had lost the Big Ten scoring lead late in the season to Chicago's Joe Stampf by four points but was voted the conference's Most Valuable Player.

When the national championship game began, Englund had his way with Lindeman, who finished with only three points and missed all five of his field goal attempts thanks to the Badgers' pesky double-teaming of him in the post. Englund scored 13 points, and Kotz—the tournament MVP—added 12, as Wisconsin defeated Washington State 39–34 to capture the title in front of 9,350 fans. The game was an ugly affair, with UW shooting 23.9 percent from the field and Washington State connecting on only 22.2 percent of its field goal tries.

"Boys in other sections of the country seem able to shoot better than boys in the middle west," *Milwaukee Journal* sports writer Oliver Kuechle wrote in his title game recap. "Boys in other sections handle the ball just as well. In team defense, however, they still have a lot to learn."

Kuechle noted that Wisconsin's ride home from the championship game "was like the awakening from a pleasant dream which has suddenly become a reality."

A crowd estimated by police at 12,000 people was at the railroad station shortly after midnight to congratulate the team upon its arrival back in Madison. Only Englund was missing when the squad arrived. He left the team in Chicago to return to his home in Kenosha, Wisconsin, where he would appear before his local draft board.

Though the Wisconsin boxing team returned aboard the same train from its NCAA tournament in State College, Pennsylvania, the reason so many people showed up was clear.

"The crowd began gathering at the state capitol at 11:00 PM, pushing and crowding for vantage points while police good naturedly sought to keep order," the *Journal* wrote. "The train was late, but that did not discourage the students and townspeople who were still cheering three hours later when a red fire truck carried the cagers from the station to the campus."

Although the university's 12:30 AM curfew for female students was pushed back to 1:30, even that deadline was forgotten as hundreds of students trailed with the crowd until nearly 3:00 AM. The train, which was scheduled to arrive at 12:50 AM, did not pull in until 1:30. Shouts of "No school Monday!" went up along the line of the march, but classes continued as scheduled the next day.

"If we had tried to plan a season with the connivance of our opponents, we couldn't have arranged a happier one," Badgers coach Harold "Bud" Foster said. "Nobody gave us a tumble in December. Then we started to develop and win, and frequently, which added spice to the season. We had to win the hard way. These boys really had heart. They deserved everything they won. I am prouder of them than I can say."

12 Wisconsin Topples Unbeaten Kentucky

The vision of 2015 crystallized a year earlier in a somber locker room in Arlington, Texas, where only throbbing heaves of weeping teammates disturbed the silence. Wisconsin's basketball team had lost to Kentucky by a single point in a national semifinal game at the 2014 Final Four, and through the pain, a resolute determination rose above the surface.

"After that loss, we really didn't speak much," Badgers forward Nigel Hayes said. "But we all looked at one another saying we would definitely be back."

Thus began a long and arduous process. Wisconsin's two best players, Frank Kaminsky and Sam Dekker, announced they would bypass the NBA draft and return for another year. And with the knowledge the Badgers would possess perhaps the most talented and experienced team in school history, the entire group rallied around the idea that it could achieve something truly meaningful by banding together and playing for each other.

Players wanted their moment, craved another chance to prove their worth in the postseason. And that moment finally arrived on April 4, 2015, in a highly anticipated Final Four rematch against unbeaten Kentucky—a team on the verge of a season unlike any in decades.

But in quite possibly the program's most significant game, Wisconsin's players delivered a masterpiece, coming from behind in the final minutes to edge Kentucky 71–64 at Lucas Oil Stadium in Indianapolis to derail perfection. UW advanced to face Duke in the national championship—the Badgers' first title game appearance since 1941.

"I truly believed that we were going to win," Badgers guard Josh Gasser said afterward. "Kentucky, they're the best team all year long. There's no denying that. But I knew on this night we were going to be better. I believed it. I told the guys that. They believed it. And when you have that mind-set, special things can happen."

Kentucky entered the night 38–0 and had its own visions of polishing off the first Division I undefeated season in 39 years. But the Wildcats also had demonstrated during the NCAA tournament they were fallible, narrowly escaping Notre Dame by two points in the Elite Eight. The magnitude of the moment, this time played out in front of 72,238 fans, seemed to seep in as the game wound toward a close.

"They had everything to lose, really, being unbeaten," Wisconsin point guard Bronson Koenig said. "But we didn't really look at it like that, as them never being beaten before. They've been in such close games, so we just looked at it as another game, another opportunity to prove ourselves."

For a stretch, it appeared the Wildcats would do what they had done all season—find a way to pull away from a team that managed to hang close for more than 30 minutes. When Kentucky center Karl-Anthony Towns buried a turnaround inside with 6:37 remaining, the Wildcats led 60–56, and the wheels on Wisconsin's magical season wobbled.

That's when Dekker scored on a strong drive to the hoop to bring UW to within two points—the start of an 8–0 run that changed the entire course of the game and history. Hayes followed by tying the score at 60 on a layup as the shot clock expired in one of the more controversial calls of the game. Kentucky players pleaded for a shot-clock violation, but 2:35 remained, and video reviews on plays couldn't be made until the clock ticked under two minutes.

For five consecutive possessions, Kentucky's high-powered offense came up empty, three times forcing shots late in the shot clock. During that stretch, Dekker, the West Region's most outstanding player, buried a straight-on three with 1:44 left to give Wisconsin a 63–60 lead—the Badgers' first advantage in nearly eight minutes.

"Off my hand, I knew it was down," Dekker said. "I was waiting for a good look like that all night."

Kentucky's talented team would not go away, of course. Guard Aaron Harrison—the late-game hero in Kentucky's Final Four win against Wisconsin one year earlier—trimmed the deficit to 64–63 on a three-point play with 56.2 seconds left. But Kaminsky was fouled on a spin move to the basket with 24.5 seconds remaining and buried two free throws. Kentucky could not inch closer than two points, and Wisconsin washed the game away at the free throw line.

The fact Badgers players were involved in a similar scenario a year earlier and couldn't close the deal was not lost on them.

"Being in this situation before, we knew what to expect," Badgers forward Duje Dukan said. "Last year we were I guess babies to the situation. We didn't know how to handle it. I think this year we were more so on a mission."

Kentucky head coach John Calipari pointed out his team committed only six turnovers, shot 90 percent from the free throw line, 60 percent from the three-point line, and 48 percent from the field—statistics that likely would have been good enough to beat any other team in America.

"And we lost?" he said. "What does that mean they did? We struggled to guard them… It was the rebounding and the toughness and the plays around the goal."

One of the central themes entering the game was the stark contrast in styles between Kentucky and Wisconsin. The Wildcats possessed a starting five with height that rivaled most NBA teams and had nine more McDonald's All-Americans than Wisconsin—which is to say the Badgers did not have any on their team. Calipari had made a habit of bringing in the best players in the country for a single season as a stopgap between the NBA, while Badgers coach Bo Ryan's methods focused on development of players over four and five seasons.

"People can say what they want about we don't have X number of All-Americans, we don't have this," Ryan said. "I've never in life looked at what you don't have. I've always looked at what we do have and what can we do with it."

As the final seconds ticked off, Wisconsin's student section behind the south basket began chanting "Thirty-eight and done." Dekker raised his arms to the Wisconsin fans, as did Kaminsky and Hayes, who leapt up and down as though he were performing jumping jacks. The entire team burst off the bench and onto the raised court platform to revel in a monumental victory.

It was a performance one year in the making. And though the Badgers would fall one game short of winning the championship, ultimately losing to Duke two days later, the Kentucky game would prove to be the defining victory in the most memorable Wisconsin basketball season in history.

13 Mark Johnson

Navigating an adolescent life as a coach's son required patience and mental fortitude. Possessing plenty of talent didn't hurt Mark Johnson, either. Still, no matter what Johnson achieved as a high school standout in Madison, there were opposing fans across the Midwest who couldn't wait to taunt him upon his arrival as a freshman on Wisconsin's men's hockey team.

Johnson had grown up around the game, watching his father, known as "Badger Bob," revitalize the Badgers' hockey program as head coach. It was the only college Mark ever seriously considered, and when he showed up on campus in 1976, he had earned the opportunity to play for Bob based entirely on merit as a hockey player.

Fans, however, were dubious. Or, at the very least, they wanted an excuse to jeer someone they believed represented an easy target.

"Especially my first year, a lot of the visiting fans would always indicate that the only reason I was around was because my dad was behind the bench coaching the team," Johnson said. "The best way to offset those things is to go on the ice and play well and help your team win."

Over the next few months, that's exactly what he did. Johnson became the first Wisconsin player ever to win Western Collegiate Hockey Association rookie of the year honors and was essential in helping the Badgers capture the 1977 national championship. He scored two goals in Wisconsin's 6–5 overtime victory against Michigan in the title game, solidifying his status as one of the most clutch players in program history.

By the time his three-year Badgers career was over, Johnson had become the school's second all-time leading scorer with 256 points on a program-record 125 goals and 131 assists. He was the conference's most valuable player in 1979 and a two-time first-team All-American. He was later selected as one of the WCHA's Top 50 Players in 50 Years.

Johnson opted to bypass his senior year to pursue the opportunity of a lifetime— becoming a member of the 1980 U.S. Olympic men's hockey team under coach Herb Brooks. It was a dream Johnson had been chasing for four years. He had played in 11 training games for the 1976 Olympic team as a high school senior on a squad coached by his father. He wasn't quite ready for the challenge of international competition, however, and Bob cut him from the team over dinner one Sunday night.

"I wouldn't say it was a very good meal," Mark Johnson said. "The food might've been good. It certainly was the right choice. The pressure of coaching an Olympic team is in itself a challenge. So to have one of your kids a part of that team would make it much more challenging."

By 1980, Johnson was a force few countries could reckon with. And as he did during Wisconsin's 1977 national title run, he became an important piece to a team that made international sporting history. In one of the most famous contests of the last century, a United States team filled with amateur players defeated the seemingly unbeatable Soviet Union team full of professionals 4–3 in the semifinal of the Olympic Games held in Lake Placid, New York. The ending prompted a well-known call by television broadcaster Al Michaels, who exclaimed, "Do you believe in miracles? Yes!"

"It's tough to forget the magnitude of the game and of the event," said Johnson, who scored two goals against the Soviets. "It just became bigger than life."

Johnson scored a goal and assisted on the game-winning score against Finland two days later to help the United States capture an improbable gold medal. In total, Johnson led the Americans with 11 points (five goals, six assists). Team captain Mike Eruzione told the *New York Daily News* that Johnson was "the best player and most important player on our team. We don't win without Mark…. In order for us to win, Mark had to be Mark. And he was. When we needed big goals, Mark scored them."

That United States team inspired the 2004 Disney movie *Miracle*, which vaulted Johnson into greater fame than he had ever experienced.

"When the movie came out, it went to a whole new level," Johnson said. "Because now people that weren't even of age to watch those games in 1980 see it on the big screen. Kids of all ages and actually parents, too, will come up and indicate that they've watched the movie 50 or 60 times and just love it. They think it's a great piece of work. It happens pretty regularly."

Johnson eventually played professional hockey for five NHL teams and retired in 1990. From 1996 to 2002, he served as an assistant coach for the Badgers men's hockey team. When Johnson was overlooked for the head coaching job in 2002 in favor of former Badgers hockey great Mike Eaves, he took a new path. Wisconsin's women's hockey program needed a head coach, and Johnson was the person for the job—a position he continues to hold.

Like his father, Johnson is molding the talents of college hockey players at Wisconsin. And, like his father, he is doing so while helping teams play at their highest level. Since Johnson became the women's coach, the Badgers have won four NCAA championships.

"As I look back on it now, it's been nothing but wonderful memories," Johnson said. "I'm certainly very happy that I was able to get a chance to do it."

Athlete Profile: Mike Eaves

As 1–2 scoring combinations go, you'd be hard-pressed to find a better hockey duo than Mike Eaves and Mark Johnson, whose careers overlapped for two successful seasons from 1976 to '78. Eaves and Johnson were the catalysts for the Badgers' 1977 national title, and they remained connected for years afterward.

During that 1977 championship season, Eaves was a junior and Johnson a freshman. Eaves finished with 28 goals and 53 assists for 81 points, while Johnson tallied 36 goals and 44 assists for 80 points. Eaves assisted on three goals in the title game, including the game winner just 23 seconds into overtime, a 6–5 victory against Michigan. In 1978, Eaves totaled 89 points to Johnson's 86.

Eaves finished his four-year, 160-game career as the school's all-time leading scorer with 267 points (94 goals, 173 assists), and he still holds that mark today. Johnson played in 125 games over three years and is second on the all-time list with his 256 points.

Eaves played 324 games over eight seasons in the NHL with Minnesota and Calgary. He returned to Wisconsin to take over as the men's hockey coach in 2002, earning the job over other candidates that included Johnson. Although many thought Johnson and Eaves might become bitter rivals, the two forged a strong bond. Their sons, both named Patrick, were even baptized together.

"There's great history there and we've been able to work through what some may have perceived as an awkward situation," Eaves told the *Wisconsin State Journal* in 2006. "Our friendship has continued on."

Eaves coached the Badgers from 2002 to '16, winning a national championship in 2006 and returning to the title game in 2010.

14 1999 Rose Bowl: "We're at Least the Second Worst"

A defining characteristic of the Barry Alvarez era at Wisconsin was his ability to create motivational ploys before a big game.

He certainly didn't have to look far in the days leading up to Wisconsin's Rose Bowl appearance against UCLA in 1999.

Thanks to an unusual and antiquated tie-breaking rule, Wisconsin was awarded the Rose Bowl over co–Big Ten champions Michigan and Ohio State because the two other teams had played in the game more recently. All three teams finished 7–1 in league play, with Ohio State beating Michigan and Michigan cruising past Wisconsin. UW and Ohio State did not play each other that season. Many believed the Badgers were only the third-best team in the Big Ten, and they entered the Rose Bowl as double-digit underdogs.

For those reasons, CBS college football analyst Craig James famously uttered a line that would stick with the Badgers long after the game ended: "Wisconsin is the worst team to ever play in the Rose Bowl."

Why did any of the Badgers care what an announcer with no affiliation to Wisconsin said?

"Respect," defensive end Tom Burke said. "Full respect."

It was a week full of slights for the Badgers, and Burke was in the center of the storm. UCLA head coach Bob Toledo inadvertently referred to Burke, a Badgers All-American lineman, as "Tom Barnes," prompting some Wisconsin players to interpret the slip as a sign nobody was taking them seriously.

"I apologized to him," Toledo said before the game. "He said, 'That's okay, Coach Rogers.'"

Fifth-year Badgers senior safety Leonard Taylor told the *Los Angeles Times* his Rose Bowl experience had been soured by ignorance about Wisconsin and rudeness on the part of Californians he had met. Taylor said he had to defend himself at a club when a patron tried to pick a fight with him. And he noted when the Badgers attended a luncheon for both teams at Universal Studios, they had to wait 15 or 20 minutes for the Bruins to arrive—then watched hungrily while restaurant staffers served the Bruins first.

Even after players from both sides toured Universal Studios, the bus driver told his passengers, "I'd like to thank UCLA for being here and I'd like to thank the other team."

As if those stories weren't enough, Alvarez recalled another one that particularly irked him in the build-up to the game. Actor William Shatner stood up and rooted for UCLA to beat Wisconsin at a black-tie event in which both teams attended.

"Damn it, you can't say something like that," Alvarez relayed years later to reporter Mike Lucas for the school's website, *UWBadgers.com*. "I was ticked. The next day at a luncheon, Shatner walked up to me and handed me his autographed picture. I didn't ask for it, and I didn't want the damn thing. So I crumpled it up and threw it at his feet and walked away."

Needless to say, Wisconsin was ready for a football game when kickoff arrived. The Badgers certainly played accordingly, and their top-rated defense excelled in the fourth quarter with the game on the line. UCLA set a Rose Bowl record with 538 yards of total offense but could not capitalize late.

When Badgers freshman Wendell Bryant sacked UCLA quarterback Cade McNown on fourth-and-3 at the Wisconsin 47-yard line with 59 seconds left, Wisconsin finally preserved a 38–31 victory. Earlier in the quarter, Badgers cornerback Jamar Fletcher intercepted McNown for a game-clinching 46-yard touchdown, which made the score 38–28.

"I think we proved that we can play with the big boys," Fletcher said, "and are good enough to deserve to be in the Rose Bowl."

In the game, Badgers running back Ron Dayne played through the pain of a torn pectoral muscle and bone chip to destroy the UCLA defense. He finished with 27 carries and 246 yards, a yard short of Charles White's Rose Bowl rushing record set for USC in 1980. Dayne also scored four touchdowns on runs of 54, 7, 10, and 22 yards to tie a modern Rose Bowl record.

Toledo joked earlier in the week that the Bruins' defense practiced defending Dayne by tackling pickup trucks. But nothing could slow the "Dayne Train."

UCLA had been in the hunt for a national championship less than a month earlier, until losing 49–45 against Miami in a rescheduled game to end the regular season. Instead, the once 10–0 Bruins finished the season 10–2. Wisconsin, meanwhile, closed the season 11–1 with a No. 6 Associated Press national ranking and captured its second of three Rose Bowl victories under Alvarez.

As for that charge James had made about Wisconsin's place as the worst team in Rose Bowl history? Alvarez was quick to offer a rebuttal.

"We're at least the second worst!" he quipped.

15 2000 Rose Bowl: Dayne Goes Out with a Bang

By the time Wisconsin arrived to play Stanford in the 2000 Rose Bowl, much of the pomp and circumstance surrounding Ron Dayne's Heisman Trophy–winning season had subsided. He'd faced intense media exposure the past two months in the buildup to the announcement, and now, the national media had turned its attention to championship contenders in the Sugar Bowl and the Fiesta Bowl.

Finally, 49 days after Wisconsin's last game, Dayne could focus strictly on football. And Stanford could focus strictly on him.

"No one to my knowledge has stopped Ron Dayne," Stanford coach Tyrone Willingham said before the game.

For one half, the Cardinals managed to pull off what had seemed impossible. Stanford's defense, which ranked as the fifth-worst in the NCAA, held Dayne to a mere 46 yards rushing, 20 of which came on one carry. The halftime score: Stanford 9, Wisconsin 3. For a Badgers team that had averaged 38 points per game the past seven contests on their way to seven straight wins, the result was stunning.

"We had a nice talk, a nice little calm talk at halftime, and everybody got more motivated," Dayne deadpanned afterward. "I think that really gave us momentum, and we just carried on. It would have been nice if we could have scored some more, so we wouldn't have had to bite our nails at the end."

Dayne's storybook career would not end without him writing one more magical chapter. He broke loose for a 64-yard run on the second play after halftime and scored a 1-yard touchdown two plays later, as Wisconsin came back to beat Stanford 17–9. He simply could not be stopped, gaining 154 of his 200 yards in that second half on his way to picking up a second straight Rose Bowl MVP award. In doing so, Dayne joined USC's Charles White and Washington's Bob Schloredt as the only players to win consecutive Rose Bowl MVP honors.

The game proved to be the lowest-scoring Rose Bowl since 1977, and Badgers coach Barry Alvarez attributed some of Wisconsin's inconsistent play to rust. Wisconsin had not played a game since November 13, when Dayne broke the NCAA career rushing record in a 41–3 victory against Iowa at Camp Randall Stadium.

"We had a long layoff after that last game, and it took us a little while to get in a rhythm," Alvarez said. "Big 33 [Dayne] got lathered up a little bit, and that seemed to help a little."

The fourth-quarter drive that put the game away for Wisconsin began with Dayne at Stanford's 40-yard line. Dayne gained six yards on his first carry and two on his second before Stanford's Marc Stockbauer stopped him short of a first down on his third run. On fourth-and-two, Wisconsin quarterback Brooks Bollinger rolled out and hit tight end John Sigmund for a seven-yard gain and a first down. Dayne then helped Wisconsin reach inside the 1, when Bollinger kept the ball on a quarterback sneak for a touchdown.

Stanford had a chance to tie the score with 2:19 left, but the team's two-minute offense sputtered amid a flurry of penalties. Stanford quarterback Todd Husak slipped and fell on fourth down on the team's final offensive play. Wisconsin finished the season 10–2 and became the first Big Ten team to win back-to-back Rose Bowls.

"There is nothing like doing something no one else has done," Alvarez said. "Not many people have an opportunity in their lifetime to do something like that. To do it really makes me proud."

Dayne's college football career came full circle that day. Four seasons earlier, the breakout game that turned him into an eventual star came as a freshman against Stanford on September 21, 1996. He gained 75 yards on 12 carries in a 14–0 victory and quickly became the Badgers' featured tailback. He had opened the season third on Wisconsin's depth chart behind Carl McCullough and Aaron Stecker.

Dayne admitted years later at a Big Ten Fanfest event before the 2011 Big Ten championship game that he considered transferring to Michigan State his freshman season because of his initial lack of playing time. According to the *Milwaukee Journal Sentinel,* an uncle convinced him to stay.

"I guess it worked out pretty good," Dayne said.

16 Bucky Badger

The name William "Bill" Sachse might not ring a bell with the modern-day University of Wisconsin student or fan. Without his contributions, however, Wisconsin's school mascot might still be a real-life badger, small in stature, antisocial, and replete with all the charisma and charm of a cheese curd.

Sachse (pronounced *Socks-e*) is the man responsible for replacing the animal with Bucky Badger, a costume worn by humans who have pumped up Wisconsin's crowd at sporting events since 1949. As homecoming chairman at UW-Madison that year, he sought an alternative for the furry fellow who simply didn't do much to inspire fans and often escaped the control of handlers.

"Once you dragged him out of the runway [in the stadium], he'd immediately start burying into the turf on the field to hide," Sachse said of the original mascot in a 1999 *Wisconsin State Journal* story. "That was the badger's disposition, and we couldn't change that."

Then Sachse hatched an idea while eating dinner in the student union one day.

"I saw a display of papier-mâché African masks and I thought, *Why not a papier-mâché head of a badger?*" he said.

Sachse tracked down an art student named Carolyn [Connie] Conrad, who designed the first modern Bucky mascot with chicken wire and papier-mâché. Initially, Bucky also donned a pair of boxing gloves to honor the school's national championship boxing program. When Bucky was first introduced at a pep rally, which included new football coach Ivy Williamson, more than 1,000 people showed up for support.

Gymnast and cheerleader Bill Sagal, a Plymouth, Wisconsin, native, was directed by Sachse to wear the outfit at the homecoming game. At that time, the badger went by names like Benny, Buddy, Bernie, Bobby, and Bouncey. But following a contest staged to name the mascot, Buckingham U. Badger, or Bucky, was selected as the winner. The name may have come from a song lyric that encouraged the football team to "buck right through that line."

The nickname Badgers dates back well before Bucky came into existence. Wisconsin was named the "Badger State" because of an association of lead miners in the 1820s, who were said to have lived like

Bucky Badger is a fan favorite whether he's cheering on men's and women's hoops or doing pushups at a football game. Interacting with Bucky Badger is an essential part of the Wisconsin experience.

badgers in tunnels burrowed into hillsides in the winter. The badger has been Wisconsin's official mascot since the inception of intercollegiate football in 1889. And the version that is currently known as Bucky, wearing a cardinal-and-white sweater, was first drawn in 1940 by professional illustrator Art Evans of Garden Grove, California.

In the years since Sachse's decision, one failed attempt to overthrow Bucky Badger as the school mascot has been made. In 1973, assistant attorney general Howard Koop suggested Bucky be replaced by Henrietta Holstein, a lovable and productive cow. Koop argued that "kids love cows. A generation could grow up supporting the university and Henrietta Holstein."

Fortunately for everyone else, the cow idea was put out to pasture. The Badgers remained. Sachse graduated with a business degree from the university in 1950 and died in 2012 at age 85, and his legacy continues to endure.

17 Dick Bennett

For years, Dick Bennett clung to a dream of some day coaching the Wisconsin Badgers basketball program. He had spent most of his life in the Badger State—he was raised in Clintonville, graduated college in Ripon, and had coaching stops at high schools in West Bend, Mineral Point, Marion, New London, and Eau Claire and at colleges in Stevens Point and Green Bay.

It was a path, Bennett had always hoped, that would help lead him to Madison. Instead, despite all of his coaching success, the dream he held simmered. It sputtered. It darn near died.

"I sorta gave up on it," Bennett once told the *Chicago Tribune.* "I just assumed I would not ever get the job."

Bennett had first applied for the vacant Badgers coaching position in 1976, after he led Eau Claire Memorial High to a runner-up finish in the state tournament. Bill Cofield was hired instead. Bennett applied again in 1982 after helping to turn around the University of Wisconsin–Stevens Point from a nine-win NAIA team his first season to a 22-win team that tied for first place in its conference. Steve Yoder was hired instead.

Bennett applied once more in 1992 after guiding UW–Green Bay from a four-win season the year before he arrived to the program's first NCAA tournament appearance. Stu Jackson was hired instead. In 1994, after Jackson left to become general manager of the NBA expansion Vancouver Grizzlies, Stan Van Gundy was hired as his replacement. Bennett was not considered for the job.

At that point, Bennett and his wife, Anne, assumed they were destined to remain in Green Bay. They built a dream house together and settled in for the long haul. But that was before Van Gundy underachieved in one season at Wisconsin with future NBA standout Michael Finley in 1994–95. Wisconsin finished the season 13–14, with a 7–11 Big Ten record only good enough for ninth place in the league. Van Gundy was fired, and suddenly Bennett had become athletics director Pat Richter's top choice for the job.

Bennett wasn't sure he could take the job because of his rapport with players at Green Bay. He had won at least 18 games in six of his last eight seasons there. His 1994 team upset Jason Kidd's California team in the opening round of the NCAA tournament, and the Phoenix returned to the big dance again in 1995, losing 49–48 to Purdue in the opening round.

Purdue coach Gene Keady's praise for Bennett's possible ascension into the Big Ten coaching ranks was effusive. "We'd be in trouble," Keady said. "Now, instead of having nine, 10 teams go for the title, you'd have to add another one.... He would make them a contender."

Richter, who noted, "Keady's reaction said it all," refused to take no for an answer from Bennett. He told Bennett to speak to his Green Bay players, who helped convince him to make his long-time dream of coaching at Wisconsin a reality—finally.

"I told myself if I didn't take the opportunity, I'd have to live with it," Bennett said. "If I went down there and failed, at least I did what I wanted to do. Put your money where your mouth is."

Bennett's style never was about flash or an up-and-down game, and it took time for Badgers players to understand the importance of his principles. He preached defense more than most and demanded players to be patient offensively, to set screens and milk the shot clock for quality shots. Though some of his players were initially resistant to the change—one player once told Bennett in a closed-door meeting he was a scorer, not a screener—the system began to take shape.

Wisconsin reached the NCAA tournament in Bennett's second season. The Badgers returned again in 1999—the program's first year with at least 20 victories. But Bennett's crowning achievement came in 2000, when Wisconsin's grind-it-out style saw the Badgers make a magical run to the Final Four as a No. 8 seed in the NCAA tournament.

"I've always been happy coaching basketball and being a part of my players' lives in Wisconsin," he said during that Final Four week. "I always said that I hoped they would let me coach somewhere in Wisconsin. As long as I could find a job, I'd be happy."

Bennett contemplated retiring after the Final Four run but opted to return. Three games into the 2001 season, however, he retired, citing burnout. He was drained and had begun to notice he could not put forth the effort necessary to keep Wisconsin successful, noting he no longer called players in their dorm rooms or was willing to spend extra hours in the gym with them. Assistant Brad Soderberg, who played for Bennett at UW–Stevens Point in the early 1980s, was hired as acting coach.

"Like a musician who first knows himself when that ability to play that instrument is suffering, it doesn't take long for his audience to realize it," Bennett said upon retirement. "And I thought it was going to be obvious pretty soon that I don't have the drive that I once did.

"But I got caught up like everyone else did in the euphoria of the Final Four, and I thought maybe I could just kind of keep rolling along here."

In five-plus seasons at Wisconsin, Bennett's record was 93–69. Wisconsin went to three NCAA tournaments in his five years after going just three times in program history before he arrived. His final two teams were the two winningest in school history at the time.

18 Melvin Gordon

It was a sunny mid-June day, and Melvin Gordon lounged on the patio at Wisconsin's Union South, wearing a Badgers football T-shirt, shorts, and sandals. He placed his cell phone on a table and briefly put the world on hold while he discussed what it was like living in a football purgatory of sorts.

Gordon, Wisconsin's standout running back, had spent his summer watching NFL Network on television daily, and when he heard the names of the league's latest rookies, he couldn't help but wonder what would happen when those pundits were talking about him. Each new mock draft prediction for 2015 trickled into Gordon's Twitter mentions because followers notified him whenever his name was included. Sports agents continued calling his mother, Carmen, to be first in line when he finally required representation.

It was too late to turn back on his decision to forego the NFL draft, too soon to prove on the field why he returned in 2014 for his redshirt junior season. Fall camp hovered in the distance, more than a month and a half away. All Gordon could do was try and block out the noise ahead of one of the most highly anticipated seasons by a running back in school history.

So much potential. So much hype. So much at stake for a career and a life.

"I want to leave something here," Gordon said that day. "I just don't want to be another guy that comes through Wisconsin. I want to be remembered like Montee [Ball], James [White], and Ron Dayne. All those other guys behind them. It's all about leaving a legacy."

In the end, it's hard to fathom Gordon could have achieved any more than he did. In 2014, he put together one of the finest seasons

Melvin Gordon, who was drafted by the San Diego Chargers in the first round of the 2015 NFL draft, finished second in the Heisman Trophy voting during his junior season.

in the history of college football—one that will be remembered long after his NFL career concludes.

With a blend of power, speed, and agility never before seen at Wisconsin, Gordon ran for 2,587 yards, a Big Ten record and the second-most in Football Bowl Subdivision history (trailing only Barry Sanders, who gained 2,628 yards for Oklahoma State in 1988). He led the nation in rushing at 184.8 yards per game and became the fastest player in FBS history to reach 2,000 yards, doing so on his 241st carry of the season.

So many games stood out in Gordon's career. As a redshirt freshman in 2012, he famously ran for 216 yards with a touchdown on only nine carries against Nebraska in the Big Ten championship game. In 2014, he ran for 254 yards and five touchdowns against Bowling Green, 259 yards against Northwestern, and then briefly set the FBS single-game rushing record with 408 yards against Nebraska in only three quarters.

Gordon would set the FBS career rushing average record with 7.79 yards per carry behind the strength of 22 100-yard rushing games and seven 200-yard games. He also would finish runner-up for the Heisman Trophy, only the fourth finalist in Badgers history.

It's no wonder, then, why Barry Alvarez heaped on so much praise for Gordon before the team's Outback Bowl game against Auburn.

"I'll remember him as probably the best back that ever came through here, and that's saying a lot," Alvarez said. "But he can do it all. He combines power with a great burst. He can make you miss. He's one of a kind. All the great ones that we had, had different styles. He's got his own style of running. Great kid. Somebody that's just fun to be around."

Alvarez, who coached Dayne during a stellar four-year career that resulted in a Heisman Trophy and two Rose Bowl victories, said he had no problem acknowledging Gordon was even better than Dayne.

"I have no reservations," Alvarez said. "Ronnie would probably tell you, too."

In his final game before officially entering the NFL draft, Gordon once again showed why he was as good as anybody in the nation. He ran for an Outback Bowl–record 251 yards and three touchdowns to help Wisconsin beat Auburn 34–31 in overtime, the Badgers' first bowl victory since 2009. Gordon was named the game's most valuable player, and Wisconsin closed the season 11–3.

Gordon certainly could have left school one year earlier and been rewarded with a nice NFL contract. Some scouts, in fact, surmised he would have been the very first running back taken in the 2014 NFL draft. Instead, Gordon chose to stay after submitting his name for a grade with the NFL's draft advisory board. It wasn't about the Heisman Trophy chase, he said, or the pursuit of records. He wanted to earn more credits toward his degree, to be a team leader, to become an even better player and, ultimately, to help Wisconsin win.

After he had finished his last game, Gordon could check nearly all his goals off the list. Not a single regret lingered. He had left a legacy few could ever match.

"Looking back, a lot of people probably thought it was the wrong decision and a lot of people thought I should have left," said Gordon, who would be taken No. 15 overall in the first round by the San Diego Chargers in the 2015 NFL draft. "I think I became a better player overall, so I did the things I needed to do, and I feel like this year was a success."

19 The 2000 Final Four Run

Ohio State coach Jim O'Brien perhaps best summed up what it was like playing Wisconsin's 1999–2000 basketball team when he compared the experience to "a trip to the dentist—without anesthesia."

Over the years, Wisconsin's basketball program has developed a reputation as hard-nosed, blue-collar, tough-as-nails and every other clichéd term you can think of for an underappreciated, overachieving group of players. But Badgers coach Dick Bennett's 2000 team epitomized all those traits better than just about any UW bunch before or after, taking a perfectly mediocre group at mid-season all the way to the school's first Final Four in 59 years.

On February 19, 2000, Wisconsin lost 59–54 at Michigan State to drop to 13–12 on the season. A third NCAA tournament appearance in five seasons under Bennett seemed highly unlikely with the Badgers mired near the bottom of the Big Ten at just 5–8. But Wisconsin closed the regular season with three straight wins to finish sixth in the league, and two more victories in the Big Ten tournament helped the Badgers squeeze into the NCAA tournament as a No. 8 seed at 18–13.

Then, over the course of two weeks, UW made history, using a suffocating defense to fuel the team to four straight wins in the Big Dance. First, Wisconsin handled Fresno State 66–56. Badgers defensive stalwart Mike Kelley held Fresno State's Courtney Alexander, the nation's leading scorer, to 11 points—nearly 15 below his average.

In the Round of 32, Wisconsin lured another fast-paced team into playing its methodical, slow-down style and upset top-seeded Arizona 66–59 to advance to the Sweet 16. To that point, the Badgers hadn't won a second-round game since the NCAA tournament went to the 64-team format 15 years earlier.

"They accepted the game plan and employed it as close to perfect as humanly possible," Bennett said afterward.

When Wisconsin toppled LSU in the Sweet 16 and Purdue in the Elite Eight—holding the Boilermakers without a field goal for nearly six minutes late in the game—the Badgers became the lowest-seeded team to advance to the Final Four since 1986.

"I've always preached defense and felt it was supposed to be at least 50 percent of the game," Bennett said after Wisconsin stunned Purdue 64–60. "But the focus and attention almost always goes to offense. You learn to live with that and eventually you have your day in the sun like this, and you enjoy it."

Wisconsin's team was by no means a typical Final Four squad. Only one player, 6'9", 235-pound junior forward Mark Vershaw, averaged double figures in scoring that season. Andy Kowske was the only other player to average even nine points. Wisconsin's go-to scorer in the Elite Eight game, Jon Bryant, was a Division II transfer from St. Cloud State who arrived at Wisconsin as a walk-on and wondered whether he'd ever earn a chance to play in that kind of game. He scored 18 points and drilled five three-pointers against Purdue.

"What we're proving is that basketball is a team sport," Vershaw said. "If it were an individual game, I think a lot of us would be playing in the YMCA right now."

One of the faces of the team—Kelley—was someone who would much rather force an opposing player into a poor shooting effort for the good of the team than earn individual praise. Kelley, once the Big Ten's defensive player of the year, held Purdue shooter Jaraan Cornell to just 1-of-9 shooting to help Wisconsin reach the Final Four.

"I don't set out to get into anybody's head, but I do set out to be a pest," Kelley said. "I want to be there in front of you as much as I can so that you're so sick of me, you'll pass the ball."

In the week leading up to the Final Four game against Michigan State, the Badgers were described as a throwback team to a different era that didn't have the star power of the remaining teams in the field. There was no Wisconsin player on any of the six media and coaches' all-conference teams. There wasn't even a Badgers player listed among the honorable mentions. They were labeled in the *Pittsburgh Post-Gazette* as "old school, playing the game the way your grandfather did. Bounce passes, teeth-rattling screens, high-percentage looks at the basket and defense with pride, passion, and purpose. They are Princeton with more talent."

"There's no one on this team that the best programs in the country would waste a recruiting visit on," wrote *Post-Gazette* writer Bob Smizik. For that reason, Smizik also noted Bennett deserved to be the coach of the year.

"He has taken an athletically challenged team and made it play his way, which is the only way the Badgers could have made it this far."

Bennett, for his part, made no apologies for his style of play, which many considered to be boring.

"I've always coached the same way," Bennett said during Final Four week. "It was not until recently that I learned I had set basketball back."

Added Kelley: "Nobody wants to lose to Wisconsin. Nobody thinks they will lose to Wisconsin. There's not a lot of glory beating us."

Wisconsin ran out of magic in the national semifinal, falling 53–41 to Michigan State. It marked the Badgers' fourth loss that season to the Spartans, who would go on to capture the championship two nights later.

20 Bo Honors Butch

He would've danced the night away in the team locker room like a college kid, tears welling over his eyes and spilling uncontrollably down his cheeks. Those who knew William "Butch" Ryan well were certain of it. He would've embraced his son, tussled his hair, and told him how proud he was of perhaps the greatest accomplishment of his lengthy coaching career.

During the minutes after No. 2 seed Wisconsin had outlasted No. 1 seed Arizona in overtime 64–63 in the most thrilling, back-and-forth, edge-of-your-seat game of the 2014 NCAA tournament, Bo Ryan's thoughts were a muddled mess. In his 13th year at Wisconsin, the Badgers had finally advanced to the Final Four, relinquishing Ryan of the title as the best active coach never to reach the last weekend of the college basketball season.

It was a moment in time Ryan had always hoped to share with his closest friend and confidant. But Bo's biggest fan was not in the stands. His father had passed away at age 89 the previous August.

So Wisconsin players danced without him, surrounding Bo on the Honda Center court in Anaheim, California. They donned gray hats and T-shirts that read "Net Worthy," as champions of the West Region, and took turns cutting down strands of the hoop. They saved the last snip for Ryan, while the crowd chanted, "Bo, Bo, Bo."

Up in the second deck, someone held a sign that read simply: "This one's for Butch."

As he walked off the floor, Bo Ryan clutched the net tightly in his left hand, pumped his right fist and strolled to the locker room. He told his players, as he did often during the Badgers' remarkable run to their first Final Four since 2000, of his pride in their performance and thanked them for allowing him the opportunity to coach for another 40 minutes.

And then, Bo couldn't help but think of Butch.

"Just so you guys know," he said to his team, "this would have been my dad's 90th birthday."

"He had a little tear in his eyes," Badgers forward Sam Dekker said afterward. "So you know his dad was smiling down on him at that time."

If one truly believes in cosmic forces beyond the control of human beings, Wisconsin's Elite Eight performance on March 29, 2014, seemed to represent a pretty good example of such a case. Arizona, which entered the game 33–4, possessed more athletes and, on paper, presented the toughest defense Wisconsin's 29–7 squad would see to that point of the season.

Yet it was the Badgers who proved up to the task in the biggest game of the year, overcoming an intensely pro-Arizona crowd and the play of standout big men Aaron Gordon (eight points, 18 rebounds) and Kaleb Tarczewski (12 points), along with Pac-12 Player of the Year Nick Johnson (16 points).

Wisconsin never led in the first half but managed to enter halftime trailing just 28–25. UW took its first lead at 36–34 with 15 minutes left in the game on a Bronson Koenig jumper, and the teams engaged in a seesaw battle the rest of the way.

Badgers point guard Traevon Jackson had an opportunity to win the game in regulation but missed a jumper from the left wing over Gordon, sending the game to overtime tied at 54. And the tension in the arena ratcheted up even more for the extra session.

"It was a fight," Dekker said. "If I wasn't wearing my mouth guard, my teeth would have been gone."

In those five minutes, Wisconsin played with the kind of passion and excellence Ryan knew his team was capable of seven months earlier. Later in the night, Ryan acknowledged in a moment of reflection that he saw things in his team during an August trip to Canada for five exhibition games—just weeks before his father died—that made him believe this group could finally reach that elusive Final Four. And he pushed them to believe in themselves, too.

"I was a lot tougher on this group than I was on last year's group," Ryan said. "I just wasn't going to accept them not understanding that they could be pretty good."

The Badgers pushed ahead for good in overtime 61–59 on center Frank Kaminsky's layup with 2:21 left and clung for dear life down the stretch. UW led 64–63 when Jackson lost the ball out of bounds with just 2.3 seconds remaining, setting up one last opportunity for Arizona to win.

But Johnson caught the inbound pass running away from the basket and couldn't get a shot off as time expired, sending Wisconsin's entire team into hysterics—and sending Badgers fans flooding State Street back in downtown Madison.

"It really feels like we won the lottery," said Kaminsky, who finished with 28 points and 11 rebounds and was named the West Region's Most Outstanding Player. "If I were to describe it, I would celebrate like that if I won the lottery, but this was 10 times better."

The final sequence sealed Ryan's trip to the Final Four and provided even more symbolism for the man who had devoted his entire life to basketball.

Butch Ryan—a pipefitter, decorated World War II serviceman, and former youth sports league coach—became a fixture at every Final Four when his son earned an assistant coaching job at Wisconsin in 1976. That first Final Four was held at the Spectrum in Philadelphia, a short drive from their hometown of Chester, Pennsylvania. From that point on, Bo and Butch rarely missed a Final Four, with Butch bringing along his RV. And over the years, the stories of Butch's Final Four exploits and his gregarious nature grew.

He would bypass security guards and fans to shake hands and swap stories with the likes of North Carolina coach Dean Smith. He once held an impromptu dance-off with MC Hammer in a hotel lobby. In 1994, Butch noticed all the other RVs in his row had team flags, and he did not. He tied an orange UW-Platteville sweatshirt on the line and pulled it up the flagpole to support his son, who was on his way to coaching the Division III program to four national titles. After one such national title that resulted in a perfect 30–0 mark in 1998, Butch famously held a sign during the postgame celebration that read, "Bring on Duke."

In 2013, Bo and Butch watched one more Final Four together in an Atlanta hotel. Butch was too ill to attend the festivities at the arena, but Bo flew him out so they could enjoy the games, away from Bo's coaching buddies and former players.

Bo didn't know at the time it would be their last Final Four together.

"He was always about the kids that he helped mentor growing up, and that's why I do it," Bo Ryan said late in the night after the Arizona victory. "To be able to see the faces on these guys, to see the genuine excitement, I can remember some of the great teams that he had of kids and their first championships and how they acted and just had the joy."

That joy lasted well into the next morning for Wisconsin, which advanced to play Kentucky in the first of two consecutive national semifinal matchups. And for the first time, Bo Ryan wouldn't be watching the Final Four from the stands. He would have company on the bench, in more ways than one.

21 Recapping Six Men's Hockey Titles

March 17, 1973:
Wisconsin 4, Denver 2

Wisconsin came within five seconds of never even reaching the 1973 national title game. That's how much time was left on the Boston Garden clock when Wisconsin tied Cornell 5–5 to send the semifinal game to sudden-death overtime. The Badgers had made an incredible comeback after Cornell jumped out to a 4–0 lead midway through the second period. With 33 seconds left in overtime, Dennis Olmstead centered the puck to freshman Steve Alley. Alley's shot was blocked, but the rebound came to sophomore Dean Talafous, who scored the game winner.

In the national title game, captain Tim Dool tied the score at 2–2, and then Talafous again scored the goal that proved to be the winner, giving UW a 3–2 advantage. Senior Jim Johnston added an insurance goal in the third period. Talafous was named the MVP of the tournament. UW finished with a school record for wins in a single season at 29–9–2.

Wisconsin seniors Lloyd Bentley, Dool, Norm Cherrey, Johnston, and Doug Kelso, who participated in three NCAA tournaments in their four years, finished 99–43–4 in their careers.

March 26, 1977:
Wisconsin 6, Michigan 5 (overtime)

Wisconsin fans streamed onto the Olympic Stadium ice in Detroit, chanting "We're No. 1" and mobbing players in bright red jerseys following a dramatic victory. Senior Steve Alley scored just 23 seconds into overtime to give the Badgers their second national title in four seasons in front of 14,437 people, the second-largest crowd in the NCAA tournament's 30-year history.

"Maybe we lost, but it sure was the best show in town," Michigan coach Dan Farrell said afterward.

The underdog Wolverines surged from a three-goal deficit to tie and send the game to sudden-death overtime. Michigan defenseman John Waymann forced the extra session with a slapshot goal at 14:42 of the third period. That offset Wisconsin freshman Mark Johnson's second goal of the night, which looked like the game winner.

After the game, Wisconsin coach Bob Johnson called his Badgers "the finest college team I've ever been associated with."

UW finished the season 37–7–1, a school record for wins in a season, and became the first team to win the Big Ten, WCHA, and NCAA titles in the same season.

"We were tired, and they had the momentum," said Johnson, whose team had struggled to a 4–3 overtime win against New

Hampshire in the semifinals. "But in overtime, all you can be is lucky, and we were lucky."

March 28, 1981:
Wisconsin 6, Minnesota 3

Well before the Badgers knocked off the heavily favored Gophers, they had to sweat out whether they would even earn an NCAA tournament opportunity. Earlier in the month, Wisconsin had lost to Colorado College in the Western Collegiate Hockey Association playoffs and had to depend on an at-large berth in the tournament for a shot at the title.

Wisconsin sneaked into the tournament anyway and made the most of its time. UW slipped past Clarkson College with a two-game, total-goals victory and then defeated Northern Michigan 5–1 in the national semifinal before dominating Minnesota. The team some thought didn't deserve to be in the NCAA tournament famously became known as the "Backdoor Badgers."

"I guess we did come in through the back door," said John Newberry, Wisconsin's standout freshman center. "But we're going out the front door."

Newberry and Ed Lebler each scored two goals against Minnesota, while Dan Gorowsky and Ted Pearson scored one. Wisconsin goalie Marc Behrend made 30 saves and was named the tournament's most valuable player.

"People can call us what they want," Lebler said, "but we're No. 1."

The two WCHA rivals had met four times previously that season, with Minnesota winning three of those games on its way to a league title. But Wisconsin scored the first four goals of the NCAA championship game and never looked back.

"We felt like we were uninvited guests at a party," coach Bob Johnson said. "We certainly deserved to be here."

March 26, 1983:
Wisconsin 6, Harvard 2

Wisconsin dominated Harvard and led 3–0 early to put the game away in one of the team's most unlikely national titles. Pat Flatley and Paul Houston each scored two goals for the Badgers.

First-year Badgers coach Jeff Sauer came to Wisconsin with a losing record at Colorado College and was not expected to produce a winner in his first season.

"I've waited a long time for that," said Sauer, a onetime Badgers assistant who would coach the team for the next 20 seasons and win two national titles. "I am so happy I came back to Wisconsin. It worked out."

UW goalie Marc Behrend was named the tournament's most valuable player, the same honor he won when the Badgers captured the title two years earlier in 1981. Wisconsin finished the season 33–10–4, the third-most victories in school history.

"There's no way I thought at the start of this year that we would go all the way," Behrend said. "I thought that this would be a transition year and that I would simply have to be happy with it."

April 1, 1990:
Wisconsin 7, Colgate 3

Seven seniors, six drafted by NHL teams, propelled the Badgers to a dominant victory in the NCAA title game before 15,034 fans at Joe Louis Arena in Detroit. One of those seniors, John Byce, scored three goals, including two before the game was four minutes old, to lead the Badgers to their first title since 1983.

"I knew this group of seniors deserved to win it somewhere along the line, and it's great to have them go out this way," said Badgers coach Jeff Sauer, whose team finished 36–9–1.

The Badgers took a 4–1 first period lead on three power play goals and one short-handed score and held off Colgate the rest of the way. Senior Chris Tancill, who scored both Wisconsin goals in the Badgers' 2–1 semifinal win against Boston College, was named the tournament's most valuable player.

"We weren't going to be denied," Tancill said. "This is everything we've worked for, for four years, and it's just an unbelievable feeling."

Byce, a Madison native, scored 90 seconds into the final to set the tone and scored again at the 3:23 mark. Tancill rifled in a hard slapshot for another power play goal and a 3–1 lead at 7:33 of the first period. Wisconsin went 18–1–1 over its final 20 games.

"Growing up in Madison, you dream about playing for the Badgers, and it's natural that you'd dream about winning it all," Byce said. "Tonight the dream came true."

April 8, 2006:
Wisconsin 2, Boston College 1

Senior Tom Gilbert's goal 9:32 into the third period proved to be the winner for the Badgers at the Bradley Center in Milwaukee, marking the only title of the Mike Eaves coaching era.

Junior Robbie Earl added UW's other goal as the Badgers (30–10–3) won their sixth national championship and first in 16 years. Earl earned the Frozen Four Most Outstanding Player Award with three goals and one assist.

Fellow junior Brian Elliott made 22 saves and was named to the All-Frozen Four Team. He was joined by Earl, Gilbert, and Adam Burish.

"This is the best group of guys," Gilbert said. "The best university. The best fans in college hockey. The best coaching staff. It's a dream come true."

The title game did not start off particularly well for Wisconsin, when Boston College took a 1–0 lead 9:01 into the first period. The Badgers had grabbed leads in 32 of their 42 previous contests.

But Earl tied the score at the 1:17 mark of the second period after he redirected a Burish pass across the slot into an open net. Gilbert gave the Badgers their first lead of the game in the third period with a power play goal.

The moment was sweet for Eaves, who played for UW from 1974 to 1978 and returned in 2002 after coaching the U.S. National Team Development Program. He told his players to enjoy the title run.

"Relish this time because it may not happen again," Eaves said.

22 Ed Nuttycombe

When Ed Nuttycombe arrived in Madison with his wife, Diane, to serve as an assistant track coach at Wisconsin in 1980, the two figured they would remain in the area for only three to five years. He was from Virginia and his wife from New York, and their assumption was they'd move back to the East Coast to be closer to family and friends.

Somewhere along the way, however, Ed Nuttycombe fell in love with a town, a university, and a track program and couldn't pull himself away. Five years became 10. Ten became 20. Twenty stretched past 30. Until, finally, Nuttycombe retired in 2013 after 33 years, the last 30 as the Badgers' record-setting head coach.

"I think the city of Madison and then the quality of the university and the young people that I had a chance to work with just grabbed a hold and didn't let go," Nuttycombe said.

During those years, his accomplishments were unparalleled in the sport. No coach in conference history, in any sport, won as many Big Ten titles as the 26 Nuttycombe's teams collected.

Add in cross country—a program for which he was responsible but didn't directly coach—and UW earned 52 Big Ten championships under Nuttycombe's watch. As a point of reference, that number was 15 more than the rest of the league combined (37) since he took over the Badgers program in 1984.

On 10 occasions under Nuttycombe's direction, the Badgers swept the cross country and indoor and outdoor track titles in the same season to earn the Big Ten "Triple Crown."

"Looking back upon my career as a whole, probably what I'm proudest of is being able to keep both the cross country and track programs at a very high level of conference and national competition over 30 years," Nuttycombe said. "One specific event, I don't think that makes for anything other than you had a fantastic team."

One of Nuttycombe's most monumental achievements occurred when Wisconsin became the first Big Ten school to win an indoor track national title by claiming the top spot at the 2007 NCAA championships. It marked the first national championship for a UW track program. Wisconsin crowned an individual national champion as well with Chris Solinsky (5,000-meter run), and the Badgers picked up 10 All-American honors.

In all, Nuttycombe coached five Olympians, 11 NCAA individual champions, and 165 Big Ten individual winners. He earned Big Ten coach of the year honors 22 times and was named the national coach of the year in 2007. He also hired three cross country coaches during his tenure at Wisconsin, and each went on to win a national title: Martin Smith (1985, '88), Jerry Schumacher (2005), and Mick Byrne (2011).

"He was an amazing coach, and I don't know if it's for the Xs and Os that he obviously knew," Solinsky said of Nuttycombe. "I think it's how he carried himself. He was there for 30-some years. As time went on, he didn't age, if you will. He always was able to relate with anyone and everyone on the team. I think that's how a program can thrive.

"That brought that extra little one percent out of the athlete that makes and breaks a championship team. If you're winning championships by slim margins, an athlete is going to be more willing to invest in suffering in their event and really getting the best out of themselves if they know there's a reason they're doing that."

Nuttycombe, a native of Newport News, Virginia, was a track star in college at Virginia Tech and won six collegiate pole vault titles. He graduated in 1977 and spent the next two years as an assistant coach while earning his graduate degree at Northern Illinois. In 1980, then-Badgers track coach Dan McClimon asked if he would join Wisconsin's staff, and Nuttycombe moved to Madison, where he has remained ever since. Nuttycombe served as interim coach after McClimon tragically died in a plane crash in 1983, and Nuttycombe officially became head coach before the 1984 season.

There was symmetry to Nuttycombe's career. His father, Charles, coached high school football and track for 34 years in Virginia. In 2005, Charles was inducted into the U.S. Track and Field and Cross Country Coaches Association Hall of Fame, and Ed was there to present him with the honor.

In 2014, Charles, at age 84, was there to return the favor to his son. They became the first father-son duo to be inducted into the hall of fame.

"When I presented him, there were people who came up and said, 'Well, your day may come some day,'" Nuttycombe said. "And I knew we were doing well, never knowing whether that would come true or not. But I have to say that, as the years ticked along, if it was going to happen, I was really, really hopeful that my father was going to be there to share it with me. He was the biggest influence, teacher, mentor to me as a coach. And to share that with him was magical."

Even after Nuttycombe retired in 2013 at age 61, he couldn't stay away from the program. Instead, he became a volunteer assistant with the men's and women's track programs, spending five days a week helping to mentor the next generation of Badgers track athletes.

It is a gift his runners are no doubt happy to receive.

"Laying it all on the line for the coach, laying it all on the line for teammates, he created that atmosphere," Solinsky said. "I 100 percent attribute that to the kind of man and coach that Nuttycombe was."

23 Stu Jackson and the NCAA Tournament

Wisconsin's basketball players convened in nervous silence, an unsettling uncertainty building like a tidal wave in the pit of their collective stomachs. Selection Sunday, as it's come to be known, is supposed to be a celebration for the teams that qualify for college basketball's most prestigious event, the NCAA tournament. Of course, a celebration only occurs once a team knows it has actually qualified.

The Badgers didn't have that luxury on March 13, 1994, when they met at head coach Stu Jackson's house. All players could do was sit and wait, the fate of an entire season—and five decades of failure—having boiled down to a tournament selection committee and one 30-minute national television special to reveal its decision.

"Everybody was pretty worried that we'd walk out of that Selection Sunday with no bid," said Andy Kilbride, a guard on the 1993–94 Badgers team. "I thought, *Man, it's really going to suck if we don't get in.*"

Perhaps 47 consecutive years without a tournament bid had prepared the Badgers for further disappointment. But just minutes before the TV announcements, Jackson—wired for sound on the broadcast from his home—received the good news in his ear from old friend Dick Vitale in the studio: Wisconsin was in the NCAA tournament as an at-large bid.

"I remember my heart dropping in my stomach," Jackson said. "I was so happy. I didn't say anything for that next minute or two, and then I sat back and watched the team's reaction when it was announced on television. It was literally an explosion in my house. It was unbelievable."

Mass hysteria ensued in Jackson's living room, a sea of paper plates and snacks splattering across the floor as players and coaches embraced. There it was in block letters on TV for all to see: Wisconsin vs. Cincinnati in a first-round game in Ogden, Utah.

"Pizza and soda and popcorn and chips were flying all over the place," former Badgers forward Howard Moore said. "It was a great moment and a tremendous celebration for everybody.

"All the work was validated by when you see your school name on that screen and you see where you're going. We didn't care if it was Pluto. I had never heard of Ogden, Utah, before that. We didn't care if it was Siberia. We were just glad to be dancing."

Since that time, Wisconsin's basketball program has become a staple on Selection Sunday. But the 1993–94 season is the one most remembered for changing the culture of a Wisconsin program that had been a perennial cellar dweller, even if Jackson, the man behind the transformation, sometimes gets forgotten.

Jackson was hired to replace former coach Steve Yoder a year earlier, for the 1992–93 season, and he brought a different swagger to a dormant program. Over the previous 47 seasons, Wisconsin had finished with a losing record 30 times—a number that didn't sit well with Jackson.

"At the time when our staff came to the program, it was a program that didn't have a very good reputation within the Big Ten and certainly not throughout the country," said Jackson, who had coached the New York Knicks from 1989 to 1991.

"My expectation was to try to build a program that was sustainable going forward as a winning program, one that had a brand of basketball that was attractive for recruiting. And to change the culture of the program that, at least in my mind, didn't have the mentality for winning."

Among his most significant moves was installing an up-tempo offense that perfectly suited the Badgers' players, particularly stars Michael Finley and Tracy Webster, who combined to average 36 points that first season.

Although the Badgers didn't make the NCAA tournament that year, they did qualify for the NIT, losing 77–73 to Rice in the first round at the UW Field House. In the immediate aftermath of the defeat, expectations rose even higher with Finley and Webster returning the following season.

"I remember how broken up and heartbroken we were as a team in that locker room after the loss to Rice in the NIT at home," Moore said. "All of us as a group just made a vow that we were going to push each other that spring, that summer, and the goal was to get to the [NCAA] tournament that next year."

While players strengthened team chemistry by working harder and spending more time together off the court, what helped push Wisconsin over the top was Jackson's ability to recruit top-level talent. His most notable recruiting achievement before the '93–94 season was landing Rashard Griffith, a 6'11" center who earned the Mr. Basketball honor in Illinois as the state's best prep player.

"He just added that inside presence that we needed," Webster said of Griffith. "He was so strong and had so much weight on him that he would wear guys down. He was one of those guys that could dominate a game without even touching a basketball because he demanded attention."

With Finley, Webster, and Griffith leading the way, Wisconsin opened the 1993–94 season with 11 consecutive victories and a high-octane offense that eclipsed 100 points three times. On November 22, 1993, Wisconsin entered the Associated Press poll ranked No. 25 in the country, the first time the Badgers had been ranked in the AP poll since January 1976.

Wisconsin stumbled down the stretch of conference play, but the Badgers finished the regular season 17–10 overall and 8–10 in the Big Ten—just good enough to squeak into their first NCAA tournament since 1947. Motivation to perform well was not an issue after a TV analyst picked against Wisconsin leading up to the first-round game with Cincinnati.

"Digger Phelps made a bold prediction that the Cincinnati-Missouri game in the second round was going to be a great game," Moore said. "I was like, 'Wait a minute!' I remember the team really taking that personally, and [they] had some choice words for Digger when we went to bed."

Determined to make Phelps eat his words, and with Jackson trumpeting the disrespect card, No. 9 seed Wisconsin knocked off No. 8 Cincinnati 80–72 in the opening round of the NCAA tournament—exactly one year to the day of its NIT loss against Rice.

Griffith produced a monster game with 22 points and 15 rebounds, and Finley also scored 22 points, including four three-pointers.

"The players, to their credit, were not daunted at all by being in the first NCAA tournament in 47 years," Jackson said. "They were feeling good about themselves, and they thought they could win."

The dream season came to an end just two days later, when top-seeded Missouri outgunned Wisconsin 109–96 in a wildly entertaining second-round game. Finley, who left Wisconsin as the program's all-time leading scorer, tallied a game-high 36 points.

Wisconsin closed the season 18–11 and averaged 77.9 points per game. It remains the highest-scoring Badgers team in the three-point era. Jackson's two-year stint in charge ended in July 1994 when he resigned to become general manager of the NBA expansion

Vancouver Grizzlies and was replaced by Badgers assistant coach Stan Van Gundy. But Jackson's presence left a lasting impact.

"I think that, for whatever reason, Stu hasn't been given nearly enough credit," Van Gundy said. "He's the guy that turned it around. He's the guy that started the winning back. But because he didn't stay for very long, and because of the success the program had afterward, he hasn't gotten the credit that he deserved."

Jackson, meanwhile, remains proud of what his teams accomplished and the foundation it laid for raising expectations in Wisconsin's basketball future.

"I think it was a huge milestone and a stepping stone for the program," Jackson said. "There's no question that was the beginning of something. People in the basketball circles began to look at Wisconsin basketball differently."

24 Montee Ball

A wave of euphoria washed over Madison the night of October 16, 2010, after Wisconsin had secured a historic 31–18 upset against No. 1 Ohio State at Camp Randall Stadium. The Badgers hadn't defeated a top-ranked team since 1981, and a party raged in the city.

Badgers running back Montee Ball didn't feel much like celebrating. Wisconsin had called 38 rushing plays for its running backs that night, none of which were for Ball, who stood on the sideline and did not play a single snap as the third-string tailback. Instead, teammates James White and John Clay took all the carries in the backfield.

It was the first time in Ball's football career in which he did not play while being healthy enough to go, a devastating blow to his psyche. Ball, then a sophomore, decided he'd had enough and told his father, Montee Sr., he wanted to switch to linebacker to get on the field. If not for some harsh truth from Dad, it's possible Ball never would have broken the NCAA's all-time Football Bowl Subdivision touchdown record.

"If you go to that team right now and say you want to switch positions just to contribute, how do you think those other running backs are going to feel?" Montee Sr. told his son. "How do you think that coach is going to feel with you bailing on them? You stick with it. That's what we do as a family. When something comes up, you fight. You go back and you practice twice as hard as everybody else. When the opportunity arises and your chance is given to you, don't give it away."

One week later against Iowa, White and Clay were injured during the game. Ball entered and scored an eight-yard touchdown to win the game with just more than a minute remaining. He averaged 155.4 yards rushing and scored 14 touchdowns in the final five games that season. The rest, as the saying goes, is history.

Ball, a native of Wentzville, Missouri, would lose 26 pounds during the offseason on a cottage cheese and baked potato diet and transform himself into a Heisman Trophy finalist. His 2011 season will be remembered as one of the most prolific in college football history. That year, Ball scored 39 touchdowns to equal Barry Sanders' FBS record. He rushed for 1,923 yards and earned consensus All-American honors while playing alongside quarterback Russell Wilson on a team that finished 11–3.

Many assumed Ball would leave Wisconsin after his junior year. But after receiving a grade from the NFL draft advisory board that suggested he would not be selected any higher than the third round, he opted to return and further his legacy at UW.

"Kind of sitting back and thinking about it, I knew there were better running backs in front of me," Ball said. "I knew that if I stayed, I'd have the opportunity to get my degree, I'd have the opportunity to play another year with my teammates, get another Big Ten championship if possible, and also be one of the top running backs in the next draft."

Ball's senior campaign began slowly and took time to gain steam. Just before the season began, Ball was assaulted in downtown Madison, a block from his off-campus apartment. Five men knocked him to the ground, kicked his chest and face, and fled into the night, leaving Ball with a concussion that would stall his progress to open the season.

But when challenged, Ball seemed to make his best moves, and he would rally with a strong late-season push. On a chilly late November Saturday afternoon in 2012, Ball took a toss play 17 yards around the right side of the field at Penn State to break the all-time touchdown record in the final regular season game of the year. The touchdown, his 79th overall at Wisconsin, moved him past Miami (Ohio) running back Travis Prentice, who established the mark in 1999. Ball would go on to win the Doak Walker Award as the nation's best running back, rushing for 1,830 yards and 22 touchdowns.

In his Wisconsin career, Ball carried 924 times for 5,140 yards and an FBS record 77 rushing touchdowns. His six receiving scores gave him 83 total and set another career FBS mark, though Navy quarterback Keenan Reynolds would surpass both scoring records in 2015. Ball eventually was selected 58th overall in the second round by the Denver Broncos in the 2013 NFL draft. But he'll be best remembered for his determination in the face of adversity at Wisconsin.

"If he'd come in and told me he wanted to switch to linebacker, I probably wouldn't have let him, as bad as he might have pleaded," former Badgers coach Bret Bielema said. "I do think we always knew all along he was going to be pretty special."

25 Baseball Shuttered

They arrived on a warm spring Friday afternoon symbolically dressed for a funeral. Black hats. Cleats. Stirrups. Undershirts. The gesture, while futile in the big picture, represented a declaration of mourning. For history, and for themselves.

Yes, they were there to play a college baseball game. But they also were there to find a cathartic release, to cope with the unthinkable and spend just a few more hours lingering by the field they had called home.

Arrogance and youthful naivety had convinced each player this day would never come. How could a Big Ten athletics department drop one of the signature sports in American culture? How could the University of Wisconsin cut baseball, the oldest athletics program at the school, after 116 years?

"As an athlete, it's kind of the last thing you think that could possibly happen," said Kris Hanson, a freshman pitcher for the Badgers during that final season. "You fear getting injured. You fear potentially being cut from the team. But the last thing you fear is that the entire program itself is going to be cut out from under you."

Yet here they were, 34 baseball players and a handful of coaches at Guy Lowman Field, trying to fend off the inevitable during a doubleheader against Purdue. Badgers players desperately hoped the games would somehow push past darkness and force a continuation the next day, however remote the possibility.

But when Wisconsin third baseman John Vanden Heuvel's fly ball nestled into the glove of Purdue's center fielder in the ninth inning, the end of a doubleheader and a program had unceremoniously arrived with a 1–0 defeat.

It was 5:40 PM on May 10, 1991. Wisconsin's players cried and hugged in the dugout.

"Nobody wanted to step outside the lines into reality," recalled Jason Beier, the Badgers' first baseman.

Reality hadn't been kind to Wisconsin baseball. One month earlier, a plan to drop baseball and four other nonrevenue sports was approved 8–3 by the athletics board for financial reasons. The cuts helped eliminate an athletics department debt that approached $2 million. Dropping the five sports would save $3.3 million over a four-year period, create a $500,000 reserve for other sports, and go a long way toward satisfying the needs of meeting Title IX demands for gender equity in athletics at Wisconsin.

Decades later, the decision remains one of the most controversial moves the Wisconsin athletics department has ever made. Each spring, there are pleas to bring back baseball, but hope dims as the years pass. Instead, the lasting image of the program continues to be that somber group of players silently shuffling off the field in black, grieving and protesting to no avail.

Wisconsin is one of just four power-five conference schools without a baseball program, along with Syracuse, Colorado, and Iowa State. The Badgers also are the only Big Ten school without the sport. It was a decision then-athletics director Pat Richter did not take lightly. Richter, a three-sport letter winner at Wisconsin in football, basketball, and baseball in the 1960s, had taken over a floundering athletics department in 1989, and a move needed to be made.

At the time, Wisconsin offered the third-most sports in the Big Ten with 25 but had a budget that ranked only sixth in the conference. Given that the department was so far in debt, a proposal began circulating to drop baseball, men's and women's gymnastics, and men's and women's fencing. The idea was that Wisconsin would be better prepared to fund 20 sports instead of 25.

"We were just kind of limping along," said Richter, who served as Wisconsin's athletics director from 1989 to 2004. "We were able to compete, but we weren't competitive. So that just isn't right. They believed we needed a smaller program with better resources for those remaining."

In the years since, Wisconsin's athletics department has recovered significantly thanks to the success of revenue-generating operations with football, men's basketball, and men's hockey. In 2013–14, Wisconsin's total revenues and operating expenses each exceeded $125 million, according to a *USA Today* study. Still, the idea the Badgers might bring back baseball remains slim given the operating cost and the likelihood of having to add a women's sport to balance Title IX requirements, which would double costs.

"Let's put it this way," Richter said. "It's possible. But it's not probable."

Reichardt Changes MLB History

Rick Reichardt left Wisconsin in 1964 as an All-American outfielder who batted .443 overall and .472 in Big Ten games. He became only the second player since 1939 to repeat as the conference's top hitter, and his talents were in such high demand that he set off a huge bidding war for his services among Major League Baseball teams. What followed was a move that would alter the course of the sport's free-agent signing deals.

Reichardt ultimately signed with the Los Angeles Angels, who offered him a staggering $205,000 contract. The amount was higher than the salary of any other player in the pros despite the fact he had never played a game. Paying that much for an amateur was considered so absurd that MLB changed the system it had used for years to acquire young players. In 1965, MLB held its first amateur player draft. When the Kansas City Athletics selected Rick Monday with the first pick, he signed for a bonus of $100,000, more than half of what the Angels had rewarded Reichardt with a year earlier.

In 1966, Reichardt was in the midst of his best season when he had to have his kidney removed. Despite not performing quite at the same level afterward, he managed to play seven more seasons.

"I never had the resiliency after that," Reichardt told MLB.com in 2008. "Who's to say how I would have done. I was one of the most sought-after free agents in history. I was on my way when that happened. But I played 10 seasons, and I'm very thankful."

Reichardt played with the Angels, Washington Senators, Chicago White Sox, and Kansas City Royals and batted .261 with 116 home runs and 445 runs batted in. He retired in 1974 after one at-bat with the Royals—a base hit. He was inducted into the College Baseball Hall of Fame in 2015.

26 J.J. Watt

Outside of Green Bay Packers quarterback Aaron Rodgers, there is perhaps no professional football player more beloved in the state of Wisconsin these days than J.J. Watt. His hulk-like feats of strength on the field, coupled with his unyielding work ethic, have made him a force in the NFL as a defensive end for the Houston Texans. And his down-to-earth charm and aversion to celebrity status make Wisconsinites even more proud to call him one of their own.

Watt has worked for everything he's ever earned as a football player, and maybe there is no better example of that devotion to his craft than when he left Central Michigan to chase a dream of playing college football at Wisconsin, his home-state school. The Pewaukee, Wisconsin, native took classes at a local community college for six months, worked at Pizza Hut, and trained four days a week with Brad Arnett, a trainer who began transforming Watt's body during his junior year of high school.

Arnett said when he first met Watt, he weighed 212 pounds and could barely maintain a timed body plank hold for 30-second

Wisconsin native J.J. Watt, who won the Lott IMPACT Trophy in 2010, has had one of the most celebrated careers of any Badger, winning the AP NFL Defensive Player of the Year Award three times.

increments. But Watt returned to Arnett's gym multiple times every week, and by the time he arrived at Wisconsin in 2008 as a transfer without a scholarship, it became clear Watt could be a special player. During his redshirt season, he was named the defensive scout team player of the year.

In 2009, he started all 13 games at defensive end and finished second on the team in tackles for loss, pass breakups, and fumble recoveries. His 2010 season was so spectacular that he declared for the NFL draft a year early after leading the Badgers in tackles for loss, sacks, quarterback hurries, forced fumbles, and blocked kicks while earning consensus first-team All-Big Ten and second-team All-American honors on a Rose Bowl squad.

As his fame increased, Watt never lost sight of his ultimate goal to be the best football player he could become. In 2011, he was rewarded when the Texans selected him No. 11 overall in the first round of the NFL draft.

"This is a story I've always told people about J.J.," Arnett said. "He was in working out one time. There were some other guys from Madison, former players, talking about a bar up in Madison. J.J. had never been to it. Somebody made a comment, 'Well, what do you mean you've never been to it?' He goes, 'I was busy becoming a first-round draft pick.'

"He knew what he wanted, and he was going to do everything he had to do to get it."

Watt's athletic feats continue to amaze. He earned Associated Press NFL defensive player of the year honors in 2012, 2014, and 2015 and was so versatile that he even caught three touchdown passes for the Texans in 2014. Watt, who bulked up to 289 pounds, still found ways to push the limits of his body. He was seen flipping huge rubber tires during workouts and set a new personal record by recording a 61-inch box jump.

"The second that I start looking back and I start thinking about what I've already done, I kind of lose that edge and I lose what I'm looking forward to," Watt said. "And there's still so much left for me to accomplish that someday I'll be in a rocking chair hanging out by the lake somewhere and I'll think about, 'Wow, all that stuff was pretty cool.' But for right now, there's way too much left to accomplish. I can't think about it yet."

Watt also has taken the time to personally brighten the days of many of his adoring fans. He handwrote a fan a "get out of work" letter so she could attend his celebrity softball game, he assisted a fan who had been bullied by helping him join a YMCA flag football team and giving him a pair of game-worn cleats, and he bought pizza for both the Houston Police Department and Houston Fire Department, attaching another handwritten note of thanks. Additionally, he started the J.J. Watt Foundation, which has provided funding in excess of $1 million to sixth through eighth grade after-school athletics programs and organizations.

Watt's mother, Connie, said watching her son develop so many fans has been nice. But watching how he carries himself, supports younger brothers Derek and T.J. (who followed in his footsteps as Badgers football players), and remains true to his upbringing has been even more rewarding.

"That hasn't changed him as a person, and that is one of the things I'm most proud of," she said.

Added Arnett: "He's a very loyal person from the standpoint of he never forgets his roots, where he came from, his school, people that were a part of his journey to where he's at. That's just the type of kid that he is. He's just a wholesome person."

27 Bo Schembechler and Bob Knight Could've Been Badgers

In many ways, decisions made by Wisconsin's athletics department mirrored the mediocrity of its teams during part of the school's sports dive into irrelevancy in the 1960s and 1970s. And the stories of coaches Bo Schembechler and Bob Knight serve as prime examples of the department's clumsy approach. If not for the mishandling of both situations, each legendary figure could have made his name as a Badger.

The story begins with Schembechler, an up-and-coming coach at Miami (Ohio), who wanted to be the head football coach at Wisconsin in 1967. UW needed to replace Milt Bruhn, and the top candidate for the job was Bruhn's assistant, John Coatta. In the 1974 book *Man in Motion*, Schembechler recalled that he and Notre Dame assistant Johnny Ray were brought to Madison to interview on a Sunday night, primarily as a dog-and-pony show, with neither having a real chance at the position.

"They brought in all the candidates at the same time but put us up at different hotels," Schembechler said in the book. "Real secret agent stuff. They asked Johnny Ray and me to come down together, and he goes in first before the committee. I guess it's about 10 [PM] before it's my turn.

"You have to picture this. They've got 20 guys sitting around, and one of them—a board member, I guess—is sound asleep. He is sitting there asleep. I mean, how the hell would you feel? I'm mad. Really mad. I don't even want to be there. I don't want to answer any of their questions."

According to John U. Bacon, the entire interview lasted all of 40 minutes. Schembechler also wasn't thrilled that a student seemed to relish asking smart-aleck questions during the interview.

He promptly walked out the door, found the nearest pay phone, and called Wisconsin athletics director Ivy Williamson to withdraw his name from consideration.

"I really got miffed when I got there," he said.

Schembechler coached two more seasons at Miami (Ohio) before taking the Michigan job in 1969. He would beat Wisconsin 18 of 19 times during his tenure at Michigan, the only loss coming in 1981, when Dave McClain led the Badgers to a 21–14 upset of No. 1 Michigan in the season opener. Schembechler's career record at Michigan was 194–48–5. Coatta, who was offered the Wisconsin job, lasted three seasons and went 3–26–1.

In Schembechler's first season at Michigan, he faced Coatta at Wisconsin for the only time. Michigan hammered Wisconsin 35–7.

The story behind Knight's near-hire is equally maddening for Badgers fans. In 1968, he was a coach on the rise at Army and arrived in Madison as one of seven candidates to appear before the athletics board for the vacant men's basketball coaching position. The previous coach, John Erickson, had resigned to become general manager of the Milwaukee Bucks.

Knight wowed the board and was offered the Wisconsin job. There is some dispute as to whether he outright accepted the position or whether he asked simply for more time to think about it upon his return to West Point—which he claimed was the case in his book, *Knight: My Story.* Either way, he was not prepared for school officials to leak any news of his hiring to a local newspaper. That move, however, is exactly what happened.

"Almost as soon as I left, they announced me as their new coach," Knight said in his book. "When I arrived home at West Point, I heard what they had done. Now, I was in a hell of a spot. I was up all night trying to figure out what I should do."

The only person Knight could think of to run his decision by was Schembechler, who was still coaching at Miami (Ohio).

Schembechler had served as an assistant to Woody Hayes when Knight was in school at Ohio State, and Knight was aware of his situation one year earlier at Wisconsin.

"I told him how Wisconsin had released my name as the new coach before I'd had a chance to talk to them about what was necessary for them to do—that I'd have liked to take the job but I didn't think I could, under those circumstances," Knight said. "He listened to everything I said, then told me, 'Just call them and tell them you have no interest in the job.' I did."

John Powless, an assistant under Erickson and a compromise choice, was given the Wisconsin job on the same day Knight turned it down. Knight returned to Army for three more seasons, then moved on to Indiana in 1971.

Powless coached at Wisconsin from 1968 to '76 and posted a record of 88–108 (.449 winning percentage) in eight years. During the same eight-year period, Knight's teams went 176–49 (.782 winning percentage). And in 1975–76, Powless' final year at Wisconsin, Knight's Indiana team finished 32–0 and won the NCAA championship. No Division I team has completed a perfect season since.

Knight would win 902 games over his hall of fame coaching career, capturing three NCAA championships while with Indiana.

Knight recalled that about 20 years after he spurned the Badgers, an alumnus of Wisconsin approached him at a golf course and asked for his version of what happened when he almost became Wisconsin's coach. He told the man about his situation and the one a year earlier with Schembechler

"If Wisconsin had handled both situations a little better, Bo and I might have been coaching there together for a long time," Knight told him.

After relaying the story, Knight could sense disgruntlement on the alum's face. "I think the football part bothered him the most," he said.

28 After 28 Years, a Hockey Revival

It's difficult now to picture a time when the Wisconsin men's hockey program wasn't an intercollegiate sport. As the team's arena space has grown, from the Hartmeyer Arena to the Dane County Coliseum to the Kohl Center, so too has the fan base. Popularity was such that, from 1999 to 2012, Wisconsin led all Division I programs in average attendance each season. And during the 2009–10 season, UW's average attendance of 15,048 represented the highest mark in NCAA history.

Yet for 28 years, fans had no place to cheer on the Badgers. That's because there was no sanctioned hockey program from 1935–63 until a revival changed how the state viewed the sport for good. Wisconsin did sponsor hockey as an intercollegiate sport in the 1920s and early '30s, but it died out after the 1935 season. Students continued to play intramural hockey on an outdoor rink situated on the lower campus, now the Library Mall that sits between State and Langdon streets.

Thanks to the efforts of V.W. Meloche and Ivan "Ivy" Williamson, hockey was brought back on a freshman basis for the 1962–63 school year, with an understanding that it could become a full intercollegiate sport the following season if interest remained strong enough. Meloche was a hockey fan who had been a spectator at Badgers games in the 1920s and '30s. He also was a longtime member of the Blue Line Club, the team's hockey booster organization. Williamson, meanwhile, had taken over as athletics director in 1955. The school was looking for a sport to add after boxing had been discontinued in 1960 following the death of Wisconsin boxer Charlie Mohr.

The sport was officially reactivated as an intercollegiate program for the 1963–64 season under co-coaches Art Thomsen and John Riley. Thomsen had coached the last Wisconsin team in 1934–35, and Riley was a coach for several youth teams in the Madison area. In fact, Riley said, it was the success of those youth teams that convinced Williamson that college hockey in Madison was feasible.

Riley coached an area 18-and-under team, the Hawks, to a national championship, beating a team from Minnesota 6–2 in the finals. Another area hockey enthusiast, Fenton Kelsey, also coached youth teams and built the Madison ice arena, which became the Hartmeyer Arena when it was sold to the city.

"Ivan became interested when he saw what could be accomplished," Riley told the *Milwaukee Sentinel in* 1967. "Actually, the kids winning that national championship did it. At first, Ivan didn't think [hockey] could be self-sustaining. There wasn't enough high school hockey to give any reason to believe you could get players from the state.

"Of course, if Kelsey hadn't built that arena, we wouldn't have had hockey at the time, either."

Wisconsin played a 16-game schedule the first season and finished 8–5–3. Riley noted 14 candidates showed up for the team's first organized practice.

"I had kids report for hockey on figure skates and speed skates, and some couldn't stand up on them," Riley later told the school's athletics website in 2013.

Wisconsin's schedule continued to grow, and so did the talent level. UW finished 14–9 in Year 2 and 12–9 in Year 3, as Riley took full control of the program. Riley said it was in the 1965–66 season when Badgers hockey came of age. Wisconsin upset Minnesota, a perennial power, 5–4 in overtime in Madison on a goal 10 minutes into the sudden-death period. UW also played two close games against a Michigan State team that went on to win the NCAA title.

"Those were important," Riley told the *Sentinel.* "The kids knew then they could compete."

Riley, a Madison attorney and 1940 Wisconsin graduate, guided the Badgers through their first three seasons before resigning because of his law practice obligations. His departure opened the door for coach Bob Johnson, who would lead Wisconsin to spectacular success over the next 15 seasons.

Both Johnson and Riley shared a philosophy about building those early teams largely around in-state talent or from surrounding states rather than Canadian imports, as most members of the Western Collegiate Hockey Association did. For example, there was only one Canadian on the Badgers' 1964 team, sophomore defenseman Don Addison of Winnipeg, Manitoba, and he came to the school unsolicited. Riley insisted his 18-year-old freshmen could hold their own with Canadian players of the same age.

"The spirit of these boys is simply great," said Norm Bolitho, Riley's assistant coach. "These players are more eager to learn than Canadian boys of the same age. And being newer to the game, they haven't picked up as many bad habits."

Johnson, too, made a point of scouring the state for the best players he could find.

"Our aim is to have home-grown talent," Johnson said during his first season with the team. "That calls for development at the grassroots level, starting with preteen-age youngsters and moving on into high school competition. Milwaukee naturally looms big in this program because of its population and concentration of high schools. We want to do everything possible to stir up youngsters' interest in playing the game and adults' interest in providing the necessary facilities."

The combination of local talent and solid recruiting quickly made hockey one of the most popular sports on campus. With the football program in the midst of a 23-game winless streak from 1967 to '69, fans were looking for a sport to be proud of, and hockey filled that void. In 1967, the Badgers moved from the 3,500-seat Hartmeyer Arena to the roughly 8,000-seat Dane County Coliseum. UW's attendance rose from 3,384 to 6,651.

In 1969, Wisconsin joined the WCHA, becoming the ninth member of the most prestigious league in Division I college hockey. Wisconsin finished fourth that season under Johnson. All previous first-year teams in the league had finished last.

By 1972, Wisconsin hockey games were the place to be. During the 1971–72 season, average home attendance reached 7,857, setting a school and collegiate record and leading the nation for a third consecutive year. Fourteen of the team's 20 home games were sellouts. *Michigan Daily* reporter Frank Longo likened the fan support at Wisconsin hockey games to that of Ohio State football spectators.

"You have to see it to believe it," he wrote.

"I've seldom seen a group of fans like we have at our hockey games," Wisconsin athletics director Elroy Hirsch said in December 1972. "Their enthusiasm for the Badgers is what we want to see throughout our athletic program.... Those Coliseum sellouts and the record turned in by Coach Johnson's squad are among the high points of these last three years."

Added student manager Gary Ciepluch, "This year, all the seats are reserved. Last year, when some of the seats were sold on a general admission basis, people would start standing in line at 10:00 AM. They'd let them stand inside, so people came in and made a party of it all day long."

Fans certainly had plenty of reason to party. During that 1972–73 season, Wisconsin captured its first men's hockey national championship.

"The big thing is, of course, that everybody loves a winner, and at Madison they sure have one," Longo wrote. "And it shows no signs of stopping now."

408!

The chant began from the highest seats of Wisconsin's student section, slowly trickling downward until it spilled into the front rows and spread—expansively, triumphantly—across Camp Randall Stadium. On a day in which 80,539 people witnessed perhaps the greatest display by a running back in the history of college football, acknowledging the man responsible seemed the only appropriate thing to do.

With No. 20 Wisconsin well on its way to a 59–24 decimation of No. 16 Nebraska on November 15, 2014, the rhythmic calls poured forth.

MEL-VIN GOR-DON! MEL-VIN GOR-DON!

Moments earlier, Gordon had zipped into the end zone on a breathtaking 26-yard touchdown run as the third quarter expired, a heavy snowstorm pounding the turf around him. The play call, Fire Zulu Curve, was designed for Gordon to wade through a small hole behind his fullback on the weak side of the field. In typical Gordon fashion, however, he made the ordinary look magnificent, cutting across the field past three would-be tacklers, leaping toward the end zone and into the record books.

When the play was over, Gordon—a fourth-year junior from Kenosha, Wisconsin—had broken the single-game Football Bowl Subdivision rushing record and earned his last carry. The final total: 25 carries, 408 yards, and four touchdowns. Former TCU running back LaDainian Tomlinson's record of 406 yards, set November 20, 1999, against Texas–El Paso, was now only second best.

Gordon jumped into the arms of teammates. He smiled wide. Then he heard the announcement declaring the record over the public address system. He stuck his red mouth guard in his teeth, pumped his left fist and held up the Wisconsin "W" with his hands as the camera panned on him. The chants continued.

MEL-VIN GOR-DON! MEL-VIN GOR-DON!

It was, quite simply and without hyperbole, an evening and a performance for the ages.

"I didn't even know I was close to a record like that," Gordon said afterward. "I was kind of just running to win.... I knew they would all sell out going to the left, so I just pressed it a little bit, cut back, and just made it happen."

Badgers coach Gary Andersen, sitting next to Gordon at the postgame podium as he described his record-setting run, quickly interjected.

"Yeah, just made it happen," Andersen deadpanned. "See how easy it is?"

Few players, if any, could make something look as easy as Gordon did against a Cornhuskers team that entered with one of the best run defenses in the nation. And given the circumstances, the opponent, and the mind-numbing cold, it made Gordon's performance somehow seem even more remarkable.

The winner of the game would be in prime position to capture the Big Ten West division with two regular season games remaining—a feat the Badgers ultimately achieved. On top of that, the game-time temperature of 26 degrees was the coldest Badgers game at Camp Randall Stadium in 50 years—since a November 21, 1964, contest against Minnesota (11 degrees). Snow flurries began dancing through the stadium early in the second quarter and never relented.

It was exactly the type of game Gordon envisioned for himself when he bypassed the NFL draft a year earlier, and it represented his signature moment at UW. Gordon would go on to be a Heisman Trophy finalist and finish second behind Oregon quarterback Marcus Mariota for college football's highest honor. Gordon rushed for 2,587 yards—second-most in FBS history—with 29 touchdowns and averaged 7.5 yards per carry.

Against Nebraska, Gordon ran for gains of 42, 62, 44, 43, and 68 yards. He powered past the first wave of defenders, only to juke or leap over the second wave. Nebraska had not allowed more than 188 yards rushing in a game the entire season, but Gordon eclipsed that mark in the first half and entered halftime with 238 yards rushing.

"I give Wisconsin a lot of credit," said Nebraska coach Bo Pelini, who described his team's tackling as atrocious. "Gordon is a hell of a back, but we played a big part in that, too."

That day, Gordon knocked down longstanding records with ease. He surpassed former Badgers Heisman Trophy winner Ron Dayne's 1996 single-game program rushing record of 339 yards. He then beat Indiana tailback Anthony Thompson's Big Ten record of 377 yards established in 1989. That set the stage for the final carry, with Gordon sitting on 382 yards, to break Tomlinson's mark.

"Here comes Melvin to the 25, to the 20, Gordon 15, 10, 5, touchdown, Wisconsin!" Badgers radio announcer Matt Lepay screamed on the live broadcast. "Record-breaking run. Melvin Gordon. Four-oh-eight!"

Soon after, Tomlinson himself couldn't help but marvel at Gordon's achievement and chimed in on Twitter: "That kid [Melvin Gordon] bad!! Congrats on breaking the NCAA single game rushing record. #respect"

"It's a great feeling to see your hard work pay off," Gordon said. "My teammates were so excited, too, they got me amped up. I was trying to hold back a little bit. But after they told me, man, I felt so good."

Oklahoma running back Samaje Perine would break Gordon's record one week later with 427 yards rushing against Kansas. But it couldn't diminish a stunningly dominant performance from Gordon, whose totals could have been even higher if not for the blowout victory.

Andersen pulled Gordon for the fourth quarter, hugged him, and told him how proud he was of the accomplishment. And when the game was over, Gordon soaked in the scene at midfield, snow clinging to his dreadlocks. Teammates patted Gordon on the back, then fell to the turf and made snow angels.

"I'm glad the atmosphere was the way it was with the snow falling," Badgers left tackle Tyler Marz said afterward. "It was a beautiful scene."

Nothing more beautiful, of course, than Gordon galloping his way into the record books.

Racking Up Yardage

Wisconsin fans have been privy to some of the best tailbacks in college football history. But certain individual performances stand out above the rest. Here is a look at the five highest single-game rushing outputs in school history, three of which have occurred against rival Minnesota.

Player	Yardage	Opponent	Date
1. Melvin Gordon	408	Nebraska	November 15, 2014
2. Ron Dayne	339	Hawaii	November 30, 1996
3. Billy Marek	304	Minnesota	November 23, 1974
4. Anthony Davis	301	Minnesota	November 23, 2002
5. Ron Dayne	297	Minnesota	November 9, 1996

30 Elroy "Crazylegs" Hirsch

Elroy Hirsch's exploits on the football field created quite a stir around Wisconsin's campus during the first month of the 1942 season. The Badgers stood 3–0–1, with a tie against mighty Notre Dame serving as the only hiccup in the early season. Hirsch, a sophomore running back from Wausau, Wisconsin, had burst onto the scene with a bevy of speedy and powerful maneuvers, and word of his talent had begun to spread.

When Hirsch tore apart Missouri at home during a 17–9 Wisconsin victory on October 10, the *Chicago Tribune* took notice. He scored both Badgers touchdowns and ran 22 times for 174 yards—an average of nearly eight yards per carry.

"Outstanding man on the field all day before he left the game in the fourth quarter was Elroy Hirsch," the newspaper's account read. "The writing gents who are inclined to describe ball carriers as 'dervishes,' 'swivel-hipped,' and such, would have a field day watching Elroy today....

"When they're rounding up all-American sophomores for 1942, it would be well to include Master Hirsch, unless you don't plan to visit Madison, Wis."

But the game that cemented Hirsch's legacy—and earned him a nickname that would follow him forever—took place one week later in his first game away from Camp Randall Stadium. On October 17, Hirsch scored the decisive touchdown with an eye-popping run to help Wisconsin knock off Great Lakes 13–7 at Chicago's Soldier Field. Chicago sportswriter Francis Powers' account of the game noted, "Hirsch ran like a demented duck. His crazy legs were gyrating in six different directions all at the same time during a 61-yard touchdown run that solidified the win."

Hirsch, no doubt, was thankful "demented duck" didn't stick. Instead, the legend of "Crazylegs" was born.

"It was better than being called Elroy," Hirsch told the *Chicago Tribune* in 1986. "Yes, the nickname has been good to me. Close friends still call me Legs."

Hirsch finished the 1942 season with 786 yards rushing, 226 yards passing, and 390 yards receiving on the way to third-team All-America honors from *Look* magazine. Wisconsin completed the year 8–1–1, including a 17–7 victory against No. 1 Ohio State—a game in which Hirsch threw one touchdown pass and accounted for more than 200 yards of total offense. UW finished the season ranked third nationally by the Associated Press. Hirsch became such a standout player that he eventually portrayed himself in the 1953 movie *Crazylegs, All-American*.

Following the season, Hirsch entered the Marine Corps during World War II, a commitment that forced him to transfer to the University of Michigan. The 1942 season would be his only campaign in a Badgers uniform, and he went on to even greater success with the Wolverines. He became the only athlete in Michigan history to letter in four sports (football, basketball, track, and baseball). He helped the 1943 football team finish third in the final AP poll.

In 1944, Hirsch performed double duty in two sports that would make even Deion Sanders and Bo Jackson blush. At the Big Ten outdoor track championships held at Illinois, he broad jumped 22 feet, 5¾ inches during the preliminary round, then drove 150 miles to Bloomington, Indiana, and pitched the second game of a doubleheader for Michigan—a four-hitter in a 12–1 victory. Hirsch finished third at the conference track meet despite not participating in any final round.

Hirsch became a 1945 first-round NFL draft choice of Cleveland. He then played for the Chicago Rockets (1946–48) and the Los Angeles Rams (1949–57). He was a three-time Pro Bowl selection, a two-time Associated Press first-team All-Pro, a 1951 NFL champion, and a member of the NFL's 1950s All-Decade team, and was elected to the Pro Football Hall of Fame in 1968. In his pro career, he caught 387 passes for 7,029 yards and 60 touchdowns.

Yet it is Hirsch's contributions during an 18-year stint as Wisconsin's athletics director that solidified his Badgers legacy. When he started the job in 1969, the football team had gone 0-19–1 over the previous two years, the athletics department was $200,000 in debt, and the best Wisconsin high school players were playing for other Big Ten programs.

During his time in charge, athletics expanded from 12 men's sports to 25 men's and women's programs. The Badgers captured numerous Big Ten team titles and won national championships in men's hockey, men's and women's crew, and men's and women's cross country. Hirsch, noting that "85 percent of the department's income is from football," helped raise attendance at home games from 43,000 in 1968 to more than 70,000 per game four years later.

"The main reason football came back at Wisconsin was all the good people who rallied around me," said Hirsch, who held the athletics director position until 1987. "Even with a doggone handful of rowdies always trying to spoil it, we get together and enjoy ourselves, win or lose."

Wisconsin retired Hirsch's No. 40 and named him to the school's all-time football team in 1969. He also was inducted into the Wisconsin Athletics Hall of Fame (1965), the College Football Hall of Fame (1974), the Madison Sports Hall of Fame (1977), and the National High School Sports Hall of Fame (1988). His nickname, Crazylegs, has been celebrated as part of an annual spring run in Madison that attracts thousands of participants.

Hirsch died January 28, 2004, at age 80.

"There has never been a more loved and admired ambassador for Badger sports than Elroy Hirsch," UW athletics director Pat Richter said. "Anyone who came into contact with him enjoyed a special treat."

31 National Title Slips Away

Belief is a powerful tool. It can lift the spirit from the depths of despair and will the human body to a place that may not otherwise seem possible. And when that conviction diffuses through an entire basketball team, coupled with a level of talent unmatched in school history, a truly special unity can happen.

It was this combination of skill and faith that convinced Wisconsin's players months earlier they would be playing for a national championship the night of April 6, 2015, in Indianapolis. They were certain they would beat any team in their path, sure they would capture the program's first title in 74 years because nothing could stop them. Not North Carolina in the Sweet 16. Not Arizona in the Elite Eight. Not even undefeated Kentucky in the Final Four.

But the coronation, the celebration of the single greatest team the program had ever seen, did not take place. Instead, when the final buzzer sounded and the confetti dropped around Lucas Oil Stadium, the party raged for someone else. The Badgers were suddenly unwanted guests in the bash they believed would belong to them.

Moments earlier, Duke had squeezed past Wisconsin 68–63 to capture the national championship before 71,149 fans in a game that lived up to expectations, a blow-for-blow affair that came down to the final minutes. It ended with Badgers players walking off in silence amid the deafening rumble of music, heads staring at the ground or into the vast expanse of the arena, a space in the distance that did not contain the answers they were seeking.

"I couldn't even believe what I was seeing," Badgers forward Duje Dukan said afterward. "It almost felt like a bad dream."

Sam Dekker tugged his jersey up near his mouth. Frank Kaminsky hugged Josh Gasser and pulled his head in close as the confetti floated around them, two seniors who had done so much for the program, only to see it end in devastating fashion in their final college game. Gasser stood there near Wisconsin's bench, his hands on his knees, bent over in shock, while teammates tried unsuccessfully to console him.

How could he explain the feeling? He had seen the program's rise from Big Ten contender to national power, seen up close the effort required to reach this level, and approached the mountaintop only to watch it slip away in a flash. It was all so hard to swallow, he said, because the team *knew* a win was there for the taking thanks to a trust so strong it could not be broken.

No, it wasn't supposed to be over like this.

"Life's not fair sometimes," Gasser said, tears having given way to red, glassy eyes in front of his locker. "You work so hard. You believe you're going to win it. You put so much blood, sweat, and tears into it that no one else understands except for the 16 guys in the locker room."

The idea of belief had become part of the team's mantra. *Make 'Em Believe*, they uttered again and again back in October when the season began—believe that the previous season's Final Four run wasn't a fluke, that they could push over the hump and be as good as any team in the country. And it became such a rallying cry that the team wore the phrase on pregame warm-up shirts all season.

Where did everything career off the championship path? Wisconsin led 48–39 with 13:25 remaining in the title game after Kaminsky, the national player of the year, freed himself under the basket for an easy layup off an in-bounds pass. The highly partisan Wisconsin crowd, taking full advantage of Kentucky fans' ticket dump after the Badgers polished off the Wildcats in the national semifinal, roared with approval, and UW seemed poised to take down Duke.

During the entire NCAA tournament, this was exactly the place where Wisconsin had shined. The Badgers never faltered in tight, late-game situations, demonstrating a resolve and an undeniable camaraderie that had formed over years together. They were a group that could not be separated between practices that season. Often they would spend hours in the locker room playing video games, cracking jokes, and simply loving life. It was a near-perfect blend of players: fun loving, free of ego, and exceptionally talented, and it manifested on the court in remarkable ways.

This time, however, the moment players expected escaped them. They could not grind away and demoralize their opponent with the same beautiful, crisp basketball that had come to define them.

"They said what they wanted to do, they put themselves into that position, and they won't forget this for a long time," Badgers coach Bo Ryan said. "I told them that's life. Wait until you get a job. Wait until you start the next 60 or 70 years of your life. It's not always going to work out the way you would like it to. But you measure a person by what it takes to discourage them."

The game began to change when Duke guard Grayson Allen buried a three-pointer from the right wing and then converted a three-point play at the rim, drawing a foul on Dekker, to provide the Blue Devils life. A nine-point lead had been cut to 48–45, and the teams remained razor-close from there.

Dekker finished a layup off Bronson Koenig's pass to break the last tie and give Wisconsin a 58–56 edge with 4:25 remaining. But it proved to be the Badgers' final lead. On the ensuing possession, Duke guard Tyus Jones drained a three from just left of the key, and the Blue Devils pulled ahead 59–58—the start of a decisive 12–5 run to close the game.

When freshman center Jahlil Okafor put back Justise Winslow's miss, Duke led 63–58, and the result was all but certain. Wisconsin could not creep closer than three points from there, and Duke (35–4) pulled away for its fifth national championship under head coach Mike Krzyzewski.

Wisconsin finished the year 36–4, the program's single-season record for victories. But perspective would have to wait. In the locker room, there was only silence, interrupted by sobs for the second straight season in the Final Four. The Badgers had come one step closer, but that hardly resonated amid the gloom.

"This is one that no one's going to be able to take away from us," said Dekker, who would declare for the NBA draft days later. "All 16 guys as a whole know that this is the closest team we've ever been a part of. It's all right to show emotions. We're still men, but when something's taken from you like this, it's hard not to show them."

Kaminsky closed his college career with 21 points and 12 rebounds. Nigel Hayes finished with 13 points, Dekker 12, and Koenig 10. And though Wisconsin had played well enough to win for long stretches, it wasn't enough on a monumental night players wouldn't soon forget.

"All of us felt like we were the best team in the country," Dukan said. "All year we talked about that, that we were the best team in the country. We were going to be national champions."

They believed it until the very end.

32 Walk-On Tradition

Barry Alvarez's affinity for the way Nebraska's football program operated came from firsthand experience. As a linebacker under Cornhuskers coach Bob Devaney from 1965 to '67, he saw the formula required to maintain a consistent level of success. So when Alvarez earned his first head coaching opportunity at Wisconsin, it was no surprise he borrowed many of the same tactics that made the Cornhuskers such a force for decades.

Among the similarities Alvarez noticed between Nebraska and Wisconsin was that both schools represented the only major Division I program in the state, with kids growing up dreaming of playing for their respective in-state schools. Generally, there were more players than there were scholarships. But that didn't stop

Nebraska from bringing in talent as walk-ons—non-scholarship players who craved the opportunity to earn a coveted scholarship down the road.

Devaney won or shared the Big Eight crown in eight of his 11 seasons at Nebraska, with two national championship victories. Over the next 25 years, Tom Osborne won 12 Big Eight titles, one Big 12 crown, and three national championships. From 1962, when Devaney arrived, to 2009, 442 Nebraska walk-ons became letterwinners, and 131 walk-ons became starters.

If it worked at Nebraska, Alvarez decided, it could work at Wisconsin.

"Almost everything we did at Wisconsin, we stole from Nebraska, including the fabled walk-on program," Alvarez said before a Nebraska Football Coaches Clinic in 2009.

"I used the Nebraska blueprint. We analyzed what we could do and what we could consistently have, and then we implemented our strategy. First, we kept the best in-state kids at home. Then we recruited the best players we could recruit to be a very physical, run-oriented team. And finally, when we realized no one in the Big Ten was doing what Nebraska was doing with walk-ons, we went after it."

The model became vital to Alvarez's success and has continued at Wisconsin ever since. From 1990 to 2014, the Wisconsin football team's walk-on program produced 141 letterwinners, 11 team captains, and 16 NFL players. Two of its biggest stars included defensive end J.J. Watt, the 2012, 2014, and 2015 Associated Press NFL defensive player of the year, and wide receiver Jared Abbrederis, who received the 2013 Burlsworth Trophy as the best college football player to begin his career as a walk-on.

Other notable names of players who started their Wisconsin careers as walk-ons include Jim Leonhard, Joe Panos, Matt Davenport, Chris Maragos, Luke Swan, Joe Schobert, Alex Erickson, Rick Wagner, Mark Tauscher, Bradie Ewing, Joel

Stave, Ben Strickland, Donnel Thompson, Joe Stellmacher, Jason Doering, and Chad Cascadden, among others.

Alvarez and his successor, Bret Bielema, have called walk-ons "the ultimate erasers" because they help to erase mistakes made in recruiting. Walk-ons, Alvarez generally found, were among the most consistent and productive players on the team because each felt he had something to prove and would stop at nothing to achieve his goals.

"When I was coaching, we'd bring 20 to 25 walk-ons in every year," Alvarez said. "At least four or five of those walk-ons would turn out to be really good players."

It is a tradition that Badgers coach Paul Chryst, who took over the team before the 2015 season, felt important to maintain. In the 2011 Rose Bowl, nearly 20 percent of Wisconsin's starters began their college careers as walk-ons—the last year in which Chryst served as the Badgers' offensive coordinator.

"I don't know if it's because I've been here longest or know the history of this place better than any school, but it sure seems like it's special and unique with the walk-on program," said Chryst, who awarded scholarships to three walk-ons his first season in charge. "I think it is a place, though, where guys come and see that they are treated fairly, they will be given opportunity, and I think that helps us."

Wisconsin's walk-on system is unique because there isn't any other option for an in-state athlete who wants to play Division I football in the state. The Wisconsin Intercollegiate Athletic Conference offers quality Division III football but cannot provide athletic scholarships under NCAA rule. Many Wisconsin high school players from small towns often fail to gain recognition from other Division I programs and maintain the hope they can succeed if provided a chance with the Badgers.

"When you're younger, you'd watch the Badgers on TV and you would see success," former Badgers walk-on defensive lineman

Ethan Hemer told *Sports Illustrated* in 2012. "I watched the back-to-back Rose Bowls [in 1999 and 2000]. Small town kids across the state get the tradition here. There's a reason why our walk-on program is so well known. It's because kids want to work hard and they want to be a part of this."

Hemer, a Medford, Wisconsin, native, eventually joined the long list of walk-ons to earn scholarships and spent time on the Pittsburgh Steelers practice squad. What did that scholarship truly mean to a Wisconsin walk-on?

"I heard once that if you get a scholarship out of high school, it proves you can play high school football," Hemer said. "But if you can earn one when you're here, it proves you can play college football."

33 Dave McClain

Whipping wind, pelting rain, mud, and brutal cold had made playing conditions unequivocally miserable for Wisconsin's football team. It was a wet December night in Shreveport, Louisiana, and 23 mph gusts had reduced the wind-chill factor to 10 degrees. Paying fans couldn't even be bothered to show up—although more than 49,000 tickets had been sold, only 24,684 watched from the stadium.

Nothing about the 1982 Independence Bowl seemed glamorous. But through the harsh elements, Dave McClain's crowning achievement could not have been more beautiful. After 97 years and only four other postseason opportunities to show for it, Wisconsin had finally won its first bowl game.

McClain stood on a bench in the locker room, his voice hoarse, and told players they didn't have to steal their new red jerseys with

Independence Bowl patches on the shoulders. They could keep them as a token of their accomplishment.

"I'm so proud of everybody," McClain told them. "You guys don't realize what you've done. You've helped build a tradition. Tradition is a great thing."

There hadn't been much in the way of football tradition for some time at Wisconsin. For the better part of 20 years, the two words had seemed mutually exclusive. But with McClain in charge, the football program carried a renewed optimism. The payoff the night of December 11, 1982, was a 14–3 Independence Bowl victory against Kansas State that ran the Badgers' record to 7–5.

When McClain took over for John Jardine in 1978, the Badgers had experienced just one winning season in the previous 14. Despite recent history, McClain remained steadfast he could turn around the program.

"We plan to do a lot of talking to the players about pride," McClain told the *Chicago Tribune* after being hired at Wisconsin. "You know when you do your best, even if it's not apparent to others. I believe long-range goals are unrealistic. We'll look at short-range goals, take each game on its merits.

"I am not that familiar with what happened here last season. Of course, I read about the fans throwing stuff at Jardine. But the fan spirit here seems great to me. Since 1972, Wisconsin has been either fourth or fifth in Big Ten attendance. The potential is here to make it go."

McClain's background proved he was a man up to the task. He'd spent time as an assistant at Miami (Ohio) under Bo Schembechler, at Kansas under Pepper Rodgers, and at Ohio State under Woody Hayes. He went 46–25–3 in his first head coaching job at Ball State, where he earned Mid-American Conference coach of the year honors in 1975.

After three rebuilding years at Wisconsin, McClain found the magic touch. He led Wisconsin to the Garden State Bowl in

1981, a 21–14 loss to Tennessee, which marked the school's first bowl appearance in 18 years. He then became the first coach in program history to reach consecutive bowl games with the 1982 Independence Bowl appearance. His team qualified for another bowl in 1984, losing 20–19 to Kentucky in the Hall of Fame Bowl. McClain was the first Badgers coach to have four consecutive winning seasons since Ivy Williamson from 1949 to '54.

In eight seasons at Wisconsin, McClain was 46–42–3, including 32–34–3 in the Big Ten. The 46 victories left him just six shy of tying Milt Bruhn as the winningest Wisconsin coach in the modern era. And although McClain's Big Ten record was under .500, some of his biggest victories came against conference powers.

His 1981 team opened the season with a stunning 21–14 upset of No. 1 Michigan and also knocked off Purdue and Ohio State. The following year, Wisconsin defeated Ohio State 6–0 for Wisconsin's first victory over the Buckeyes in Columbus since 1918. His 1984 squad, which produced 11 NFL draft picks, including three first-rounders, was 4–0–1 in its final five games and beat Big Ten champion Ohio State again.

McClain did not have an opportunity to coach a ninth season at Wisconsin. He died of a heart attack at age 48 on April 28, 1986, after working out on an exercise bicycle at Camp Randall Stadium and collapsing in a sauna. Following his death, the university named the football practice facility in his honor. The Big Ten also named its football coach of the year award after McClain. He was inducted into the UW Athletics Hall of Fame in 2011.

Wisconsin's football program would slide into the Big Ten basement following McClain's death. The team finished 3–9 in the 1986 season under interim coach Jim Hilles and then went 6–27 in three seasons under Don Morton before Barry Alvarez restored the program to the prominence McClain first began establishing.

Seven years before McClain's passing, following the unexpected deaths of McClain's mother and Badgers freshman defensive back Jay Seiler during a two-week span, McClain reflected on how the experience had changed him.

"You ask how something like this could have happened," McClain said. "But I believe very strongly that God has a plan for each and every one of us. I'm not a religion fanatic, but I do believe that God's plan is perfect, and that helps me get through trying times....

"We know about the uncertainties of life. We know we have to enjoy life as it is, because tomorrow it might not be there."

34 Lee Kemp

A large picture of Dan Gable standing in his Olympic warm-up suit was plastered to the wall of Lee Kemp's Regent Street apartment in Madison. Gable was, to nearly every American wrestler of his era, a hero. He didn't lose a high school match and plowed through his collegiate career at Iowa State, winning 181 of 182 matches. He had won a gold medal in the 1972 Munich Olympics without surrendering a single point. He was the best anyone had ever seen, a symbol of pride across the country.

And now, Kemp was supposed to figure out how to beat him on the mat.

The two were scheduled to meet in the 158-pound championship of the 1975 Northern Open, held at Wisconsin. Gable was approaching the end of his career and considering a comeback. Kemp was a sophomore wrestler on the rise for the Badgers, having placed second in the NCAA tournament at 150 pounds the previous season.

Even three years after his Olympic victory, Gable was such an intimidating figure that Kemp's wrestling coach at Wisconsin,

Duane Kleven, tried to convince Kemp to drop back down to 150 pounds before the tournament began. Kemp said no.

"We struggled over the conversation," Kemp told *Inside Wisconsin Sports* magazine in 2012. "Coach said, 'You know, Gable's at your weight class?' And all I said was, 'Okay.' I wasn't trying to be cocky, but if you were a pitcher, wouldn't you want to pitch against Babe Ruth just to see how good you really are? That's the way I looked at it."

Before the championship match, Kemp noticed people would approach and ask whom he was wrestling in the final. When he mentioned Gable's name, they simply laughed.

"It wasn't a joke to me," Kemp later recalled to the *Milwaukee Sentinel*. "But people knew his name and his credentials. A lot of guys are overwhelmed and defeated even before they start against Gable. I'd seen him wrestle in the tournament earlier, and I wanted to give him a better match than other people did."

Kemp gave Gable more than a good match. He defeated Gable 7–6 to win the title in front of one of the most raucous crowds to ever witness a wrestling match in Madison. It was a victory that validated Kemp to the wrestling world and prompted Gable, who had suffered only his second loss since high school, to drop his plans of a comeback. He became head wrestling coach at the University of Iowa the following year.

"I was very surprised," Kleven said afterward. "I didn't think anybody could beat Gable."

Kemp became arguably the most storied wrestler in Wisconsin history. He was the first, and only, Wisconsin wrestler to win three NCAA championships, doing so in his sophomore, junior, and senior seasons. His final victory, a 10–8 defeat of Iowa State's Kelly Ward, pushed his career record at Wisconsin to 143–6–1, the best winning percentage by any Badgers wrestler (.957). Kemp also was the first UW wrestler to finish a season undefeated, when he went 39–0 during the 1975–76 season.

Kemp's success continued well after his time at Wisconsin. Two months after finishing his senior year of competition, he won the World Championships for freestyle wrestling, his first of four straight titles at 163 pounds. He also won four consecutive gold medals at the World Cup of Freestyle and was a two-time gold medalist at the Pan-American Games. In 1980, he made the United States Olympics team, but a government boycott of the event in Moscow prevented him from competing. He returned to the Olympics in 2008 as an assistant coach for the U.S. freestyle team in Beijing.

Oddly enough, the impetus behind Kemp's rise up the wrestling ladder also involved Gable, though it happened three years before the two squared off in Madison. Kemp didn't start wrestling until he was a freshman in high school, and as a sophomore, his record was only 11–8–3. In the summer of 1972, he attended a wrestling camp in Logan, Ohio, in which Gable attended as well. One morning, Kemp was going to breakfast and spotted Gable wearing a rubber suit, coming out of a wooded area.

"He'd been running hard and he was all sweaty," Kemp recalled. "That really impressed me. Until then, I'd never done any extra work. But after I saw how hard Dan Gable worked, I started running every day."

Kemp did not lose a match during his junior and senior years of high school, going 55–0. But Kemp, who grew up in Chardon, Ohio, a small farming community of 3,900 people about 30 miles northeast of Cleveland, still needed to find a place to wrestle in college.

Kleven first heard about Kemp after receiving a phone call from Northwestern wrestling coach Ken Kraft in the spring of 1974. Ten minutes later, athletics director Elroy Hirsch asked to see Kleven in his office. He said he had just received a call from an Ohio State alumnus from Kemp's hometown of Chardon—whose brother and son both attended Wisconsin—about a great wrestler named Kemp.

"Have you ever heard of him?" Hirsch asked.

"Yeah," Kleven replied, having never heard of Kemp until only a few minutes earlier.

Soon enough, the entire wrestling world heard about Kemp, the man who took down the great Dan Gable to spark an incredible career.

Athlete Profile: Jim Jordan

During the 1984–85 season, a wall inside Wisconsin's wrestling room held a sign that made the team's objectives quite clear. It read: "There can be no struggle, no question, no commitment, unless there is a goal. Big Ten and NCAA championships are our goal."

Jim Jordan took that message to heart. He would go on to finish that season as the NCAA champion in the 134-pound division, defeating eventual six-time World and Olympic champion John Smith of Oklahoma State in the finals. A year later, Jordan won his second national title, setting a Wisconsin single-season record with 49 victories.

In all, Jordan was a three-time All-American, a two-time Big Ten titlist, and a 1985 National Wrestling Coaches Association All-Star. He finished his career with a 156–28–1 collegiate record and still holds the record for most career wins in school history. He was inducted into the UW Athletics Hall of Fame in 2005. Jordan eventually became a politician and served three terms as a state representative in Ohio. In 2007, he became the U.S. Representative for Ohio's 4th congressional district.

Jordan was the fourth former Badger to be elected into the National Wrestling Hall of Fame, joining Russ Hellickson, Lee Kemp, and former head coach George Martin. His sons, Ben and Isaac, both went on to become All-American wrestlers with the Badgers.

35 1963 Rose Bowl: A (Near) Comeback for the Ages

USC quarterback Pete Beathard connected with his tight end, Fred Hill, on a 13-yard touchdown pass just six seconds into the fourth quarter of the 1963 Rose Bowl. For all intents and purposes, the outcome appeared certain, and Trojans players began acting accordingly.

"Some of our guys were congratulating each other, like the game was over," USC coach John McKay recalled after his team took a 42–14 lead against Wisconsin.

"We were already on the bus to the hotel and the party," Beathard would say.

Overcoming a four-touchdown deficit with less than one quarter to play against the No. 1 team in the country? Impossible. Preposterous. The stuff of fantasy.

A fantasy that second-ranked Wisconsin nearly made a reality in one of the greatest comebacks in program history—a 42–37 loss that spawned the legacy of Badgers quarterback Ron Vander Kelen.

"I've thought about it many times what exactly happened to me that day," Vander Kelen told the *Milwaukee Sentinel* in 1993. "And all I can say is it was just one of those times in an athlete's career when everything all of a sudden came together and just went right. It didn't matter what play I called, whether we had blocking or not—I just couldn't do anything wrong. I just happened to pick the right time in history."

Wisconsin's magical comeback in the first No. 1 vs. No. 2 bowl game matchup began when halfback Lou Holland took a pitchout 13 yards for a touchdown. USC's Ben Wilson fumbled the ensuing kickoff, and Wisconsin converted the mistake into a four-yard touchdown pass from Vander Kelen to halfback Gary

Kroner that trimmed the deficit to 42–28. A bad USC snap in the end zone on a punt attempt resulted in a Wisconsin safety to make the score 42–30. Then, with 1:19 remaining, Vander Kelen threw another touchdown pass, this time to Pat Richter, to bring the score to 42–37.

A USC attempt to stall backfired when the Trojans were forced to punt after their tailbacks intentionally lost yardage on runs to keep the clock moving. Badgers co-captain Steve Underwood distinctly recalled teammate Elmars Ezerins having a free lane to the punter but pulling off at the last instant. When Holland caught the punt at his own 44-yard line, USC tacklers met him immediately and time ran out on Wisconsin.

"He said after the game that he didn't do it because he thought he saw somebody else was going to block it, so he backed off," Underwood said. "Well, there wasn't anybody there, and he could've done it. That's the way the game is. We could have very well won that game in the last 30 seconds."

Wisconsin certainly had more than its share of chances to spring the victory. With the Badgers trailing 42–28 and at the USC 4, Vander Kelen called a short flat pass to the back corner of the end zone that USC's Willie Brown picked off when Wisconsin's receiver ran the wrong route.

"That game was the worst victory that I have ever experienced," USC's All-America end Hal Bledsoe told sportswriter Michael K. Bohn. "In the locker room afterward, you could hear a pin drop. That said, however, I have to give Wisconsin credit for not giving up. They didn't quit."

Vander Kelen set four Rose Bowl records that day: completions (33), pass attempts (48), passing yards (401), and total offense (406). Richter caught 11 passes for 163 yards, two yards shy of the Rose Bowl high set in 1935 by Alabama's Don Hutson. Vander Kelen and Beathard (8-for-12, 190 yards, and four touchdowns) were named co-MVPs of the game.

Vander Kelen had also been a member of Wisconsin's 1960 Rose Bowl team, which was embarrassed 44–8 by Washington in the game.

"Vandy had a certain air of confidence," Badgers fullback Ralph Kurek told the *Sentinel.* "He was the only one on the squad who had been to the Rose Bowl before, and he helped us get rid of the jitters.

"Once we caught on and saw we could do it, it got so contagious that we put extra effort into everything we did. We probably could have passed like that earlier if we realized how we could pick them apart. We still would have won except for that interception by Brown. It was so dark that Vandy couldn't see him."

As Badgers players sat in the locker room fighting back tears, they couldn't have known the impact their performance would have on so many people who watched the game around the country and appreciated their efforts.

"I was really let down after the game," Vander Kelen later said. "I had my head down, I was dejected—I had no idea how great a game it was until I got into the locker room and a lot of dignitaries came in. People were saying how proud they were of us, and how happy they were that we didn't embarrass anybody.

"Then as I was getting up the next morning, everything started to fall in place. The papers absolutely raved about us. The publicity we got as a losing team was phenomenal. I don't know how much more we could have gotten if we'd won."

Vander Kelen, a 6'0", 175-pound quarterback from Green Bay, Wisconsin, even received a call from legendary Green Bay Packers coach Vince Lombardi at 3:00 AM congratulating him and expressing an interest in him playing for the Packers. Vander Kelen ultimately played for the Minnesota Vikings.

"Ron and I left the next day to go to the Hula Bowl, and we were guests on a local TV show there with a couple of USC players," Richter recalled in Vince Sweeney's book *Always a Badger:*

The Pat Richter Story. "And all the people could talk about was this great comeback by Wisconsin. At some point, the USC guys said, 'Hey, wait a minute. We won the game!'"

The contest is still considered one of the greatest Rose Bowls in history. Authors David Wallechinsky and Amy Wallace even placed the game at No. 6 on their top 10 sporting events of all time in their *Book of Lists.*

"It's something that you look back on over time and you say, 'Did I really play in that game?'" Vander Kelen said.

36 Hoops Takes Down No. 1, Part I: 1962

Wisconsin basketball coach John Erickson could feel the need for a brief pep talk to his players. Five days earlier, he had watched his team lose a thrilling—and exhausting—92–90 shootout at home against archrival Minnesota. Next on the docket? Only a matchup against one of the best college basketball teams the Big Ten had ever seen.

On March 3, 1962, No. 1 Ohio State was set to arrive at the UW Field House for the Badgers' home finale. It was a Buckeyes team that featured All-American Jerry Lucas and second-team All-American John Havlicek—and a reserve named Bob Knight. Ohio State stood 22–0 on the season, including 12–0 in the Big Ten. The Buckeyes had won 27 consecutive Big Ten games and 47 straight regular season games. Simply put, they were a ruthless force bent on reaching the NCAA championship game for a third consecutive season.

To understand Ohio State's recent dominance against Wisconsin, one needed to only consider this statistic: over the previous two seasons, the Buckeyes had beaten the Badgers in all four games by a combined total of 117 points—an average of 29.3 points per contest. Wisconsin had not lost by a margin closer than 23 points.

Erickson gathered his players and left them with a simple message: "You'll always remember playing a great team like Ohio State. But you'll remember more if you beat them."

There would be plenty to remember indeed.

Wisconsin stunned Ohio State 86–67 with a devastatingly efficient offensive performance and a determined defense in a game considered among the most memorable the Badgers have ever played. It marked the first time UW defeated a top-ranked team in program history.

"This is the greatest thing in my life, outside of my wife and baby," Erickson famously said afterward.

How had Wisconsin pulled off the upset of the ages? The Badgers finished the game shooting 50.6 percent from the field (39-for-77). Ohio State, meanwhile, could only muster 32.0 percent (24-for-75). The Buckeyes entered the game leading the nation in field goal accuracy at 50.7 percent.

"I don't think they missed any shots at all," Ohio State coach Fred Taylor said. "Everything went in."

Don Hearden scored 29 points for Wisconsin, while Ken Siebel added 22. Havlicek, who went on to a hall of fame career with the Boston Celtics, made only 3-of-15 field goal tries. Lucas scored 23 points but was held to a relatively pedestrian 8-of-18 shooting. Though Ohio State out-rebounded Wisconsin 43–41 behind the efforts of Lucas' 15 rebounds and Havlicek's 14, it was considered something of a victory for the Badgers.

Erickson praised the Badgers for their incredible rebounding effort and singled out Tom Hughbanks, Siebel, and Tom Gwyn; the latter was celebrating his 21st birthday and "became a man in more ways than one," the coach noted, pointing to his defense on Lucas.

Wisconsin held its own from the outset and took a 37–30 halftime lead. The advantage ballooned to 15 points, 60–45 with a little more than 10 minutes left. Lucas, who scored 11 points in the first half, did not make his first basket of the second half until more than 11 minutes had elapsed. By that time, Wisconsin was ahead 64–50.

"We wanted to run them," Erickson said. "I'll tell you a secret—that's the only way we can play. On defense, we felt we had to stop Ohio State from spurting on us. We knew we would have a chance if we could keep them from getting a string of points on us."

When the game was over, the Field House crowd of 13,545 people cheered wildly, with many spilling on the court to celebrate the monumental achievement.

"Pandemonium broke loose at the final horn," *Wisconsin State Journal* sports writer Bob Hooker wrote in his game recap. "One would have thought Wisconsin had won the NCAA championship, and chances are the torrid Badgers would have won the national crown Saturday had it been at stake."

Ohio State closed the season 26–2 overall, losing in the national championship game. In three years together, that Ohio State group finished 78–6 overall and 40–2 in the Big Ten, winning the NCAA title in 1960 and losing to Cincinnati in the final in 1961 and 1962. Wisconsin finished the season 17–7 overall and 10–4 in the Big Ten to capture second in the league for the first time since 1950. The Badgers lost their final game of the season a week later to Iowa and did not qualify for postseason play.

For one night, however, they felt like champions. *Milwaukee Journal* sports writer Bill Letwin called the Ohio State victory "the biggest day in Wisconsin basketball in many a year."

"Although they were tiring fast, the Badgers kept on running to the very finish," Letwin wrote. "They did not have to walk to the dressing room, though. The enthusiastic crowd carried them there."

37 Alando Tucker

Of all the characteristics that defined Alando Tucker's basketball career at Wisconsin—scorer, leader, All-American—one seemed to stand above the rest: friend.

Tucker scored more points than any men's basketball player in Badgers history and is widely considered among the very best to ever play there. Yet the stories his teammates returned to during their careers were about Tucker's infectious zest for life, a rare standout who felt no sense of entitlement and genuinely cared for teammates as brothers.

"He's always around," former Badgers guard Michael Flowers told the *Milwaukee Journal Sentinel* in 2007. "He always wants to do stuff. He's the type of guy who gets two hours of sleep and comes in energized at 6:30 in the morning, laughing and joking around when we're lifting weights. He's the spirit and heart of this team."

Tucker routinely took time to make all of his teammates feel appreciated, from the starters down to the walk-ons, by inviting them to hang out and taking an interest in their lives. One of the defining stories about Tucker came one day when teammate Joe Krabbenhoft thought he suffered a foot injury and had no one else to turn to—the team trainer was off for the day. So, he called Tucker.

Krabbenhoft assumed his season was over, and Tucker spent nearly four hours with him as he broke down in tears. Tucker drove Krabbenhoft to the hospital and waited with him until the X-rays came back negative.

"No matter if he has known you for five years or meets you for the first time, he greets you with the same smile and the same personality," then-Badgers assistant coach Greg Gard told the *Wisconsin State Journal.* "He always has time for people. He doesn't big-time anybody."

Tucker also was a pretty darn good basketball player during his time with the Badgers. His final tally of 2,217 points was 70 points ahead of Michael Finley's previous record. He finished his career ranking first in made field goals (798), first in offensive rebounds (314), and first in minutes played (4,247).

As a freshman, Tucker started 27 of 32 games and averaged 12.0 points and 5.9 rebounds. He persevered after missing all but four games of the 2003–04 season with a foot injury and was granted an extra year of eligibility from the NCAA. He returned to lead the Badgers in scoring for three consecutive seasons. In 2006–07, his 19.9 points per game marked the highest single-season scoring average for any player during head coach Bo Ryan's tenure. For his efforts, Tucker was named the Big Ten Player of the Year and a first-team All-American—the first at Wisconsin since Don Rehfeldt in 1950.

Tucker told *Sports Illustrated* he traced his leadership instincts to a day in seventh grade when his older half brother, Antonio, left their hometown of Lockport, Illinois, to join the Army and serve in Kosovo. Alando, alongside his mother and grandmother, then helped to raise his three remaining siblings.

Alando made a pact then to not drink, smoke, or get tattoos, to be a good role model for his community and achieve as much as he could. Antonio had encouraged Alando to read books such as *The Iliad* and the Bible and stimulated his intellectual curiosity, which thrived in college. He wrote a 19-page proposal as part of a class at Wisconsin in which he outlined how he would build a new youth center in Lockport that would include baseball and football fields, as well as an academic learning center.

"The whole concept of academics has been lost in my community," Tucker said during his senior year at Wisconsin. "I want to re-teach that to kids…. I go back and talk to schools in my community. I tell them I happened to be a student first. I grasped that concept early in high school. I use my basketball success to further my point. I got here through academics."

Tucker was selected 29th overall in the first round of the 2007 NBA draft by the Phoenix Suns and later enjoyed a successful professional career overseas. Everywhere Tucker went, he left quite an impression—one his former Badgers coach certainly won't forget.

"He's just a good person," Ryan said. "Gosh, it's nice to be around just good people that don't have a lot of other agendas. When I come in and I'm around Alando, it's like being at home. It's like a family. There are people that make you feel like that when you're around them."

38 Jim Leonhard

Jim Leonhard's story is one every overlooked Wisconsin high school football player either knows or aspires to replicate. It is the story of a 5'8", 180-pound athlete from a small town who didn't receive a single Division I scholarship offer. It is the story of perseverance, determination, and hard work. It is the story of a player who joined the Badgers program as an unknown walk-on and left as one of the best defensive players in school history.

Leonhard is considered among the most revered players to come through Wisconsin's program, and his talent and humility make it easy to see why. He was a legendary athlete in his hometown of Tony, Wisconsin (population 110), where he attended Flambeau High School and earned All-State honors as an option quarterback. During his stellar athletic career as a three-sport star, he once gained more than 500 total yards in a football game, buried

10 three-pointers in a basketball game, and struck out 19 of 21 batters in a baseball game.

Offers to play college football were scarce, and Leonhard had always wanted to test himself in the Big Ten. He finally made an impression on Badgers coaches at a summer camp before his senior year of high school, when he ran a 4.4-second 40-yard dash. When Badgers coach Barry Alvarez asked him to run it once more, Leonhard again clocked 4.4. He was offered a preferred walk-on spot at Wisconsin and happily accepted.

Still, a fast 40 time hardly equates to playing time in the Big Ten. Leonhard had to prove he belonged. He made his way onto the special teams unit as a freshman in 2001. As a sophomore, he began returning punts and also earned the starting free safety job. Opposing teams, not surprisingly, thought they might be able to pick on Leonhard as an undersized player. He wound up leading the country with 11 interceptions and a Big Ten–best 25 pass breakups in 2002. He added seven more interceptions in 2003 and three in 2004 to tie a school record with 21.

"I know for sure they were testing me my sophomore year," Leonhard told the *Chicago Tribune*. "Not only was I a 5'8" safety, I was also a sophomore who had no starting experience.... I knew that and I loved it."

In addition to Leonhard's defensive prowess, he became the school's best punt returner. He holds the school record for punt return yards with 1,347 in a career, and no other player is within 340 yards. He also owns the three highest marks for single-season punt return yards and returned three touchdowns in his career. Leonhard, who started his final 39 games, was named first-team All-Big Ten in each of his final three seasons. He earned at least one first-team All-America nod in each of those years, though it wasn't until Leonhard's junior season that he finally earned a scholarship.

"For me, there have been people who doubted me in athletics since I got here, even before I got here," Leonhard said during his senior season. "You always take that underdog mentality. That sticks with you. Just because you get a scholarship check, I don't think that changes who you are."

One reason for Leonhard's success was his incredible natural ability. At Wisconsin, he had a 33-inch vertical jump and was the football team's slam-dunk champion. People often asked Alvarez to explain how someone so unassuming could be such a force for his program.

"He looked like an altar boy," Alvarez told the *New York Times*. "Behaved like one, too. But on the field, wow, he was something else."

Former Minnesota football coach Glen Mason once saw Leonhard riding up an escalator at a Big Ten media day event before the 2004 season. He complimented Leonhard as a tremendous football player. He also did a double take at Leonhard's size. "Are you really Jim Leonhard?" Mason asked. "I have managers bigger than you."

Over the years, Leonhard never allowed perception to impede his goals. No NFL team drafted him in 2005 despite his spectacular Wisconsin career. By the fall, he was the only undrafted rookie on the 53-man opening day roster for the Buffalo Bills. He would play 10 seasons in the NFL with the Bills, Baltimore Ravens, New York Jets, Denver Broncos, and Cleveland Browns before retiring in 2014. He was inducted into the Wisconsin Athletics Hall of Fame in 2015 and returned to the Badgers football program as the defensive backs coach in 2016.

Back in his hometown of Tony, Leonhard is a hero—as he is to many walk-ons who continue to rise through Wisconsin's football program. In the center of town, a billboard celebrates his college accomplishments, complete with a giant painting of Leonhard wearing a Badgers uniform.

Welcome to Tony, Hometown of Jimmy Leonhard, the sign reads. Walk-on to All-American.

His stature was small, but no one could deny Leonhard's big talent.

39 Hard Rocks Defense of 1951

Wisconsin has produced nine different Rose Bowl teams over the years, and each has earned a special place in the program's lore. Oddly enough, however, the one team many believe was most equipped for a Rose Bowl opportunity fell painstakingly short despite possessing the finest defensive unit in school history.

It became known as the "Hard Rocks" defense of 1951, a group so dominant that it still holds its place atop the Badgers' record books. That UW team led the nation in total defense (154.8 yards per game) and ranked second in rushing defense (66.8). Both marks continue to rank first at Wisconsin and are likely to endure for years to come.

No other Badgers defense has ever allowed fewer than 231.0 yards per game for a season. The Hard Rocks also maintain the single-season school record for scoring defense (5.9 points per game) and lowest opponent average per rushing attempt (1.74). In total, opponents gained 601 yards on 345 carries.

Three of Wisconsin's top nine games all-time in total defense occurred during the 1951 season. In one game against Iowa, the Hawkeyes finished with minus-18 yards rushing and only 82 total yards—the fifth-best effort in program history. Ohio State gained 106 total yards and Northwestern managed 113 yards, only 23 of which came on the ground. For 32 years, the defense held the school record of 139 interception yards after picking off Pennsylvania three times in one game. The Badgers also recovered a fumble for a touchdown and forced a safety that day.

In total, Wisconsin outscored opponents 206–53. But the defense was so talented that it actually outscored its opponents 58–53. Perhaps it's no surprise that, after the season, the defense challenged the offense in a charity game and let the offensive team keep the ball all the time. The defense believed it could outscore the offense even without the ball.

Eight of the nine seniors on the Hard Rocks defense scored in their careers. The ninth, Bill Lane, came close. According to the school's fact book, with Indiana backed up deep in its own territory for a punt, the seniors told Lane they would refrain from rushing in order to form a wedge, or "meatchopper," for him to run behind and score. Instead, freshman Don Voss missed the call and blocked the punt.

Given all of those achievements, how in the world did the 1951 Wisconsin team not reach the Rose Bowl? Thanks to a stunning—and controversial—14–10 loss to Illinois in the second game of the season. Wisconsin led Illinois 10–7 at halftime and took the second-half kickoff all the way to the Illini 1-yard line. But the Badgers failed to register the final yard in four tries.

Former player Gene Felker told the *Milwaukee Journal* in 1981 that Rollie Strehlow lost a yard, the team was penalized for five yards back to the seven, tailback Alan Ameche gained four yards, and then the Badgers were penalized 15 yards for holding. By the time Wisconsin reached fourth down, Ameche couldn't punch the ball into the end zone. After the game, Badgers coach Ivy Williamson was peeved at the referee's calls.

"Ivy swore that guy would never officiate in the Big Ten, and he didn't," Felker said. "I don't remember his name, but they said he didn't want us to get into the Rose Bowl."

Illinois halfback Johnny Karras then helped his team gain some breathing room with a 30-yard run, and the Illini completed a 98-yard drive for the winning touchdown. Wisconsin outgained Illinois 274–142 that day, but the Badgers couldn't score when it mattered most. Illinois finished the year 5–0–1 in conference play, while Wisconsin went 5–1–1—including a 6–6 tie against Ohio State the week after the Illinois game.

UW closed the season strong, with blowout victories against Purdue (31–7), Northwestern (41–0), Iowa (34–7), and Minnesota (30–6). But it wasn't enough to earn the Rose Bowl berth.

"At the end of the year, we were so much better than Illinois that it wasn't funny," Badgers linebacker Deral Teteak said. "They were hanging on by their nails, and we were killing everybody."

Added Felker: "They beat Stanford in the Rose Bowl 40–7. We would've beaten Stanford 60–0. There probably wasn't anybody who could have beaten us by that time."

40 1953 Rose Bowl Is Badgers' First

It was a different era of college football when Wisconsin reached its first Rose Bowl. There were no television updates, incessant pundit analysis, or immediate knowledge of a team's bowl destination. In fact, not until two days after the Badgers played their regular season finale did anyone on the team know for certain a trip to Pasadena would happen.

During the final game of the 1952 regular season, Wisconsin tied Minnesota 21–21 at Camp Randall Stadium to close 6–2–1 overall and 4–1–1 in the Big Ten. Purdue also finished 4–1–1 in Big Ten play but stood 4–3–2 overall, which seemed to indicate the Badgers would garner the Rose Bowl opportunity. But nobody could be sure until the league's athletics directors decided the representative in a Monday morning vote. Even then, players had to attend classes and sweat out the decision until the afternoon.

"We didn't find out for two hours because we didn't have the communication we do now," nose tackle Charles Berndt told the *Milwaukee Sentinel* in 1993. "Then we had a big rally in front of Memorial Union."

Given that Wisconsin had earned its first-ever Rose Bowl berth, the news was met on campus with considerable enthusiasm.

"I remember being in class on Bascom Hill about 1:00 PM when the announcement was made," Kent Peters, a senior end on that team, told the *Sentinel.* "All the doors of the buildings opened, like a big fire drill. The students poured out, and the celebration went on into the night. It was as exciting a moment as we'd had in our college careers."

The 1952 season proved to be significant because it marked the only time in which Wisconsin reached No. 1 in the history of the Associated Press Top 25 poll, which began in 1936. Wisconsin spent one week in the top spot before losing 23–14 to Ohio State in the third game of the season. It also marked the only Rose Bowl appearance during head coach Ivy Williamson's successful seven-year tenure, though his teams would finish the season ranked in the top 20 in five consecutive years. But the Rose Bowl result would not favor the Badgers.

Statistics are not necessarily indicative of a game's outcome. And if ever one game served as a prime example, it would be the 1953 Rose Bowl. In nearly every way, Wisconsin outplayed USC. Wisconsin finished with more total offense (353–233) and more first downs (19–16) while dominating on the ground (211–48). Still, the Badgers could not find a way to score and absorbed a 7–0 loss.

One of Wisconsin's best scoring chances came in the opening minutes of the third quarter when standout running back Alan Ameche broke free for a 54-yard run down to the USC 21-yard line. On third down, however, Archie Ray Burks fumbled on an end run and USC recovered. Ameche finished the game with 133 yards rushing on 28 carries.

USC pieced together what proved to be the decisive 73-yard drive, which ended when Trojans quarterback Rudy Bukich connected with Al Carmichael on a 22-yard touchdown. Wisconsin countered with a 13-play, 84-yard drive that ended at USC's 2-yard line. Jerry Witt was stopped a yard short of a first down on a fake field goal play.

USC's victory represented the first win for the West against the Big Ten since teams from both conferences began meeting annually in 1947. The crowd of 101,500 was the largest Wisconsin players had played in front of in their college careers.

"Losing was tough, but it was mitigated by the chance to participate in it," Peters said. "For the people who play in the Rose Bowl, those memories you never forget. It was one of the greatest things I've ever experienced."

41 Walter "Doc" Meanwell

The picture of a basketball revolutionary was a British-born physician who earned his medical degree from Johns Hopkins, came to Wisconsin to study for a doctorate in public health, and coached wrestling. Really.

That certainly seems like an extraordinarily odd combination for a man who would hold the title as winningest Badgers basketball coach for 80 years. But Walter "Doc" Meanwell was far from ordinary. So was the story of how he became a basketball coaching legend.

Shortly before the 1911 season, Wisconsin coach Haskell Noyes quit, forcing the school to scurry for a new coach. Efforts to find a professional coach failed, so Meanwell, then director of the men's gymnasium, volunteered his services until a coach could be found. No one knew he had any knowledge of basketball outside of what he'd gleaned from coaching playground teams in Baltimore.

Meanwell implemented a style of play that had not been seen to that point. Basketball in the early 1900s was physical, and players rarely moved quickly around the court. His teams were known for short passing, crisscross dribbles, and a tight zone defense, a system that utilized finesse and footwork from his background in boxing and wrestling. His famous "crisscross, pivot, and pass" offense involved all five players making short passes, pivots in motion, and setting screens for a shooter. Rarely did the Badgers ever dribble the basketball.

"The game got completely out of hand," Meanwell said. "It was so rough that many schools dropped basketball between the years 1905 and 1915. I decided to buck the trend and stress finesse."

Defensively, Meanwell's teams operated out of what resembled a 3–2 zone used to counter an opponent's fast break. Thanks to his medical background, he also became one of the first coaches to emphasize physical fitness and training.

Meanwell's success was both immediate and incredible. In his first three seasons in charge at Wisconsin, the Badgers won 44 of 45 games. His 1911–12 and 1913–14 teams each finished 15–0 and were retroactively awarded the Helms Foundation national championship. In the 1915–16 season, Wisconsin finished 20–1 and again earned a Helms Foundation title. Meanwell, who stood 5'6", was aggressive and demanding and earned five nicknames during his time as coach: Doc, Little Doctor, Napoleon of Basketball, The Little Giant, and The Wizard.

Following a two-year appointment at the University of Missouri, Meanwell returned to Wisconsin for his second stint as Badgers head coach in 1920. He previously coached the team from 1911 to 17 and then again from 1920 to '34, when he retired. In total, he led the Badgers to eight Big Ten championships over 20 seasons and posted a career record of 246–99 (.712 winning percentage). Following his coaching career, Meanwell practiced medicine in Madison until his death in 1953. He was named to the inaugural class of the Naismith Memorial Basketball Hall of Fame (1959) and the charter class of the Wisconsin State Athletics Hall of Fame (1991).

Meanwell's revolutionary offense, known as the "Wisconsin System," was copied for decades by coaches across the country. One of his former players, George Levis, had been an All-American center at Wisconsin. He became coach at Carleton College in Minnesota in 1917 and immediately installed the Wisconsin System. Levis then moved to Indiana and brought the style there, teaching the Hoosiers' first All-American, Everett Dean. Dean, in turn, took over as coach at Carleton and taught Meanwell's system to future coaches in the state of Minnesota, along with several others.

A 1922 article from *American Golfer Magazine* on Meanwell titled "The Miracle Man of Basketball" noted the term "Miracle Man" was extravagant and overused in the sporting world. But, in its introduction of Meanwell, the magazine wrote: "Out in the Middle West, there is a university coach whose qualification for the honor would, if generally known, entitle him to serious consideration as a real contender for the all-time place in basketball; for he has been performing miracles on the court with a consistency that has been almost monotonous since 1911."

Meanwell's final Big Ten record at Wisconsin was 158–80. It wasn't until January 7, 2015, when another Badgers coach, Bo Ryan, surpassed that win tally in league games.

"I wish I'd have been around when he coached," Ryan said on the occasion of his passing Meanwell for UW's all-time Big Ten wins record. "He's an interesting guy. Could have done a lot more than coaching. He's called Doc for a reason. But he won a lot of games. And when I got here in the '70s, there were still people around that knew him. So I did hear some stories back in the '70s, and they were all positive. Must've been a heck of a guy... He did an awful lot for the game."

42 Wisconsin 21, No. 1 Michigan 14

When Wisconsin's players glanced at the Camp Randall Stadium scoreboard two days before their season opener against top-ranked Michigan in 1981, they found an illuminated message left by their football coach. There it was, spelled out in big, bright bulbs: Wisconsin 17, Michigan 14.

It was just another tactical move from Badgers coach Dave McClain to make players believe the unthinkable suddenly was possible. What reason did the outside world have to believe the same? Not much.

In the teams' four previous matchups, Michigan had outscored Wisconsin 176–0. As a result, the Badgers—who hadn't beaten the Wolverines since 1962—were listed as 19-point underdogs. To make matters worse, then–Green Bay Packers safety Mike Jolly, a former Michigan player, had insulted Wisconsin's entire football program in a newspaper article that week. He noted Wolverines players used to talk on the sideline and predict how many points they would score on Wisconsin.

"I played against Wisconsin every year—for about a half," Jolly had said. "After that, the game always turned into a joke.... The Wisconsin players were just intimidated about playing Michigan. You could see it in their eyes."

But the 1981 edition of Wisconsin football was out to prove the Badgers would no longer be overlooked. And on September 12, 1981, they shocked the college football world with a 21–14 upset of No. 1 Michigan in front of 68,722 delirious fans at Camp Randall Stadium, many of whom chanted "We're No. 1" as the clock wound down.

"A lot of people didn't think we could beat the No. 1 team in the country," McClain said afterward. "But before the game I told the players that they were the only guys in this room who believed we could win. You've got to believe."

Many pundits had suggested Wisconsin's offense was too conservative to compete with Michigan. But McClain opened up his playbook, frequently using a shotgun formation. Badgers sophomore quarterback Jess Cole passed for 182 yards and gained 41 yards on option runs, as Wisconsin rolled up 439 yards and three touchdowns. It came against a Michigan defense that had not allowed any touchdowns and only three field goals in its final five and a half games the previous season.

Michigan took a 7–0 lead when Wolverines sophomore quarterback Steve Smith scored on a four-yard run early in the second quarter. But Cole led the Badgers to a pair of touchdowns in the final 3:47 of the second quarter for a 14–7 halftime lead. Cole threw a 17-yard touchdown pass to Marvin Neal, and tailback Chucky Davis scored a touchdown from one yard out two seconds before halftime.

The Wolverines tied the score at 14 on an 89-yard touchdown run from Butch Woolfolk with 9:11 left in the third quarter. Cole, however, helped Wisconsin re-take the lead nine plays later on a 71-yard touchdown pass to John Williams. Williams caught a screen about five yards behind the line of scrimmage and raced down the left sideline to score, giving Wisconsin a 21–14 lead with 5:13 remaining in the third quarter.

The touchdown proved to be all Wisconsin would need thanks to an ornery defense led by safety Matt Vanden Boom and nose guard Tim Krumrie, who put together one of his most memorable performances. He finished with 13 tackles and earned national player of the week honors. Vanden Boom, meanwhile, intercepted Smith three times. The third interception gave the Badgers possession at their 17 with two seconds to play. Smith completed only 3-of-18 passes for 39 yards.

When the final seconds ticked off, Badgers fans streamed onto the field and pounded players on their backs as they ran through the tunnel to the locker room. McClain's bold and improbable scoreboard prediction had come true.

"It's the greatest thing that's ever happened to me," McClain said. "I've been on some great teams, but I've never had as much fun as coaching a team that beats Michigan."

Michigan coach Bo Schembechler was stunned. The game marked Michigan's first defeat in a season opener in Schembechler's 13 seasons as coach at the school—and it would be his only loss against Wisconsin in 19 tries. He even took a conciliatory call the next day from former Ohio State coach Woody Hayes, a longtime rival.

"Obviously Wisconsin is a better team than everyone thought, and obviously we aren't as good as everyone thought," Schembechler said. "This isn't 1980."

Michigan fullback Stan Edwards lamented the fact his Wolverines didn't make the effort to come back and show they could be the dominant force of years past.

"We were impostors in Michigan uniforms," Edwards said. "I don't know if Wisconsin played above their head or if they're that good. Time will tell."

Wisconsin would go on to reach its first bowl game since 1963, finishing the season 7–5, including 6–3 in the Big Ten—the same league record as Michigan.

43 Michael Finley

The way Michael Finley tells it, he didn't know much about Wisconsin's school or its basketball team when he arrived in

Madison on a recruiting visit from the Chicago area. But two things struck him almost immediately while perusing campus: the love the community had for its sports teams and the opportunity to help turn around a program.

"Once I got here, I just fell in love," Finley recalled when he returned to campus in 2011. "I remember going to a football game and hanging with the football players. It was as if I was already here, a part of the university. I don't know if they do that to all the recruits. But at that time, I felt kind of special. I went home and thought about it and I thought this was the right place for me. I think I made the right decision."

Finley's Wisconsin career ranks among the best in program history. His time at the school, from 1991 to '95, coincided with the rebirth of the Badgers' basketball program. As a junior, Finley led the Badgers to their first NCAA tournament appearance in 47 years. He averaged at least 20.0 points per game in each of his last three seasons and is one of just two players in UW history to score more than 2,000 career points, along with Alando Tucker. Finley was a two-time first-team All-Big Ten selection and three-time Associated Press honorable mention All-American.

Finley said he was not highly recruited among Big Ten teams while coming out of Proviso East High School during the early '90s. Only conference schools Northwestern and Wisconsin had expressed an interest in his talents. His recruiting trip to Madison represented the first of five planned visits to campuses around the country, but the university quickly sold him.

In Finley's freshman season, he averaged 12.3 points per game, but the Badgers finished just 13–18. The team went 14–14 the following season before finally breaking through to reach the NCAA tournament—a feat Finley called his greatest moment as a Badgers player.

"I'm proud to say that when we did make it to the tournament after a long drought, that I was a part of that team," Finley said. "I was a part of rebuilding, so to speak, of putting Wisconsin basketball back on the map."

The path at Wisconsin wasn't always easy. Finley began his career under head coach Steve Yoder, who was fired after Finley's freshman season in 1992. Finley then played for two seasons under Stu Jackson. But Jackson left to take a front office position with the NBA's expansion Vancouver Grizzlies, and Finley's lead recruiter, assistant coach Ray McCallum, left the program during that time as well. Finley spent his final season under coach Stan Van Gundy on a team that underachieved and finished 13–14.

"It was tough," Finley said. "Not only with the coaching changes but the losing. I was coming from a prestigious high school in the Chicago area at Proviso East where we maybe lost two or three games in the four years I was there. To come here and to have not much success early on, I think it helped me grow as a man."

The lessons Finley learned in leadership at Wisconsin, he said, carried over to an NBA career that lasted 15 seasons. During that time, Finley averaged 15.7 points per game and won an NBA title while with the San Antonio Spurs in 2007. He was named to the NBA's all-rookie team in 1996 with the Phoenix Suns and earned All-Star selections in 2000 and 2001 with the Dallas Mavericks. Finley retired following the 2010 season.

Even after Finley blossomed into an NBA star, he never forgot his Badgers roots. In 2011, he returned to campus to announce that he had established an endowed scholarship benefiting minority student-athletes. The scholarship came courtesy of the Michael Finley Foundation, a not-for-profit organization he began in 2003.

Finley said he hoped the endowment scholarship, given to a minority student-athlete every year, would extend his legacy at Wisconsin for years to come.

"I think my scholarship just gives other African-Americans an opportunity to attend a big-time college," Finley said. "It's an opportunity that may not have been there without my scholarship.

The beauty of it, I think, is I'm a result of what can happen when you get out of a not-so-great environment and come to an environment like this, which is different. It can make you a better person.

"Hopefully by me having that scholarship available to African-Americans, they can experience the same things that I experienced here and make them a better person in life."

44 Dave Schreiner

He turned down a chance to become an athletics director in the armed forces to enlist in the Marines. And perhaps that's a good place to start. Dave Schreiner never was someone who wanted anything handed to him.

The pride of Lancaster, Wisconsin, Schreiner is remembered as a Wisconsin football player who was both incredibly popular and an unquestioned leader of the team, even on a unit that featured Elroy "Crazylegs" Hirsch and future NFL star Pat Harder. He was a two-time All-American in 1941 and 1942 and was named the Big Ten's MVP during his final season. So respected was Schreiner that he became one of the few juniors to captain a Wisconsin team for the Badgers' final game against Purdue in 1941.

In 1942, Schreiner put together a memorable senior season when he caught 18 passes for 386 yards and five touchdowns as a wide receiver and wreaked havoc on the other side of the ball as a defensive end. He helped Wisconsin tie Notre Dame 7–7 early in the season and made a key sack of Fighting Irish quarterback Angelo Bertelli, who had a receiver wide open at the goal line. Later in the season, Schreiner caught a 14-yard touchdown pass to help

Wisconsin defeat unbeaten and No. 1–ranked Ohio State 17–7. His defensive effort also was key in the win.

A newspaper account noted Hirsch and Harder were the backs who made the offense tick, "but it was the great Badger line led by Dave Schreiner and Fred Negus that repeatedly repelled the thrusts of the Ohio State backs who averaged [more than] 400 yards per game until today's contest."

Ohio State gained 296 total yards in the game, only 79 of which came with the Buckeyes in Wisconsin territory. It should be noted that Schreiner served as the team's acting captain in both the Notre Dame and Ohio State games. In fact, his team never lost a game with him as acting captain, finishing 3–0–1, including a 20–6 victory against Minnesota in his 1942 college finale. Wisconsin closed the '42 season 8–1–1, one of the most successful teams in school history.

His legacy, however, is about much more than football. During the 1942 season, as World War II raged, Schreiner arranged his enlistment. Upon graduation, Schreiner wanted to join the U.S. Army Air Corps but was rejected because he was colorblind. He then joined the U.S. Marines in 1943 and was commissioned as a second lieutenant. He fought on Saipan in 1944 and was wounded in the head. By 1945, he had been in combat in Guam before moving to Guadalcanal with the 4th Regiment of the Marines' 6th Division and earned a Purple Heart.

Schreiner quickly became a respected leader of his unit and moved up to company commander by the time he landed in Okinawa on April 1, 1945.

A superior sent Schreiner on a dangerous mission near the west coast of Oroku Peninsula on June 20 to check if there were any holdout Japanese troops in the area. Schreiner led a three-man trek and was shot in the upper torso. There were conflicting stories about how the events unfolded, with some suggesting he was ambushed while accepting a surrender of Japanese soldiers.

Men from the patrol rushed to get Schreiner back to the unit's lines. PFC Vern Courtnage saw Schreiner before he was loaded onto a jeep to be taken to an aid station.

"Everybody was wishing him well, and he was conscious," Courtnage said in the Terry Frei book *Third Down and a War Hero to Go*. "The last words he spoke, that I heard, anyway, were, 'If any of you guys think I'm crying, I'll get out of here and kick the [expletive] out of you!'"

Schreiner died the next day, on June 21, 1945, at age 24. Three days before his death, he had mailed his parents a letter with an update on his condition and tried to assuage their fears.

Dear Mother and Dad,

Rec'd letter of June 6 from you. Enclosed was a clipping about Johnny Walsh. No, I didn't get any bronze star on Guam. I've still got my medal. I can feel it when I put my hands behind me. We've been eating very well of late. Fresh meat, good canned food etc. And I've been sleeping a lot. Boy it's good to rest. Will write next chance I get. Don't forget a company commander is a pretty safe spot.

Much love,

Dave

His final letter arrived home in Lancaster on June 25, four days after his death. His remains were reinterred, and Schreiner was brought home to Lancaster on April 13, 1949, where he was buried in the Schreiner family lot in Hillside Cemetery.

Posthumously, Schreiner became the first Wisconsin player elected to the College Football Hall of Fame. Wisconsin retired his No. 80 jersey after his death, and the school established a memorial scholarship in his name.

Retired Numbers

Wisconsin's football program has retired the jersey numbers of six players in school history. Five of those players are widely celebrated as the best to ever put on a Badgers uniform: Ron Dayne (No. 33), Alan Ameche (35), Elroy Hirsch (40), Dave Schreiner (80), and Pat Richter (88). Fans likely know far less about Allan Shafer, a freshman quarterback in 1944 whose No. 83 will never be worn again.

Shafer, a Madison native, delayed his enrollment into the Naval Academy in Annapolis one year in order to study engineering at Wisconsin. After earning All-Conference and All-City honors as a high school center, he was asked to change positions to quarterback and was named the starter for the team's season opener against Northwestern. He recovered from a back injury and was on the field for Wisconsin's game against Iowa on November 11, 1944. Tragically, however, Shafer collapsed on the field and died an hour later after being taken to a local hospital. An autopsy revealed Shafer had died of a hemorrhage of the lungs, caused by a violent blow. When he sustained the blow is unknown. He was 17 years old.

Following his death, the Allan J. Shafer Jr. Memorial Award was created. The award is given to students, generally football players, based on high scholastic achievement and citizenship.

45 Camp Randall Stadium

There is perhaps no better campus experience than taking part in the game day atmosphere that is Camp Randall Stadium. Picture it: a sea of red-clad Badgers fans wildly cheering Wisconsin on to victory in a beautiful relic that, when filled, makes it the fifth-largest city in the entire state. More often than not these days, a good seat is hard to come by, as the Badgers make full use of a stunning home-field advantage.

The history of Camp Randall Stadium is long and illustrious. It was built in 1917, making it the fourth-oldest stadium in college football, trailing only Bobby Dodd Stadium (Georgia Tech), Davis Wade Stadium (Mississippi State), and Nippert Stadium (Cincinnati). But the story of the building's grounds dates back even before it was affiliated with the university.

In the days before the Civil War, the site was owned by the Wisconsin Agricultural Society, which held its annual state fair on the grounds. When war broke out in 1861, the society gave the land to the government for a major military training center. More than 70,000 troops attended training drills at the Camp Randall complex, named after Wisconsin's first wartime governor, Alexander W. Randall.

After peace was restored nationally, the land returned to state fair property. The fair later moved to Milwaukee, and Wisconsin's Civil War veterans urged the legislature to purchase the land. In 1893, the state presented the site to the university as a memorial athletic field. The stadium was built at its present site in 1913. A tragic collapse of the wooden bleachers in 1915 prompted the university to make plans for concrete stands, and two years later, a 10,000-seat concrete stadium was built with a grant of $15,000 from the state legislature. The stadium was officially dedicated on November 3, 1917, as part of homecoming festivities, when Wisconsin defeated Minnesota 10–7.

Over the years, the stadium continued to increase its seating capacity, from 33,000 in 1924 to 45,000 in 1940 to 55,000 in 1950. By 1965, the capacity reached 77,475. Camp Randall remained virtually untouched for more than 35 years until a renovation began in 2001. The $109.5 million project was completed in 2005 and raised the seating capacity to where it currently rests at 80,321.

Of course, filling all those seats proved to be quite a challenge, particularly during the football team's prolonged struggles in the 1970s and 1980s. Students seemed more concerned at games with being a nuisance to opposing teams. In one infamous incident, after Iowa defeated Wisconsin 34-14 during a game in 1983, Hawkeyes coach Hayden Fry said eggs were thrown at Iowa's coaches and players, and beer and peppermint schnapps were poured on them as well. Fry, whose van also was vandalized, called Camp Randall the "worst place in the world" for a visiting team to play.

When Iowa returned in 1985, one student was charged with a felony for tossing a heavy bleacher section over the top of the stadium. At least 174 people were ejected from that game. Later, fans brought large slingshots to the stadium to sling water balloons, which *Wisconsin State Journal* reporter George Hesselberg noted, "mostly hit empty seats."

On the whole, fan behavior has improved, mirroring the upgraded product on the field. Under coach Barry Alvarez, the Badgers reached three Rose Bowls in the 1990s, and that success has continued. From 2009 to '12, the football team won a school record 21 consecutive home games.

Now, few venues equal the game day experience at Camp Randall, which has become particularly well known for its playing of the House of Pain song "Jump Around" after the third quarter, working fans into a fervor every Saturday.

"There are plenty of rowdy stadiums in college football," sportswriter Pete Thamel wrote for *The New York Times* in 2011. "But perhaps no stadium rocks more than Wisconsin's Camp Randall."

Van Pelt Praises Madison

ESPN's Scott Van Pelt spent 48 hours in Madison in July 2007 to take part in a charity golf event held by on-air golf colleague Andy North. He came away from the experience in awe of everything the city had to offer. Van Pelt soon declared on his radio show that Madison was "America's greatest college sports town."

"This town has got everything," Van Pelt told listeners. "The teams are relevant. The venues are unbelievable. The setting is gorgeous. Those teams mean everything to the town."

Van Pelt, a Maryland native who attended the University of Maryland, cited many of the iconic spaces folks back in Madison had already come to know and love: State Street, Camp Randall Stadium, the Kohl Center, the state capitol building, and the lakes. Five months later, he returned to Madison as the school's winter commencement speaker.

"I stand by what I said," Van Pelt said. "I've been very fortunate to travel around the country and see many universities. There is only one [University of] Wisconsin-Madison. It is not good—it is exceptional—and sometimes an outsider's point of view can simply serve to reinforce what you already know, and that's how great you've got it."

46 Hoops Takes Down No. 1, Part II: 2011

Perhaps it was fitting that former Wisconsin basketball coach John Erickson served as the team's honorary captain on February 12, 2011, before a much-hyped home game against Ohio State. Thirty-nine years earlier, Erickson had presided over the only Badgers team to defeat a No. 1–ranked team in the country. On that magical Saturday in 1962, Wisconsin knocked off unbeaten Ohio State, and players were swiftly carried off the court into the locker room by their adoring fans.

The feat of toppling No. 1 had not been duplicated since at Wisconsin. That is, not until Wisconsin mounted a stirring second-half comeback in 2011 with Erickson in attendance to stun top-ranked Ohio State 71–67 at the Kohl Center, sending Badgers fans spilling onto the court to celebrate once again.

Like the 1962 game, Ohio State entered the 2011 edition undefeated at 24–0 overall and 11–0 in the Big Ten. The Buckeyes seemed to possess a legitimate shot at becoming the first Division I team to complete a perfect season since Indiana in 1975–76, and they did little to dispel that notion early on against Wisconsin.

When Buckeyes freshman Jared Sullinger scored an easy layup to give Ohio State a 47–32 lead with 13:21 remaining in the game, Wisconsin's chances appeared bleak. That's when Badgers point guard Jordan Taylor caught fire. He made four consecutive field goals, including back-to-back three-pointers, as part of a 15–0 run to drag the Badgers back into the game.

"They had to play for that stretch damn near perfect to get us and they did," Ohio State coach Thad Matta said. "They deserve the credit for that."

After the Badgers' spurt, Ohio State took a 55–52 lead on two free throws by Aaron Craft with 7:11 left. But Badgers forward Mike Bruesewitz tied the score with a three. Later, when Sullinger tried to collect an offensive rebound, he tripped and left Keaton Nankivil open on the other end for a jumper. Taylor then buried another 3 from the left side and added two free throws to give Wisconsin a 62–55 lead with 4:18 to play. UW never relinquished its advantage.

"We got a good, old piece of humble pie," Sullinger said afterward.

Wisconsin shot 50 percent from three-point range (12 of 24). Bruesewitz and Jon Leuer scored 12 points apiece, while freshman Josh Gasser added 11 for Wisconsin, which improved to 19–5 overall, 9–3 in the Big Ten, and won its 17th straight game at the Kohl Center. Taylor scored 21 of his 27 points in the second half in one of the finest performances of his sterling career.

"He made all the difference in the world," Leuer said. "He came down and hit those back-to-back threes and got us right back into it, and from there you could just see we had some momentum. It was unbelievable what he was able to do in such a short period of time, when we were battling adversity."

As the final buzzer sounded, there was sheer delirium in the Kohl Center. Students rushed the court and hoisted players onto their shoulders to revel in Wisconsin's second men's basketball victory against a No. 1 team. Earlier in the school year, Wisconsin had defeated No. 1 Ohio State in football 31–18 to join Florida as the only programs to accomplish the feat in the same academic year.

Badgers coach Bo Ryan was asked how he felt about UW beating the No. 1 team in basketball after beating the No. 1 team in football.

"I kind of like ours because it just happened," he said. "I loved football's because I was there for the game. It's just good for the school.... I can't tell you what it meant to get the head job here after being here as an assistant. The people, what it represents, it's all good."

47 Russell Wilson

Bret Bielema stood at a podium in the front of Wisconsin's auditorium during the Badgers' first team meeting on the opening night of fall camp 2011. As had become his custom over the years, the football coach instructed every freshman in the room to introduce himself by name, hometown, state, high school, and the position he expected to play at Wisconsin.

One by one, they nervously rattled off the brief introductory details until no freshman remained. That's when Bielema, a smile creasing his face, looked toward the first few rows.

"And somebody up here in the front," Bielema said.

The man, wearing a white polo shirt and dark-wash jeans, rose to a chorus of murmurs from his new teammates.

"I'm Russell Wilson," he said. "I'm from Richmond, Virginia. I went to Collegiate School in Richmond, Virginia, and I went to NC State before this. I'm glad to be here."

"What position?" Bielema asked.

"Quarterback," Wilson responded.

Russell Wilson's Badgers career may have been short, but he nevertheless made a big impact on the program.

The most coveted graduate transfer football player in the brief history of the NCAA's grad transfer exception rule had finally arrived in Madison. And with him, so did expectations. Wilson had spent the past three years carving up defenses in the Atlantic Coast Conference at North Carolina State. While there, he threw for 8,545 yards, 76 touchdowns—the second-best mark in school history—and only 26 interceptions.

But Wilson also wanted to pursue baseball after the Colorado Rockies selected him in the fourth round of the 2010 Major League Baseball draft rather than attend NC State's spring practices in 2011. As a result, NC State football coach Tom O'Brien named Mike Glennon the starter, and Wilson was granted a transfer release.

Under NCAA rules, players who graduated at a previous institution and still had playing eligibility remaining could pursue graduate school elsewhere. The rule allowed a onetime exception for graduate students that eliminated the need to miss a year that accompanied most transfers.

Wilson picked Wisconsin, in part, because the pro-style system could help him become a better player for the NFL. The Badgers also possessed a wealth of talent, including an eventual Heisman Trophy finalist in running back Montee Ball and an offensive line whose collective girth was bigger than most pro team O-lines.

In less than four weeks, Wilson learned an entirely new playbook, earned the trust of his teammates, won the starting quarterback job, and was named one of the Badgers' captains for the 2011 season. What Wilson accomplished over the next four months was nothing short of spectacular.

With Wilson and Ball lighting up the scoreboard, Wisconsin obliterated its first six opponents, which included a 48–17 throttling of No. 8 Nebraska in a nationally televised primetime game at Camp Randall Stadium. The dream for a national championship died, however, when Wisconsin lost consecutive road contests in heart-breaking fashion. First, Michigan State won 37–31 on the final play when Keith Nichol caught a 44-yard Hail Mary touchdown pass from quarterback Kirk Cousins at the front of the end zone. A week later, Ohio State beat Wisconsin 33–29 on quarterback Braxton Miller's 40-yard touchdown pass to Devin Smith with 20 seconds remaining.

In each game, Wilson led impressive comebacks that fell just short, and his Heisman Trophy campaign faded—he would finish ninth in the voting that season. Still, Wilson rallied the team to five consecutive victories, including a thrilling 42–39 triumph in a rematch against Michigan State in the inaugural Big Ten championship game in Indianapolis.

UW ultimately lost to Oregon 45–38 in the highest-scoring Rose Bowl in history, when Wilson ran out of time at Oregon's 25-yard line while driving the Badgers in for the potential game-tying score. Wisconsin finished the season 11–3, losing its three games by a combined 17 points.

Wilson's statistics that season will remain the stuff of legend for some time. He set the NCAA record for pass efficiency and established a school record for single-season passing yards (3,175), touchdown passes (33), completions (225), and yards of total offense (3,513). His .728 completion percentage ranked as the best at Wisconsin for quarterbacks who threw at least 300 passes, and he finished the season with only four interceptions.

Many NFL teams were afraid to take a chance on Wilson because he measured only 5'11", which would have made him among the shortest quarterbacks in the league. But the Seattle Seahawks selected Wilson with the 75th overall pick in the third round of the 2012 NFL draft. He won the starting job and made the Pro Bowl in his rookie season and then reached consecutive Super Bowls, winning the championship in 2014.

Though Wilson spent just a brief period of time in Madison, he'll forever be remembered as one of Wisconsin's own.

"I was only here for six months," Wilson said during a 2015 visit to Madison for his summer passing academy. "I was here from

July 1 to January 1, but it felt like I was here for six years. I really love this school, the education here. I love the football program. I love everything about it."

48 David Gilreath's "Footrace to the House"

Camp Randall Stadium pulsated with a type of electricity that had not been seen in a football game in at least a decade. Ohio State, the No. 1 team in the nation, was set to invade town the night of October 16, 2010, and ESPN's *College GameDay* was on campus to chronicle the buzz. For one night, Madison was the center of the college football world.

These opportunities rarely came along at UW. The game marked the first time Wisconsin had played a top-ranked team at home since facing Michigan 13 years earlier in 1997. But the Badgers hadn't beaten a No. 1 since 1981, when they knocked off the Wolverines 21–14.

Wisconsin's David Gilreath understood just how precious this moment was, for him and the team. The Badgers' 5'11" wide receiver and kickoff return man from Minneapolis had suffered a concussion five weeks earlier against San Jose State. He left the field that day in an ambulance after being knocked unconscious on a helmet-to-helmet hit on a punt return. He did not regain the starting kickoff return job until halfway through a game against Minnesota—just one week before the Ohio State game.

"I've had my ups and downs," Gilreath told the *Wisconsin State Journal.* "Some real lows, just to have the concussion a couple weeks ago and people saying, 'That's the end of that.'"

But Gilreath had returned, and now he was about to produce one of the most memorable Camp Randall Stadium moments of the decade. He fielded the opening kickoff between the hash marks at his own 3-yard line, cut back just past the 20, and scooted by the entire Ohio State team at the 30. By the time he reached mid-field, five Buckeyes were in pursuit, and none of them had a chance to catch him. Just 12 seconds into the game, Wisconsin led 7–0 against Ohio State, and the fans jumped for joy.

Here is legendary Badgers play-by-play announcer Matt Lepay's call of the moment:

"For the first time in 13 years, a top-ranked team comes to town. Kick is in the air. Gilreath will have an opportunity. He'll catch at the 3. Between the hash marks, 10. Slicing left, 15, across the 20, 25, 30. Gilreath to the 40, he's to the 50. Footrace to the house! At the 30, at the 20, 10, 5. Touchdown, Wisconsin! And this game is underway with a bang!"

Ohio State had not lost to Wisconsin since 2004, and the Buckeyes' smallest margin of victory during the 2010 season had been 11 points. But Wisconsin rode Gilreath's opening return all the way to a 31–18 upset, which sent fans storming the field with delight despite the public address announcer's best attempts to dissuade them. Wisconsin would use the victory as a springboard, winning its final seven regular season games to reach the Rose Bowl against TCU—the Badgers' first appearance there in 11 years.

During the week of the Ohio State game, Gilreath told tight ends coach Joe Rudolph, who also coached the kickoff team, he thought he could take a kick back against the Buckeyes, noting their kickoff unit was "nothing spectacular." Miami had returned a kickoff 88 yards for a touchdown against Ohio State just a few weeks earlier. But even Gilreath, who briefly held the Big Ten record for career kickoff return yards with 3,025, could not have imagined a more unforgettable moment.

"I guess I couldn't script it any better for it to happen," Gilreath told the *State Journal*. "I was always hoping it would happen and thinking, 'It just takes that one time for something to open up. I don't want to miss it.'"

Other Notable Wisconsin Wins vs. Ohio State

1942: Wisconsin 17, Ohio State 7

Sixth-ranked Wisconsin recorded its first victory against a No. 1 team in one of the most memorable wins in school history. Ohio State's lone touchdown brought the Buckeyes to within three, at 10–7. But Elroy "Crazylegs" Hirsch threw a 14-yard touchdown pass to Dave Schreiner to secure the upset. Wisconsin finished the year 8–1–1 as part of coach Harry Stuhldreher's best team in 13 seasons there.

1992: Wisconsin 20, Ohio State 16

Barry Alvarez's breakthrough moment as coach occurred when Wisconsin defeated No. 12 Ohio State to mark the Badgers' first victory against a ranked opponent in seven years. Tailback Brent Moss rushed for 80 yards and two touchdowns and quarterback Darrell Bevell passed for 214 yards. The Badgers' defense stopped what would have been the game-winning drive with less than three minutes remaining in the fourth quarter.

"We won a game and national respect today," Alvarez said. "In the past, we've found ways to lose big games. That's over now."

2003: Wisconsin 17, Ohio State 10

The defending national champion Buckeyes entered Camp Randall Stadium with a 19-game winning streak. But backup quarterback Matt Schabert's 79-yard touchdown pass to receiver Lee Evans with 5:20 remaining in the game helped the Badgers spring the upset. Schabert had just two touchdown passes in his career but was thrust into action when starter Jim Sorgi suffered an injury. Badgers running back Booker Stanley carried 31 times for 125 yards in the winning effort.

49 UW Field House

The lights of the old barn darkened one last time for Wisconsin's men's basketball team, and from the shadows, a spotlight emerged on Bucky Badger. An emotional postgame ceremony signaling the end of an era included two members of the first team to play at the UW Field House in the early 1930s. Fred Miller and Bob Poser then presented a game ball to the current crop of men's and women's basketball captains. They placed it at center court, where Bucky picked up the ball and headed for the exits.

The night of January 14, 1998, represented a symbolic passing of the basketball torch. Wisconsin had clobbered Penn State 76–57 in its final game at the 68-year-old Field House. Three days later, Bucky would return the ball prior to tipoff of the next game against Northwestern, which officially opened the Kohl Center—the Badgers' sparkling new $76 million arena of the future.

"We're still going to have wrestling and volleyball here," UW athletics director Pat Richter reminded the sellout crowd of 11,500 at halftime. "We're not losing the place. You can always come back if you miss the place."

Indeed, basketball may be gone. But the Field House continues to endure, a building that still hosts sporting events and offers a reminder of a different time in Badgers athletics.

The Field House opened in 1930 as the home to Wisconsin basketball, volleyball, and wrestling. It was the brainchild of former athletics director George Little, who proposed the plan to the athletics council and regents in 1927. Its construction cost $434,000. The first game played there was on December 13, 1930, when the men's basketball team defeated Carroll College 17–14.

Original capacity was 8,000, but an upper balcony was added in 1939 to raise the seating capacity to 12,000. The facility also had a dirt floor for several years, and an eighth-of-a-mile cinder track circled the perimeter of the building. From 1933 to 1960, the Field House was home to Wisconsin's championship boxing team. And in 1949, an all-sport record crowd of 15,200 showed up to watch Wisconsin's boxers face Washington State. The building was renovated in 1976–77 and again in 2009 when new bleachers were added to the west side.

The venue hosted the 1941 NCAA men's basketball national champion Badgers and the first two rounds of the tournament. Muhammad Ali suffered one of his few losses as an amateur boxer there during the 1959 Pan American Games trials. In 2007, the Badgers' volleyball team saw its first-ever sellout for a match against No. 1 Penn State

In addition to sporting events, the Field House has hosted commencement exercises, carnivals, entertainers, and speakers, including John F. Kennedy, Bob Hope, Bing Crosby, Jesse Jackson, and the Dalai Lama. The Field House was added to the National Register of Historic Places in 1998 and remained distinctive to so many players whose time was spent inside its doors.

"I played basketball in a lot of arenas," former Wisconsin great Kim Hughes, who played from 1971 to '74, told the *Milwaukee Journal Sentinel* in 1998. "But I never saw a place where there was a bond between the fans and the players like there was in this place.

"In the new arenas you don't have this kind of atmosphere. Here, it was like you could almost reach out and touch the fans, and you almost could. It's a very special place."

Red Gym

Walk by 716 Langdon Street on the UW-Madison campus, and a Romanesque-style red brick castle meets your eye. Today, it could barely hold the Grateful Red student section, let alone the rest of Wisconsin's rabid basketball fan base at the Kohl Center. But a century ago, before even the UW Field House, the "Old Red Gym" served as a capable first hoops home, a 2,200-seat venue where the Badgers thrilled fans with some of their finest teams.

The Red Gym, also known as the University of Wisconsin Armory and Gymnasium, was built in 1894 at a cost of $127,000, and its original purpose was as a military training facility as well as an athletic and student activity center. The first floor originally held military offices, an artillery drill room, a bowling alley, a locker room, and a swimming pool. The second floor contained a drill hall wide enough to allow a four-column battalion. And the third floor included the gymnasium, which contained a baseball cage, gymnastics apparatus, and rowing machines.

Under head coach Walter Meanwell, Wisconsin was named the Helms Foundation national champion in 1912 and 1916—both years in which the Badgers didn't lose a single home game. From 1904 to 1918, Wisconsin's home record was an astounding 109–8 (.931 winning percentage), while the Badgers earned at least a share of the Big Ten title seven times. UW's all-time record at the Red Gym was 198–37 (.843).

Wisconsin played its last game at the Red Gym in March 1930 before moving into the more spacious UW Field House. Over the years, the Red Gym survived several calls for its demolition as use for the building declined. The building endured despite an attempt by arsonists to firebomb it in January 1970, intending to target the ROTC offices. The Red Gym was declared a National Historic Landmark in 1993. It was renovated in 1998 at a cost of approximately $13 million, and it remains visible from Lake Mendota and the Union Terrace.

50 Don Rehfeldt

Kareem Abdul-Jabbar introduced the sky-hook to a generation of fans in the late 1960s and early 1970s. Years before he achieved fame, however, one University of Wisconsin basketball player was busy putting on a hook-shot show of his own in Midwest college basketball circles.

Don Rehfeldt was a 6'6", 205-pound center from Chicago's Amundsen High School who terrorized opponents with his combination of size and skill while with the Badgers. His first two seasons with the program were cut short because he left in the middle of his freshman campaign to serve in the military. Newspaper accounts indicate Rehfeldt was declared academically ineligible for the second semester in January 1945, which could have spurred the decision.

When Rehfeldt returned to the court in the 1946–47 season, he was tough to stop. He became eligible to play on February 8, 1947, and immediately helped pull Wisconsin out of a nine-point deficit to beat Minnesota 60–51. Two days later, he was on the floor when Wisconsin beat Michigan, which had been undefeated at home 52–51. Wisconsin would win the Big Ten title that season and reach its second NCAA tournament under coach Bud Foster. Over his final three seasons, Rehfeldt developed into a star.

Rehfeldt averaged 11.2 points per game as a sophomore, and then upped his total to 17.3 and finally 19.8 as a senior. He was the Big Ten's leading scorer for two straight years and was the conference MVP in 1950. He also was the first Badgers player to surpass the 1,000-point plateau, finishing with 1,169 in his career. Rehfeldt was named an All-American in 1950 for his efforts. The next Wisconsin player to earn the honor didn't come along until Alando Tucker in 2007.

During his career, Rehfeldt dazzled with an array of hook shots, and he certainly wasn't shy about shooting the ball. On February 28, 1949, in a game against Iowa, he scored 37 points on 37 field-goal attempts—a number that still stands as a Wisconsin single-game record.

"I was only a sophomore then, and I hadn't heard about a hook shot until I saw him," Ab Nicholas said of Rehfeldt in the book *Field House Echoes*. "His range and accuracy were unbelievable."

In a 66–59 victory against Northwestern on February 11, 1950, Rehfeldt dropped in 35 points in front of 18,936 fans. He made 12 of 18 field goals in the game and 11 of 13 free throw attempts. He outscored Northwestern 8–0 to open the game and dominated throughout. Of his baskets, the *Chicago Tribune* noted, "several were marvelous left-hand hook shots."

How good was Rehfeldt during his senior season?

"He's just as good as he wants to be," Foster said in December 1949, though he noted Rehfeldt didn't always play his absolute hardest.

"There are times when he puts out more than others," Foster added, "and he has spells when he dogs it in there."

During a game that season against Marquette, fans yelled, "Wait for Rehfeldt!" to the other four Badgers racing down the floor with the ball. Rehfeldt, meanwhile, "walked leisurely behind," the Associated Press wrote, noting he also rarely used his size to his advantage on the boards. Still, no one could deny Rehfeldt's incredible scoring prowess.

"Rafe has one of the best hook shots I've ever seen," Foster said.

During his senior season, Rehfeldt led Wisconsin to a 17–5 record and a second-place Big Ten finish. His 436 points stood as a single-season record at the time. He was picked second overall by the Baltimore Bullets in the 1950 NBA draft—the highest Badgers player ever selected. Rehfeldt became a charter member of the Wisconsin Athletics Hall of Fame in 1991.

51 2012 Rose Bowl: Scores Galore

Russell Wilson incredulously tossed his hands in the air, completely helpless as the final seconds on the clock and a season unexpectedly died out. A sea of sparkling confetti swallowed Wilson, Wisconsin's star quarterback, in the middle of the field. Soon after, so did the entire Oregon football team, storming from the sidelines with delight following a 45–38 Rose Bowl victory for the ages.

In the midst of the Ducks' merriment, the beautiful back-drop of the San Gabriel Mountains hanging high over Rose Bowl Stadium faded behind Wilson in the night sky. Perhaps it was fitting. For all the star power that Wisconsin's football program possessed—Wilson included—the Badgers never quite saw the mountaintop on a season that began with so much promise.

A wacky, roller-coaster 2011 campaign unique for the marquee offensive talent finally bestowed upon Wisconsin ended in exactly the same fashion as a year earlier—with a tantalizingly close loss in Pasadena.

"It's something that we'll carry with us for the rest of our lives, an entire coaching career for me," Wisconsin coach Bret Bielema said afterward. "It's never easy. I'm not saying I'd rather lose by 40 points. It just makes it that much more gut-wrenching."

A team with all the necessary pieces to achieve greatness—two top-10 Heisman Trophy finalists in Wilson and running back Montee Ball and a top-10 scoring defense—lost for the third time during the season, with each game decided in the final minute. That Wisconsin team set a school record for scoring offense (44.1 points per game) but needed one more Rose Bowl touchdown despite gaining 508 yards of total offense against Oregon.

"We lost three games basically by a total of maybe 40 seconds," Wilson said during the postgame news conference. "Pretty wild. All those situations were all unfortunate. It's pretty crazy how each one of them panned out."

The Badgers' defense entered the game allowing just 17 points per contest—the sixth-best mark in the country. But Oregon easily surpassed that number with its spread attack, tying the score at 21–21 after less than 20 minutes of play. That left Wisconsin's offense to either keep pace or be left behind.

Wisconsin led the game on five separate occasions, the last of which came on Wilson's 18-yard touchdown pass to Nick Toon at the 4:44 mark of the third quarter. The score put the Badgers ahead 38–35, although it proved short-lived. Oregon scored the next 10 points, leaving Wilson in charge for one final drive with just 16 seconds remaining in the last game of his memorable, lone season at Wisconsin.

Wilson completed two passes for 62 yards, reaching Oregon's 25-yard line with two seconds left. Because the Badgers were out of timeouts, Wilson quickly rushed the team up to the line of scrimmage and spiked the ball.

When he looked up at the clock, it read all zeroes. A replay review later confirmed that the clock ran out before Wilson's spike, ending the game as Wilson stood frozen on the field.

"I didn't think there was any way that two full seconds ran off the clock there," said Wilson, who threw for 33 touchdowns and just four interceptions that season. "It would have been nice to have a chance there. With one second left, I think we could have capitalized there. Based on my perspective right now, I snapped it as soon as he blew the whistle, and I didn't think that two seconds ran off."

Bielema said he didn't have another play in mind as Wilson went to spike the ball, which brought an end to the highest scoring game in Rose Bowl history. It was of little consolation to a Wisconsin team that lost the Rose Bowl for a second straight year.

One year earlier, TCU knocked off Wisconsin 21–19, and Badgers players openly admitted they used that defeat as motivation moving into the 2011 season. When Wilson joined the program in August after three impressive seasons quarterbacking at North Carolina State, the sky seemed the limit for Wisconsin.

But a 6–0 start and national championship aspirations were squashed by back-to-back defeats against Michigan State on a last-second Hail Mary and Ohio State on a last-minute heave.

The only choice Badgers players had was to readjust their goals toward winning the Big Ten championship and making amends for the previous season's Rose Bowl loss.

It didn't happen. And one of the most entertaining Rose Bowls in history belonged to Oregon.

"I'm tired of tears of sadness," said Bielema, who would depart to coach at Arkansas one season later. "I want to come out here and experience tears of joy at some point."

52 Lee Evans

In the quiet moments spent isolated in his apartment, Lee Evans could have sulked. He could have questioned why he was still at Wisconsin for his senior year and not in the NFL. Or why he tore the anterior cruciate ligament in his left knee during the Badgers' spring game. Or whether the impending rehabilitation would allow him to be anywhere near the same type of player he once was.

Instead, Evans provided an important lesson in the study of perseverance and perspective. By working hard and looking forward to better days, anything was possible.

"I go back to the day after the injury when I went down to see him in his apartment and I was in the tank about as bad as you can be in the tank," Badgers coach Barry Alvarez told ESPN.com in 2002. "I walk in and he's sitting there with a big smile on his face, playing video games, wanting to know how I'm doing. He's been an inspiration."

Evans didn't know where his promising career was headed when he underwent ACL surgery in the spring of 2002 and required a second surgery in the fall that ended his season before it started. But he never gave up the fight after taking a medical red-shirt, and his return in 2003 was something to behold.

Evans, the most productive wide receiver in Wisconsin football history, looked good as new. In 2001, before the injury, he set the single-season program record for receiving yards with 1,545 on 75 catches and tied the school record with nine touchdowns. His follow-up act in 2003 included the second-best single-season receiving yardage mark (1,213) with 64 catches and a new record for touchdown receptions that still stands (13).

One of his highlights from the season was a 79-yard touch-down catch in the fourth quarter that sealed a 17–10 victory against third-ranked Ohio State. His signature game, however, was one for the record books.

On November 15, 2003, Evans caught 10 passes for a school-record 258 yards and five touchdowns during Wisconsin's 56–21 blowout victory against Michigan State. He topped Al Toon's pre-vious record of 252 yards set against Purdue in 1983 and tied the Big Ten record for touchdown receptions in a game.

"It was definitely special," Evans said afterward. "I mean, I had a lot of fun out there. It is probably the best game I've ever played here.… I am glad I could celebrate it with a win and celebrate it with my teammates."

Added Alvarez: "It was vintage Lee Evans. He put on a show."

Evans was virtually impossible to cover that day. He scored on passes of 9, 75, and 18 yards in the first half as Wisconsin took a 28–7 lead. He then added a 70-yard touchdown catch and an 18-yarder, all before the third quarter had ended. It was a perfor-mance that left everybody in awe, including his opponents.

"He's the best receiver I've ever faced," Michigan State corner-back Darren Barnett said after the game. "I've never seen anyone want the ball so much. He's so fluid and talented."

The only person to stop Evans was Alvarez, who pulled him from the game after his final catch, a 9-yarder that allowed him to surpass Toon's single-game yardage record with 13 minutes remaining.

Evans left as the school's career leader in receiving yards (3,468) and touchdowns (27). In 2001, Evans was a first-team All-American and one of three finalists for the Fred Biletnikoff Award, given to the top receiver in college football. He set the Big Ten record for receiving yards in a season and ranked fourth nationally with a 128.8 yards-per-game average. But Evans also bypassed the NFL draft because he didn't believe he was mentally prepared to make the leap.

In 2003, Evans version 2.0 was named a first-team All-Big Ten selection for a second time. And he was more than ready for the pros.

"You learn a lot of life's lessons, about what's important, going through the ordeal," Evans told the *Chicago Tribune*. "My family was there for me and we've grown closer during the whole ordeal."

Evans fulfilled his NFL dreams when he was selected in the first round of the 2004 NFL draft by the Buffalo Bills at No. 13 overall. He played eight seasons with the Bills and Baltimore Ravens and caught 381 passes for 6,008 yards and 43 touchdowns.

53 Badgers Shuck Cornhuskers in '74

A decade's worth of futility had reduced outside expectations to simply fielding a competitive Wisconsin football team in 1974. Over the previous 10 seasons, there had been little reason for the fan base to celebrate. Wisconsin's record was a pitiful 27–70–5, and the only notable victory came against a mediocre Iowa team in 1969 to snap the Badgers' 23-game winless streak.

Before the 1974 season, however, a sense of renewed optimism began to permeate the program. This Wisconsin football team was close to vaulting over the hump, it seemed. So very close. Head coach John Jardine's 1973 team had lost to Purdue by a single point, Colorado by three points, Nebraska by four points, and Minnesota by two points. Those four losses by a total of 10 points prompted athletics director Elroy Hirsch to defend the decision to extend Jardine's contract that offseason by declaring, "We were damn respectable last year."

Was it all a mirage? Nebraska football coach Tom Osborne certainly didn't think so. In 1973, Wisconsin had stormed into Lincoln and nearly upset the Cornhuskers. Wisconsin's Selvie Washington returned a kickoff 96 yards for a touchdown that gave the Badgers a two-point lead late in the game. But Cornhuskers quarterback David Humm led a seven-play, 83-yard drive that helped No. 2 Nebraska escape with a 20–16 victory.

When the teams were set for a rematch in Madison the following year, Osborne warned anybody who would listen that his team faced a tall task.

"We think Wisconsin is one of the better teams we are going to play this season," Osborne said the week of the game. "They are an improved team, and last year they were almost good enough to beat us."

If there were any doubters left, Wisconsin squashed them by proving just how far it had come on September 21, 1974, with one of the program's most significant performances. Wisconsin defeated No. 4 Nebraska 21–20 in front of a stunned regional television audience and a raucous Camp Randall Stadium crowd of 73,381 people.

The game-winner came on a 77-yard touchdown pass from Wisconsin quarterback Gregg Bohlig to receiver Jeff Mack down the right sideline with 3:29 remaining in the fourth quarter. On second-and-16, Bohlig rolled to his right and found Mack behind the defense just past midfield. Mack saw Nebraska safety George Kyros undercut the route in a gamble for an interception. Mack reacted by turning up field and signaling for Bohlig that he was open before hauling in the catch.

Even in the moment, the magnitude was understood. Color commentator Duffy Daugherty, on the television broadcast alongside Keith Jackson, called it "one of the greatest plays in the history of Wisconsin football. Mack, number 39. This will go down in Badger history as one of the all-time great plays."

Kicker Vince Lamia's extra point gave Wisconsin the 21–20 lead, and Badgers safety Steve Wagner's interception of Cornhuskers backup quarterback Earl Everett with 2:40 remaining sealed the victory.

The following day, the *Omaha World-Herald* headline read: MACK'S TRUCK FLATTENS N.U., 21–20. Nebraska players, meanwhile, were left to lament the physical nature of the game. Humm, who passed for 297 yards against Wisconsin one year earlier, left in the second quarter with a hip injury and was replaced by Everett.

John O'Leary, the Cornhuskers' running back, was knocked unconscious early in the game on a hit from Badgers free safety Terry Buss and was taken to the hospital to have his jaw X-rayed. He returned to the game but suffered four chipped teeth.

Nebraska trainer Paul Schneider compared the game to "playing Missouri," a compliment bestowed on Wisconsin. "They just came out and hit," he said. "There are a lot of bumps and bruises."

Wisconsin's defense also held strong when it mattered most. Nebraska drove to Wisconsin's 2-yard line but had to settle for a 22-yard field goal by Mike Coyle that gave the Cornhuskers a 20–14 lead.

"Our defense played all day, and they turned in as fine a performance as they ever have," Jardine said after the game. "We decided that if we were going to lose, they were going to suffer for it."

The defensive stand gave the Badgers an opportunity, and Bohlig took advantage with his touchdown to Mack. For the game, he completed 14 of 21 passes for 242 yards with two touchdowns and two interceptions. The 5'11" senior was named the Associated Press All-Big Ten offensive player of the week.

Wisconsin's performance validated the university's belief in Jardine. Before the season, he had received a two-year contract extension despite his record of 16–25–2 in four seasons at Wisconsin. Jardine recognized the difficult challenge that lay ahead, particularly because of the team's brutal schedule.

"It can't take much longer or someone else will have to do the job," he said before the season. "There are only two types of coaches—the ones that have been fired and the ones that are going to be fired."

Wisconsin finished the 1974 season 7–4, the program's first winning campaign since 1963. And no victory that year was as sweet as the upset against mighty Nebraska. After the game, downtown crowds spilled out of the State Street bars. They were singing, yelling, dancing, and drinking, reveling in the fact that their team had shocked the college football world.

"The crowd would allow cars to pass, but only after urging drivers to honk their horns and take a drink of beer," the *Milwaukee Journal* wrote. "Most of the drivers happily agreed to both requests."

Trophy Game

Wisconsin's stunning upset of Nebraska in 1974 represented the teams' last meeting until Nebraska joined the Big Ten in 2011. The seventh-ranked Badgers promptly manhandled the eighth-ranked Cornhuskers 48–17 at Camp Randall Stadium on October 1, 2011, in Nebraska's first game in its new conference. In 2012, Nebraska won the regular season matchup 30–27 in Lincoln before Wisconsin embarrassed Nebraska 70–31 to win the Big Ten championship.

When the teams met again in 2014, the Freedom Trophy was created to commemorate the beginnings of a new annual rivalry. It marked the Badgers' third trophy game, joining the border battle for Paul Bunyan's Axe against Minnesota and the Heartland Trophy against Iowa.

The Freedom Trophy was designed and sculpted by Harry Weber of Wright City, Missouri, and features a bronze football stadium with an American flag extending from the center. One half of the outside of the stadium depicts the North section of Wisconsin's Camp Randall Stadium (built in 1917) and the other half the East side of Nebraska's Memorial Stadium (built in 1923). The stadium and flag sculpture sits on top of a wooden base that has dedicated space for future Wisconsin-Nebraska game scores.

54 Donna Shalala

Barry Alvarez earns the lion's share of praise for helping turn around Wisconsin's once-dormant football program, while Pat Richter is credited with having the foresight to hire Alvarez when he took over as athletics director. Both men have bronze statues of their likenesses side-by-side outside Gate 1 of Camp Randall Stadium. But one key figure, many point out, often goes overlooked in the entire process.

"The other person who deserves a statue is Donna Shalala," said former Wisconsin associate athletics director Joel Maturi, who held the position from 1987 to '96. "To me, that's where everything changed. She was frustrated and embarrassed by the performance of our football team. I remember being in the box when she attended a game at Michigan. We were behind by 50 at half. That may be an exaggeration, but it was brutal. I remember her saying, 'This will not continue.'"

Shalala served as UW-Madison chancellor from 1988 to '93. And when she arrived, Wisconsin's athletics programs were largely in disarray, particularly the football program—which was in the midst of a 3–21 stretch in Big Ten play under coach Don Morton.

Shalala understood the ways in which winning teams helped unite a campus and a community. So in 1989, she fired Morton despite him having two years remaining on his contract. Then-Athletics director Ade Sponberg also was forced to resign.

"I think people felt that football was very important," said Shalala, an Ohio native whose previous job in academics had been as president of Hunter College in New York City. "I was impressed with the fact the farmers woke up in the morning and talked about our football team and checked the scores and listened. That they stopped in their fields to listen to the Badgers play. It was important as an overall college experience for our students. But it certainly was important to the people in Wisconsin."

With Wisconsin in need of an athletics director and a football coach, Shalala turned to Richter to take over the department. It was a particularly tough sell because Richter was happy with his job as vice president of personnel at Oscar Mayer Foods Corp., a position he held for 17 years. Richter, however, also had been a three-sport star at Wisconsin in football, basketball, and baseball in the 1960s, and his ties to the university remained strong.

"The key to recruiting Pat was his wife," Shalala said. "Convincing her. Because he had to take a pay cut. They loved Wisconsin, and I played on that."

After several initial attempts sputtered—Richter would say no numerous times—Shalala eventually convinced him to take over an athletics department with old facilities, poor teams, and a $2.1 million deficit. Richter's first order of business was to hire Alvarez away from Notre Dame, where he was a successful defensive coordinator. Once at Wisconsin, Alvarez guided the Badgers to the Rose Bowl in his fourth season as coach.

"She sent a message that there was a strong commitment from the top," Alvarez said of Shalala during that Rose Bowl season. "That doesn't happen every place.... She saw the potential around here. It makes sense. If you've got the best business school, why not have the best athletic program?"

Shalala credited both Arlie Mucks and Elroy "Crazylegs" Hirsch for providing her with the confidence and support to make a move with the football coach before the 1990 season. Mucks was a 27-year head of the Wisconsin Alumni Association who served as special assistant to Shalala from 1989 to '92. Hirsch, meanwhile, served as the school's athletics director from 1969 to '87.

Ultimately, Shalala left Wisconsin in 1993 and accepted a position as U.S. Secretary of Health and Human Services under President Bill Clinton. But she did not miss Wisconsin's 1994 Rose Bowl appearance in Pasadena, and she has kept the game ball through the years.

"I still run into people from Wisconsin who thank me for turning around the football program," Shalala said. "It's said that you can walk into any bar in Wisconsin and mention my name, and they'll buy you a drink. I don't know whether it's true or not."

55 The Father of Wisconsin Basketball

Chris Steinmetz arrived on Wisconsin's campus during a time when college basketball was viewed as little more than a hobby to escape the cold winter months. His first Badgers team in 1903 had no coach, so a team captain acted in that capacity. Players purchased their own equipment because the university provided no financial backing. And the basketballs themselves were so worn that the team used ones with "lumps and corners on them," he once recalled.

Despite those hurdles, it is Steinmetz who is lauded for helping to bring credibility to the game, a reason he is known all these years later as the Father of Wisconsin Basketball.

A 1930 *Milwaukee Journal* article on Badgers basketball noted Steinmetz "had more to do with its successful launching than any other one man.… It was due to the fine play and unselfish devotion of the men, among whom Steinmetz was a leader and outstanding player, that the game was established as a recognized sport at Wisconsin."

Steinmetz came to Wisconsin from South Division High School in Milwaukee, where he starred in both basketball and track. He participated three years in each sport and helped South Division win state high school basketball championships in 1901 and 1902 as a team captain. He also was the state champion in the high jump in 1902.

The 5'9½", 137-pound Steinmetz immediately lived up to his high school reputation as a scorer on the court, playing with a style that had rarely been seen before at Wisconsin. While other players relied on underhand, two-handed shots, Steinmetz often used a one-handed shot. He could leap in the air for a rebound or shot before coming down, a feat almost unheard of during that period.

One writer who witnessed one of his performances said, "He was a human dynamo on a basketball floor. Possessed of an uncanny eye for the basket and a bulldog on defense, Steinmetz always seemed to be in the right place at the right time."

Steinmetz played in an era when basketball scoring was low and the rules of the game were far from stable, yet he thrived anyway. On December 2, 1904, Steinmetz scored 50 points to set a pre-modern, single-game scoring mark in Wisconsin's 75–10 victory against Sparta's Company C. His 462 points that season would stand as the best at Wisconsin for 61 years.

In fact, when Steinmetz died in 1963 at age 80, he still held six school records set during his final season: most points per season (462 in 18 games), most points in a single game (50 against

Sparta), most field goals in a single game (20 against Beloit), most free throws in a single season (238), most free throws in a single game (26 against Two Rivers Athletic Club), and best single-season scoring average (25.7 points). He achieved all this on a team that averaged only 37.8 points per game that year.

Steinmetz recalled reading after his 20-field-goal performance against Beloit that he had come within one basket of the national record.

"The game was stopped five minutes early so Beloit could catch a train," he said. "Otherwise I might have had another record."

His point total was enhanced, in part, because he was the only man who went to the free throw line for Wisconsin in those days, when teams could pick which player attempted the shots after a foul. He made 238 of 317 attempts (75.0 percent). Steinmetz often credited his teammates for passing him the ball because they "knew it was understood that if I was in the vicinity of the basket, I would shoot," he said.

The physicality of the game back then was especially high, particularly because teams would return to half court after every basket to engage in a center jump. The rule finally was eliminated in 1937. In his later days, Steinmetz lamented what the game had become and said he'd like to see the center jump brought back and less whistle blowing.

"Basketball in those days was football for the lighter fellows," Steinmetz said. "The officials allowed rougher play. Why, we wore moleskin pants or they would have tore them right off you the way they hung on."

Following his graduation from law school, Steinmetz moved to Milwaukee to practice law. He also coached and officiated for many years. For 19 years, he selected the All-Western Five for the *Official Basketball Guide*. He served terms as president of the Milwaukee "W" Club, and in his later years, he was easily recognized because of his cardinal tie with the Bucky Badger insignia.

Steinmetz, who became the Badgers' first All-American, was inducted into the Wisconsin Athletics Hall of Fame, the Helms

Foundation Hall of Fame, and the Naismith Memorial Basketball Hall of Fame. Despite all his accomplishments, Steinmetz said he was proudest of the fact that he had three sons who won basketball letters at Wisconsin—one as a player, and two as student managers.

"When we're all home, that makes four of us at the table," he said, "and you don't find many tables like that."

56 Ivy Williamson

Ivy Williamson's impact as Wisconsin's football coach can best be measured by examining the Badgers' win-loss records under his predecessor, Harry Stuhldreher. In Stuhldreher's 13-year coaching career, UW finished with a winning record four times, including only once in his final six seasons from 1943 to '48.

Enter Williamson, who quickly changed expectations of the entire program and became one of the most effective Wisconsin football coaches of the modern era. Williamson's 1949 team finished 5–3–1, beginning a string of six consecutive winning seasons that brought great prominence to the football program and the university.

Williamson's 1951 team, known as the "Hard Rocks" for its incredibly staunch defense, was generally considered his best but missed the Big Ten title because of a 14–10 defeat against Illinois, the Badgers' only loss that season. In 1952, behind the strength of the great tailback Alan "The Horse" Ameche, Wisconsin won its first league title since 1912 and appeared in its first-ever Rose Bowl—a 7–0 loss to USC. From 1950 to '54, Wisconsin finished no worse than third in the league and closed the season ranked in the top 20 each time.

In a 1954 article, *Sports Illustrated* noted football had earned $517,447.96 of the athletics department's total revenue of $720,921. Basketball was the only other sport to pay for itself at the school. Football would pay for a new $1.5 million field house, football uniforms, the 180-piece band, and it would send the crew team to California.

"This success is based on a winning combination of two incongruous elements," *Sports Illustrated* wrote. "One is the tall, agonizingly shy head coach, Ivan B. Williamson, a living contradiction to Dale Carnegie. The other is a likable kid, born Lino Dante Amici [sic], who now receives mail addressed to The Horse, Wisconsin."

Williamson, born February 4, 1911, in Wayne, Ohio (formerly Prairie Depot), was an outstanding athlete at Michigan from 1930 to '32 when the Wolverines lost only one football game. He was an all-Big Ten end and Michigan captain in 1932 and then became a coach. From 1934 to '41, he served as an assistant coach at Yale, spent time in the Navy from 1942 to '45 and then returned to Yale for two years.

"I guess [that's] when I took a look at myself," he told *Sports Illustrated*. "I figured as long as I was a football coach, I ought to try to be a good one."

Williamson worked a two-year stint as coach at Lafayette College in Easton, Pennsylvania, from 1947 '48 before finally arriving at Wisconsin, where he helped turn around the program. During his seven-year tenure from 1949 to '55, he went 41–19–4 overall, including 29–13–4 in the Big Ten. His .672 winning percentage was better than even Barry Alvarez's .619 winning percentage.

Williamson shared his perspective on the importance of football with the *Milwaukee Journal* in 1964.

"I believe that one of the most important things our boys learn is the value of self-discipline," he said. "Sacrifices must be made in training, time must be carefully budgeted, and the fact realized that competition is one of giving and taking in every respect. Each individual must be convinced that successful results are attained only by hard work. He needs to develop the desire, the loyalty, and the character necessary to achieve the goals he has set."

Williamson also cited the ability for football to create a common interest among students, faculty, and employees, to create links to alumni and friends of the university and to help financially balance the intercollegiate athletics program.

In 1955, Williamson stepped down as coach, and Milt Bruhn took over. He spent the next 13 years as athletics director, a time that was marked by the construction of a natatorium, expansion of the seating capacity of Camp Randall Stadium to 77,000, and the installation of Tartan turf on the football field in 1968. He took a salary cut to become athletics director, from $15,300 to $13,500—the top under university policy, which stated the athletics director couldn't earn more than the dean of the college.

He remained athletics director until he was fired in January 1969 amid a sharp decline in performance by the football team. Less than six weeks later, he died at age 58 after falling down the basement stairs at his house. Bruhn said of Williamson, "There was no man I have admired more."

"As a coach and as an athletic director, Ivan Williamson thought only in championship terms," said Charles D. Gelatt, chairman of the board of regents. "He gave the state of Wisconsin many winning teams. More importantly, he gave us outstanding young men. They are his memorials."

57 Joe Thomas

Athletic ability is not a trait generally associated with a big, burly offensive lineman. The assumption is that moving around 300-plus pounds is a chore in itself, and if it weren't for the five spots planted on the line of scrimmage in front of the quarterback, linemen wouldn't have a place to throw their weight around. Then again, perhaps it only requires a look at Joe Thomas to dispel that notion.

Thomas was a force of nature, and many Badgers fans don't hesitate to call him the best offensive lineman in the history of Wisconsin football—quite a feat considering the program has prided itself on the position for decades. But the ultimate compliment comes from former Badgers linemen, whose praise of Thomas is effusive.

"There's no question in my mind, he's the best O-lineman to leave Wisconsin," Joe Panos, a captain on the 1993 Rose Bowl team, told the *Wisconsin State Journal* in 2006. "You know what? That's a lot for me to say, because I'm a pretty proud guy. At the same time, I'm a realist. He's twice the tackle I was. He's a very special athlete, a very special football player."

Chris McIntosh, who never missed a game as a four-year starter for Wisconsin at left tackle and was a first-round NFL draft pick in 2000, called Thomas "the most complete" of any Badgers lineman.

"A lot of those players, myself included, were run blockers and could get the job done pass blocking when needed," McIntosh said. "He is a balanced tackle. He can do it all."

What couldn't Thomas do? Nothing, it seemed, if he put his mind to it. Thomas, who stood 6'8", 313 pounds as a senior, possessed a rare athletic package. He was skilled enough at Wisconsin's Brookfield Central High to be a Division I basketball recruit. At UW, he posted a 34-inch vertical jump, ran the 40-yard dash in 4.8 seconds, and held about every strength record for UW tackles except for bench press. Badgers track coaches even believed Thomas was capable of becoming an Olympic-caliber shot-putter if he concentrated on the sport.

Indeed, Thomas qualified for the 2004 and 2005 NCAA Regionals in the shot put and discus. He also set the school indoor record in the shot put.

Yet maybe the most remarkable aspect of Thomas' athletic performance at Wisconsin was his ability to be a two-way football player in an era when those hardly existed—and certainly did not happen when it involved an offensive lineman. During his freshman season in 2003, Thomas switched over to defense for Wisconsin's Music City Bowl game against Auburn because of a slew of injuries. Thomas, a stellar defensive lineman in high school, tallied seven tackles.

Two years later, Thomas again switched over briefly to defense against Auburn in the Capital One Bowl. The move prompted Badgers coach Barry Alvarez, before his final game in charge, to declare, "I think Joe Thomas could choose where he wants to be an All-American. He's a natural, whether it be blocking someone or coming up onto a linebacker or playing defense."

Thomas suffered a devastating injury in that 2006 Capital One Bowl game when he tore the anterior cruciate ligament in his right knee while playing defense. He likely would have been a first-round pick in the NFL draft had he declared a year early, but the injury meant he wouldn't have to make that choice. He returned for his senior season, though uncertainty lingered as to how effective he could be—and when he might be available.

Eight months later, Thomas defied the odds and started for Wisconsin at left tackle in the season opener against Bowling Green. He never missed a game that season. In his career, he appeared in 47 games with 38 starts. He was a two-time All-American and in 2006 became Wisconsin's first winner of the Outland Trophy, given to college football's top interior lineman. Wisconsin also finished 12–1 in his senior year, a school record for victories in a season.

The Cleveland Browns selected him in the first round at No. 3 in the 2007 NFL draft, and he became the highest drafted Badgers offensive lineman in school history. In his first nine years in the league through 2015, he made the Pro Bowl every season, becoming one of eight players in NFL history to earn that distinction. The other seven all were in the Pro Football Hall of Fame. While many of UW's best linemen under Alvarez were run blockers first, Thomas also was an exceptional pass blocker with excellent footwork—skills that made him particularly valuable in the pros.

Before Thomas closed his senior season at Wisconsin, he expressed gratitude for the opportunity to play one more season in a Badgers uniform. If not for the injury, Thomas might have left for the NFL and missed the most enjoyable year of his college career.

"If I would have come out last year, maybe I would have looked back at some point in my career and said, 'Maybe I wish I would have stayed,'" Thomas told the *State Journal*. "To be able to live out this year and just try to play every game like it was my last game, coming out and playing with such a great team, playing for new coaches I've really come to love—I wouldn't give it up for anything."

58 Suzy Favor Hamilton

She was the college superstar who could seemingly do no wrong. Suzy Favor Hamilton possessed charm, looks, and a competitive drive that could kick aside any runner in her path on her way to smashing records as the most decorated woman in NCAA track and field history. But anxiety and depression chased Favor Hamilton for years after her time at Wisconsin, affecting her career and her life. Consequently, both her soaring highs and tremendous lows became forever linked.

Favor Hamilton grew up in Stevens Point, Wisconsin, and racked up 11 state high school championships and three USA Junior 1,500 titles. She was named one of the top 100 high school athletes of the century by *Scholastic Sports Magazine* and somehow exceeded even that lofty designation in college.

She won five NCAA outdoor track titles for the Badgers, including four consecutive victories in the 1,500 meters (1987–90). She also set an NCAA championship meet record with her triumph in the 800 meters in 1990.

Overall, Favor Hamilton won nine NCAA titles and 23 Big Ten championships in cross country, indoor track, and outdoor track. She finished her collegiate career as a 14-time All-American and three times earned Big Ten female athlete of the year honors.

Favor Hamilton quickly became a United States national team sensation as a middle-distance runner while gracing magazine covers such as *Fitness* and *Runner's World* and being featured in ads for Nike and Reebok. She qualified for the Olympics in 1992, 1996, and 2000, though she didn't medal. She won seven U.S. national titles, the last of which came in 1999.

But Favor Hamilton suffered a string of mysterious problems that would take a long time to detect. She collapsed near the end of the 1,500-meter race at the Prefontaine Classic in 2000 and finished second. She would infamously collapse again at the Olympics in Sydney, Australia, in the final of the 1,500, just 200 meters from the finish line.

During that Olympics race, Favor Hamilton suffered an anxiety attack as her quest for a gold medal disappeared. She had put so much pressure on herself to win gold and honor the memory of her brother, Dan Favor, a manic-depressive who had stopped taking his medications and took his own life by jumping from a building in 1999. She also wanted to honor a close friend who was dying of cancer. But when several runners passed her as the finish line approached, she intentionally collapsed in a heap, though no one knew the truth for years.

"I was never going to tell anybody I fell on purpose," she told the *Milwaukee Journal Sentinel* in July 2012. "The media made up excuses for me. I went along with what they came up with."

Only after years of therapy was she able to admit the truth pub-licly about the race and her battle with depression, which she said began as a child and fueled her desire to succeed as a runner. After her professional running career ended, Favor Hamilton and her husband, Mark, had a daughter, and the two worked as real estate agents in the Madison area. Favor Hamilton maintained sponsorships with Walt Disney World and the Rock 'n' Roll Marathon Series.

"I feel better than I've ever felt," she told the *Journal Sentinel*, noting the antidepressant Zoloft had helped her. "I know this med-ication would have helped me as a child with my anxiety. I don't know how it would have affected my drive as an athlete. I just know I'm happier than I've ever been. My life just keeps getting better."

But in December 2012, just months after that interview, *The Smoking Gun* reported Favor Hamilton worked as a paid escort in Las Vegas under the name Kelly Lundy, charging $600 per hour. After her double life was revealed, she lost her sponsorship deals with Disney and the Rock 'n' Roll race series.

"I do not expect people to understand," she tweeted after the rev-elation. "But the reasons for doing this made sense to me at the time and were very much related to depression." Favor Hamilton noted in a series of tweets that her work as an escort provided an "escape" for her.

The Big Ten's female athlete of the year award had been named for Favor Hamilton in 1991, placing her alongside men's award namesake Jesse Owens. The recognition was bestowed upon her at an event in which she also was named the Big Ten women's athlete of the decade. "It's just a great honor," she said then. "It's hard to believe my name will always be on that award."

Favor Hamilton's name was removed from the Big Ten female athlete of the year award in 2013. In September 2015, she released a memoir titled *Fast Girl: A Life Spent Running from Madness*, recounting how manic depression and bipolar disorder drove her to excel as an athlete and contributed to her downfall after her profes-sional running career ended.

59 1960 Rose Bowl: "A Nightmare"

Wisconsin football coach Milt Bruhn was supposed to be basking in the glory of his team's achievement. Nothing had come easily for the Badgers during the 1959 season, but here they stood on the Memorial Stadium field, 11–7 road victors over rival Minnesota in the regular season finale to clinch the Big Ten crown.

It was a significant moment for Wisconsin, which had just captured its first undisputed Big Ten title since 1912—a span of 47 years. Badgers fans who made the trip to Minneapolis were throwing roses on the field to celebrate the team's second Rose Bowl berth in program history.

Bruhn, meanwhile, simply wasn't sure what to make of the whole scene that November day. He was elated, yes. He also expressed an unusual amount of frustration with the way in which his team had played.

"The whole season has been pretty much like that—frustration all the way," Bruhn told reporters after the game. "We never knew just how things were going. We were a little scared [against Minnesota]. We weren't as sharp the last two or three games as a month ago."

Perhaps Bruhn felt a premonition of what was to come. Six weeks later, on the biggest stage in college football, Wisconsin would suffer one of its most embarrassing defeats in program history at the Rose Bowl. Washington obliterated Wisconsin 44–8 in a game that was never close.

"We had gone through so much to win the Big Ten championship that when we got to the Rose Bowl, we were emotionally drained," Badgers quarterback Dale Hackbart told the *Milwaukee Journal* in 1979 on the occasion of the team's 20-year reunion. "We weren't as good a football team as we had been."

For some context, it's important to note that while Wisconsin reached the Rose Bowl that season, it was not the Badgers' most feared unit. Wisconsin finished the regular season 7–2 overall and 5–2 in the league, becoming the first team to win the title with two conference losses. UW opened with an unimpressive 16–14 victory against Stanford and closed with a come-from-behind win against a Minnesota team that finished 2–7 overall, including 1–6 in Big Ten games.

Minnesota scored 1 minute, 43 seconds into the game, after just four plays, to take a 7–0 lead on a 57-yard pass. It took Hackbart's quarterback sneak for a touchdown midway through the fourth quarter to give the Badgers the victory.

Wisconsin lost its Big Ten opener 21–0 to Purdue, which put the Badgers in a hole all season. UW also lost 9–6 to Illinois the week before playing Minnesota. Northwestern could have shared the conference crown on the last day of the regular season but lost 28–0 to Illinois.

It was no wonder, then, why Big Ten commissioner Kenneth L. Wilson said the league vote to determine the Rose Bowl participant was "not unanimous," though he refused to reveal the voting breakdown.

Wisconsin still finished the regular season in the top 10 and allowed an average of 11.7 points per game. Washington stood 9–1 and averaged nearly twice as many points per game. The Huskies hadn't allowed a point in their two previous games before the Rose Bowl, though the Badgers were inexplicably listed as 6½-point favorites. When the teams finally met, Washington established control early.

Wisconsin won the coin toss and, on orders from Bruhn, elected to kick off because of a gusty wind. Washington's George Fleming promptly returned the kickoff to midfield.

"Kicking off was our first mistake," Hackbart told the *Journal*. "We were going to be obnoxious about our defense and show them how tough we were. So we gave them the ball and they rammed it down our throats."

Washington outgained Wisconsin 352–276, and the Badgers lost four fumbles. The Huskies scored the first 17 points, including a 53-yard punt return for a touchdown by Fleming. Fullback Tom Wiesner scored the Badgers' only touchdown on a four-yard run late in the second quarter. When Hackbart completed the two-point pass to Al Schoonover, Wisconsin's scoring was done. The Huskies closed with 27 consecutive points.

"It was a nightmare," said Jerry Stalcup, a senior guard-linebacker for the team. "We couldn't accomplish much of anything."

Many spectators assumed the Badgers used the trip as a vacation to sunny California and did not take the game seriously. But Bruhn had the players running two-a-day practices, and sometimes more.

"A lot of people thought we were drinking and everything out there," Hackbart said. "That's a lot of baloney. We had curfew every night. Milt Bruhn worked the hell out of us. We had practice three times a day before Christmas.

"It finally reached the point where we got tired of working. We were going downhill, and Washington was coming up the other side of the mountain. They just beat the hell out of us."

Along with Illinois' 45–9 loss to UCLA in 1984, the 36-point margin stood as the worst Rose Bowl defeat in history until Oregon crushed Florida State 59-20 in the 2015 Rose Bowl—a semifinal game in the inaugural College Football Playoff.

"We were ready for 'em and we beat 'em, that's all," Washington quarterback Bob Schloredt said after the game. "We outhit 'em and outfought 'em all the way."

Wisconsin athletics director Ivy Williamson even heard complaints from his taxi driver after the game had ended. "What a bunch of bums," the cabbie said. "I lost a hundred on them Wisconsin guys seven years ago [in the 1953 Rose Bowl game] and I lost another hundred today. They can keep Wisconsin."

In the next day's *Los Angeles Examiner*, sports writer Melvin Durslag wrote, "Wisconsin proved itself a cheese champion yesterday. The men from Wisconsin couldn't play football for sour apples, or for that matter, sauerbraten."

60 Badgers Break Coaching Color Barrier

Bill Cofield and Edwina Qualls did not set out to be pioneers. They were simply two people who loved basketball, enjoyed coaching, and wanted to see how high up the ladder they could take their chosen profession.

But in the year of this country's bicentennial, they also became linked as part of sports history, for the University of Wisconsin and the Big Ten. In March 1976, Cofield became the first black head men's basketball coach in the league—80 years after it was founded—when the Badgers hired him. Later that summer, Qualls was hired by Wisconsin and became the Big Ten's first black head women's basketball coach.

Qualls arrived at Wisconsin after amassing an 82–15 record as a high school coach at New Haven's R.C. Lee High School in Connecticut. Her teams made several trips to the state tournament, and she was named the state high school coach of the year in 1975. She earned her undergraduate and graduate degrees in physical education from Southern Connecticut State College.

At Wisconsin, Qualls produced five winning seasons during her 10-year run, including a second-place Big Ten finish in 1983-84. The 13–5 league record still represents the most victories and the best the Badgers have finished in the Big Ten. In 1981–82, the Badgers went 21–13 and won the Midwest AIAW Regional Championship title. UW qualified for its first postseason tournament with the victory and knocked off Colorado in the first round of the tournament. Qualls closed her career with a 131–141 record before resigning in 1986.

Cofield was 36 years old when he was hired and had shown great promise as a coach. He graduated from McKendree College in Lebanon, Illinois, and went on to receive his master's degree from the University of Kentucky. His first collegiate coaching opportunity came at Kentucky State University, where he spent one year as an assistant before taking over as head coach of the Lincoln University of Pennsylvania team. Following a 38–12 record in two seasons—with two conference titles—he moved on to Prairie View A&M for four seasons. There, he compiled a 57–48 record.

Cofield became the country's first black athletics director and head coach at a predominantly white institution when he accepted both positions at the College of Racine in Wisconsin in 1973. His team finished 14–15 before the school went out of business. He then became an assistant coach for two years at Virginia, and the school won the Atlantic Coast Conference tournament his last year there.

When Cofield was hired at Wisconsin, he made no promises about how soon he could turn around the Badgers' program. The previous coach, John Powless, had resigned in February while his team was in the midst of a 14-game losing streak.

"I'm not going to say we're going to be the UCLA of the Midwest or any other nonsense like that right away," Cofield said.

Though Cofield saw it as an honor to be one of the few black head coaches in the nation, he preferred to downplay discussions about the color of his skin. When he was hired, he said, "I guess it is a historical event whether I like it or not."

"I'd rather be known as an outstanding basketball coach, regardless of color or race or anything else," he told the *Milwaukee Journal* in 1976. "On the other hand, I know that I represent a lot of black coaches who would like to have the opportunity to coach, feel they are good enough to coach, and maybe they are good enough to coach. But they may not have had the opportunity simply because of their race, which I feel is very unfortunate. Because I feel you should judge a man on his capabilities and his performance rather than what color he is.

"And I think the one thing that I have proven in coming to Wisconsin and in my relationship with my players is that I think my players have forgotten that I am black. Because I don't treat the black players any different than I do the white players. I love both sets.... They're all my players as far as I'm concerned."

Cofield was the man responsible for hiring Bo Ryan as an assistant coach at both the College of Racine in 1973 and at Wisconsin in 1976. Ryan recalled sorting through Cofield's mail at Wisconsin to keep mean-spirited letters from finding their way to his boss.

"There were some people who weren't ready for that breakthrough," Ryan wrote about Cofield's hiring in his book, *Another Hill to Climb*. "All coaches have a burden of expectations. From my perspective, there was an additional burden for Bill Cofield. It had nothing to do with winning or losing."

Cofield struggled to gain traction in the Big Ten in six seasons at Wisconsin. His teams finished with a winning record overall only once but never in league play. In 1982, he resigned under pressure from the athletics department for failing to turn the program around. Only 4,321 fans showed up to watch Cofield's final game at the UW Field House, a 77–75 loss to Ohio State. Cofield's final record at Wisconsin was 63–101. That same year, he was diagnosed with pancreatic cancer and died in the summer of 1983 at age 43.

Upon his resignation, Cofield noted it had been tough improving the program because of high academic standards and the lack of talented players to recruit from in the state. The two most notable recruits of his tenure were Claude Gregory (Washington, D.C.) and Wes Matthews (Bridgeport, Connecticut).

"This is primarily a football and hockey state," he said. "You don't have a multitude of people with great talent in this state so you can do like Bobby Knight and make four home visits, sign three people from the state of Indiana, and all of them are All-Americans. That's not a knock at the state, it's just a statement."

61 Kohl Center

At its best, the Kohl Center's raucous environment during men's basketball games provides a home-court advantage few other programs can match. There is a reason why Wisconsin's record during coach Bo Ryan's 14-plus seasons at home was an astounding 211–22 (.906 winning percentage). Good players and good coaching certainly is vital. But so is a good home court.

A 2008 ESPN.com article perhaps best summed up the plight of opposing teams who dare venture into Madison: "Good luck winning at the Kohl Center," it read. "In a league in which most of the home venues are tough, Wisconsin's stands out as almost impenetrable."

So, what makes the Kohl Center special?

The rabid fan base, for starters. During a stretch from 2003 to 2011, the basketball team had a streak of 143 consecutive sellouts. The student section, known as the Grateful Red, cheers incessantly behind the opposing team's basket. In 2007, the *Detroit News* ranked the Grateful Red as the No. 1 cheering section in college basketball.

The arena itself also is massive. The Kohl Center, with its lower bowl and two balconies, seats 17,230 for men's basketball, which includes courtside seating, and 17,142 for women's basketball. The facility accommodates 15,237 people for hockey, and between 15,000 and 17,000 for concerts.

Wisconsin's basketball team has routinely ranked among the top 10 nationally in home attendance. During the 2014–15 season, the Badgers averaged 17,279 fans per game to rank fifth in the country. They also led the Big Ten in attendance in 10 of 13 years through that season.

It's no wonder, then, why Ryan often spoke of the difficulty his longtime assistant coach Greg Gard experienced in trying to schedule non-conference opponents to visit the Kohl Center. After all, few teams leave Madison with a victory. According to RPIRatings.com, only two college programs had a better winning percentage in home games through the 2014–15 season: Gonzaga's McCarthey Athletic Center (.939) and Kentucky's Rupp Arena (.893). Wisconsin's record was 246–34 overall (.879).

Fans have been treated to plenty of memorable games at the Kohl Center. Here are some of the most notable contests:

January 17, 1998: Wisconsin opens the facility at mid-season with a 56–33 victory against Northwestern in front of 16,697 fans, including Senator Herb Kohl. Kohl, a 1956 Wisconsin graduate, donated $25 million for the project—the single largest private donation in the university's history. Former All-Big Ten basketball player Albert "Ab" Nicholas and his wife, Nancy Johnson Nicholas, pledged $10 million toward the project, which cost $76.4 million overall.

March 5, 2000: UW edges No. 12 Indiana 56–53 in Bob Knight's final visit to the Kohl Center as Hoosiers coach. Maurice Linton's basket with 1:01 remaining breaks the last tie, and Wisconsin closes the regular season 8–8 in Big Ten play and rides a hot streak all the way to the Final Four.

February 27, 2002: Wisconsin clinches a share of its first Big Ten title in 55 years with a 74–54 victory against Michigan. Devin Harris and Kirk Penney each score 21 points and hit four three-pointers. With the victory, the Badgers earn their first-ever No. 1 seed in the Big Ten tournament.

March 5, 2003: Point guard Devin Harris buries the game-winning free throw with 0.4 seconds remaining to lift Wisconsin to a 60–59 victory against Illinois and give the Badgers their first outright Big Ten title since 1947.

March 5, 2008: Wisconsin captures its third Big Ten regular season title in seven seasons under Bo Ryan with a 77–41 dismantling of Penn State, setting off a court-storming session.

January 24, 2010: UW edges Penn State 79–71 in overtime, as Ryan becomes the second-fastest coach to reach 100 Big Ten victories, doing so in 140 games. Only Indiana's Bob Knight reached the mark quicker (131 games).

February 21, 2011: Badgers junior Jordan Taylor scores 21 of his 27 points in the second half to rally No. 13 Wisconsin from a 15-point deficit and topple No. 1 Ohio State 71–67. The game marks Wisconsin's first win against an Associated Press No. 1 team since 1962.

February 9, 2013: Guard Ben Brust buries an improbable half-court shot at the regulation buzzer to tie the score against No. 3 Michigan. UW goes on to defeat Michigan 65–62 in overtime.

March 1, 2015: On senior day, Wisconsin squeezes past Michigan State 68–61 to clinch at least a share of the Big Ten regular season crown—Ryan's fourth in 14 seasons. Players high-five fans up the aisles and return for a trophy ceremony on the court. Badgers center Frank Kaminsky, the eventual national player of the year, scores 31 points. Afterward, Michigan State coach Tom Izzo calls him the best player he's seen in the league since Purdue's Glenn Robinson 21 years earlier.

December 15, 2015: Wisconsin defeats Texas A&M–Corpus Christi 64–49 in Bo Ryan's final game as head coach. He announces after the game that he is retiring, effective immediately, to allow assistant coach Greg Gard the opportunity to earn the head coaching job.

62 Devin Harris

There were 6.9 seconds remaining when Devin Harris had the ball and history in his hands. Wisconsin and Illinois stood locked in a 59–59 tie at the Kohl Center on March 5, 2003, and Badgers coach Bo Ryan trusted one man to determine the outcome with a Big Ten title hanging in the balance.

Harris, only a sophomore, already had developed into an unquestioned star. He'd started every game for Ryan since his freshman season and proved every bit the player he was when he earned Wisconsin's "Mr. Basketball" award at Wauwatosa East High School. Now, a frenzied home crowd stood on its feet, desperately hoping Harris could lift the spirits of an entire state.

Alando Tucker inbounded the ball to Harris in the backcourt. He took six dribbles toward the top of the key and blew by Illinois guard Dee Brown with a right-to-left crossover on his way to the basket. Brown stuck his hand out and altered Harris' shot, which hit the bottom of the backboard as time expired.

A whistle blew. A foul was called with 0.4 seconds remaining. Harris was heading to the free throw line for two tries with a chance to hand Wisconsin its first outright conference title since 1947.

The first shot rattled out, and the crowd moaned in agony.

"No doubt in my mind, the second one was going in," Harris said afterward.

Harris calmly released his second attempt. Swish. And just like that, No. 24 Wisconsin had beaten No. 14 Illinois 60–59. Students rushed the court to celebrate the outright championship and the Badgers' first consecutive conference titles since 1923–24.

Harris was among the most talented, clutch players Ryan ever coached at Wisconsin. He scored 20 points in his debut in the

2001–02 season opener, the second most by a freshman in school history, and never looked back. Over the course of his three-year career, he scored 1,425 points, which ranks 11th in school history. Had he stayed a fourth year rather than declaring for the NBA draft, he very likely would have been one of only three players to surpass 2,000 points at Wisconsin.

He was everything Ryan predicted Harris would be when he watched him while still coach at the University of Wisconsin–Milwaukee. After witnessing Harris play a sectional semifinal game in which Wauwatosa East beat Milwaukee King, Ryan told Harris' coach, George Haas, that Harris would be a superstar.

"Devin Harris will be an All-Big Ten player by the time he is a junior," Haas once recalled Ryan saying.

How right he was.

Harris was the Big Ten Player of the Year as a junior in 2004, earning second-team All-American honors, and averaging 19.5 points per game. His 624 points were a single-season record at the time, later topped by Tucker in 2007. During one three-game stretch his junior season, he scored 97 points to set a school record, dropping 30 on Illinois, 29 at Ohio State, and a career-high 38 against Minnesota.

In Harris' three seasons, Wisconsin went 78–28, including 35–13 in Big Ten games. The Badgers won conference titles in 2002 and 2003 and won the 2004 Big Ten tournament after finishing second in the league to Illinois in the regular season. Harris, meanwhile, became one of just two Badgers in history to start every game as a freshman, sophomore, and junior, joining Rick Olson.

After Harris' junior season, it became obvious he would be a lottery pick in the 2004 NBA draft—a scenario he simply couldn't turn down, despite his hesitation. Initially, Harris kept open the possibility of returning to Wisconsin for his senior year by not hiring an agent. But on June 3, he made the move official in a news conference after he received Ryan's approval.

"I called Coach the other day and the first thing he said to me was, 'It's your time,'" Harris said. "That's what I was waiting for, that kind of blessing that I got from him. And once I got it, I knew it was the right decision for me."

Harris developed such a high trust level with Ryan that the coach allowed him to call many of the team's plays. He rewarded Ryan's faith with an exceptional career and became the first player under Ryan to declare early for the NBA draft. Harris was selected in the first round at No. 5 overall by the Dallas Mavericks, the highest spot by a Badgers player since Don Rehfeldt went second to the Baltimore Bullets in 1950.

At his announcement ceremony, Harris thanked Ryan for all he had done to shape him.

"He's the part of the program that I'll probably miss the most," Harris said. "I don't know if in the NBA if I can talk to the coach like I can here, and come over during the game and talk strategy and he's thinking the same thing I'm thinking. I don't know if we'll be on that same kind of plane.

"I can't replace a coach like Coach Ryan. I'll probably never have a coach like him again. You can't put into words what he means to me."

Badgers' First-Round NBA Draft Picks

Wisconsin has produced nine first-round NBA draft choices. In 2015, the Badgers had two first-round selections in the same draft for the first time in school history when Frank Kaminsky (ninth) and Sam Dekker (18th) were picked. A look at the list:

Round 1, No. 2 overall: Don Rehfeldt, 1950 (Baltimore Bullets)

Rehfeldt was the Big Ten's leading scorer for two straight years and was the conference MVP in 1950. He was the first Badgers player to score 1,000 points in his career.

No. 5: Devin Harris, 2004 (Washington Wizards)

During his junior campaign, Harris earned second-team All-American honors by the Associated Press. He averaged 19.5 points per game that season.

No. 9: Frank Kaminsky, 2015 (Charlotte Hornets)

Perhaps no player improved more at Wisconsin from his freshman year to his senior year than Kaminsky. He went from averaging 7.7 minutes and 1.8 points per game to being the consensus national player of the year in 2014-15, averaging 18.8 points and 8.2 rebounds.

No. 12: Al Henry, 1970 (Philadelphia 76ers)

Henry's numbers improved drastically during his final season with Wisconsin in 1969-70, when he averaged 15.0 points and 11.0 rebounds in 24 games.

No. 14: Wes Matthews, 1980 (Washington Bullets)

Matthews left Wisconsin with a scoring average of 18.1 points per game, which ranks third all-time in program history. He was a second-team All-Big Ten selection in 1979–80.

No. 18: Sam Dekker, 2015 (Houston Rockets)

Dekker was the first Badgers player to declare early for the NBA draft since Devin Harris. His stock rose after a stellar 2015 NCAA tournament, in which he averaged 19.2 points and 5.5 rebounds on the way to a national title game appearance.

No. 20: Paul Grant, 1997 (Minnesota Timberwolves)

Grant played three seasons at Boston College before transferring to Wisconsin for his senior year. In 1996–97, he led the Badgers in points (12.5), field goal percentage (49.4), free throw percentage (71.3), and blocked shots (1.2), and he was an honorable mention All-Big Ten selection.

No. 21: Michael Finley, 1995 (Phoenix Suns)

Finley ranks second in Wisconsin history with 2,147 points scored. He was named first-team All-Big Ten in 1993 and 1995 and is the only Wisconsin player to average at least 20 points in three different seasons.

> ### No. 29: Alando Tucker, 2007 (Phoenix Suns)
> Tucker is Wisconsin's all-time leading scorer with 2,217 points and became UW's first consensus first-team All-American since 1942. He was named Big Ten Player of the Year during his senior season in 2006–07 after averaging 19.9 points per game.

63 Camp Randall Crush

One of the most significant regular season home victories in program history was marred by a postgame celebration that quickly turned ugly at Camp Randall Stadium. The aftermath became known simply as "The Crush" and altered game-day procedures in the coming decades.

On October 30, 1993, Wisconsin fans began to rejoice following a 13–10 victory against Michigan that put the Badgers on a legitimate path to capture the Big Ten regular season crown and a possible Rose Bowl berth. Amid the euphoria, students prepared to storm the field. But fans at the top of the stands pushed on those in front of them, causing pressure to build up at the chain-link fence designed to keep people off the playing field.

"Literally 70 rows of people in the student section compressed into 40 rows of students," said Susan Riseling, UW's police chief. "So essentially 30 rows of people marched right on down toward the field, compressing all the people that were in front of them."

Then, disaster struck. The railings that were supposed to prevent people from falling out into aisles or rows gave way under the immense pressure. Bolts that were fastened into the concrete buckled, and iron railings tangled "almost like spaghetti," Riseling recalled.

What followed was a mass of humanity that piled up on the field. And while many Wisconsin players already were back in the locker room, those who remained on the field rushed to offer their assistance. That included team captain Joe Panos, who said students were "literally blue" and described the moment as the scariest thing he had ever seen.

"We start leaving the locker room and seeing kids coming down the tunnel with tears in their eyes screaming, 'There might be some students dead out there,'" former Badgers defensive coordinator Dan McCarney recalled. "We were in the locker room celebrating. We didn't know. It was an unbelievable swing of emotions."

A quick response by on-field police and paramedics prevented any deaths. About 70 students, most of them female, were hospitalized. Of that number, 10 were unconscious and not breathing when first treated at the scene.

"Thank God nobody got killed or very seriously injured," Badgers center Cory Raymer said. "It wasn't the way you wanted to celebrate a victory after coming off the field. It was pretty scary."

Wisconsin went on to win the Big Ten and the Rose Bowl that season. Several players admitted the incident helped to galvanize the team and further illustrated how special their fan base was to them.

The incident also provided a reminder of what can go wrong when thousands of people try to storm the field and exposed flaws in the design of a stadium constructed in 1917. It then led to changes that made Camp Randall Stadium safer. For instance, the chain-link fence on the field was removed, and students are now assigned to specific sections to prevent overcrowding. The previous system used general admission seating and often led to too many students seated in one particular area.

"There were 11,800 seats in the student section back then," Riseling said. "That was the motion of probably 11,000 people. Maybe 800 didn't participate. I pretty much think they all did."

The best news to emerge from the stadium changes: no similar incidents have occurred since.

64 Paul Bunyan's Axe

On a cool mid-November evening, two strange men sneaked through the doors of Wisconsin's football practice field curiously clad in maroon and gold helmets and uniforms with mischief on their minds.

The men, faintly resembling University of Minnesota football players, bolted toward the sideline where the indelible symbol of the century-old rivalry between Wisconsin and Minnesota's football teams rested. Before players could react, the two dashed off with the precious prize known as Paul Bunyan's Axe—six-foot handle and all—in front of a stunned Badgers team.

"Everybody is looking around like, 'What the hell just happened?'" former Wisconsin football coach Bret Bielema recalled before the teams' 2011 game.

Turns out, the heist was all a ruse. Two of the Badgers' strength coaches had been assigned the task at a practice a few years earlier from Bielema himself. Amid the confusion, an important message emerged.

"They had never seen the trophy lost before, most of them," Bielema said. "I wanted them to feel what that was going to be like."

Several Badgers classes, as it happened, never knew the pain of losing the trophy. Wisconsin was able to keep possession of the axe every year from 2004 to 2015 during the longest winning streak by one team in series history. One of the most famous games in that streak took place in 2005, when Jonathan Casillas blocked a punt and Ben Strickland recovered it in the end zone with 30 seconds left to give Wisconsin a 38–34 victory in The Miracle at the Metrodome.

"When you think you've seen it all," then-Badgers coach Barry Alvarez said, "you haven't seen it all."

Maintaining bragging rights in the annual border battle remains the same source of pride for players and coaches now as it has throughout the decades. The winner runs toward the sideline to unearth the axe, and players take turns "chopping" at the opposing team's goalpost. In years in which Wisconsin retains possession of the trophy, one of the team managers holds it upright so players can touch the axe as they enter and exit the practice field the week of the game. It is near the players at all times, including during team meetings.

Wisconsin's players also listen to history lessons from former players and coaches and watch videos of previous games to gain a better understanding of its true meaning. One story relayed to players—though its truth remains in question—involved a Wisconsin football player in the 1930s or '40s who asked that his injured finger be cut off so he could play against Minnesota.

The moral of the story? *Better to lose a finger than a fumble to Minnesota.*

Not surprisingly, history runs deep in the rivalry, which dates to 1890. From 1923 to '25, there were three consecutive ties. In 1962, the teams met in the regular season finale, and Wisconsin won 14–9 at Camp Randall Stadium when Ralph Kurek scored on a 2-yard run with less than two minutes remaining to clinch a spot in the Rose Bowl. It wasn't until 52 years later, in 2014, when Wisconsin and Minnesota played with a title on the line again. This time, UW edged Minnesota 34–24 in the regular season finale at home to win the Big Ten West division and advance to the conference championship game.

Minnesota won the first game in the series 63–0, and the scores of each subsequent game have been printed on the axe—though it hasn't been around from the start. Before Paul Bunyan's Axe, there was merely the Slab of Bacon.

That name became attached to the first trophy, created in 1930, with the idea being that the winning team each year would "bring home the bacon." The trophy was a piece of black walnut wood carved by R.B. Fouch of Minneapolis. In the middle, a football carving read either "W" or "M" depending on how it was held. Scores of each year's game were painted on the back. And when the Slab of Bacon changed teams, a sorority from the losing school presented it to the winning school.

But in 1943, the Slab of Bacon mysteriously disappeared after a Gophers victory. As a way to continue the trophy tradition, the Wisconsin "W" Club in 1948 created Paul Bunyan's Axe, named after the mythical giant lumberjack. The same trophy changed hands until the turn of the century, when the axe became unsteady and the six-foot long handle ran out of space for scores. In 2000, a new axe was created, and the old one was donated to the College Football Hall of Fame three years later.

In an odd twist, the Slab of Bacon was found in 1994, more than 50 years after it disappeared, by an intern from the Wisconsin men's sports information office while cleaning out a storage room. Despite being deemed lost in the 1940s, every score of the Minnesota–Wisconsin football game from 1930 to '70 was engraved on the back of the trophy, adding to the mystique of the annual rivalry. The discovery prompted Alvarez to famously remark, "We took home the bacon and kept it!"

Other Notable Games for Paul Bunyan's Axe

1952: Wisconsin 21, Minnesota 21

The Badgers earned a tie with the Gophers in the regular season finale, which helped Wisconsin secure its first-ever Rose Bowl bid. UW finished with the same 4–1–1 Big Ten record as Purdue, but conference athletics directors voted in favor of Wisconsin. They believed the Badgers provided the league with the best chance to win in Pasadena. USC would go on to defeat Wisconsin 7–0.

1961: Wisconsin 23, Minnesota 21

Quarterback Ron Miller's 21-yard touchdown to Pat Richter on the last play of the third quarter gave Wisconsin a lead it never relinquished, and the Badgers deprived the third-ranked Gophers of winning a Big Ten title.

In the final month of the season, Gophers quarterback Sandy Stephens famously remarked his team had "three tough games left—Michigan State, Iowa, and Purdue," omitting Wisconsin. Badgers tackle Dick Grimm held up a sign after the game containing Stephens' quote, good-naturedly taunting the Gophers.

1999: Wisconsin 20, Minnesota 17 OT

No. 20 Wisconsin edged No. 25 Minnesota when kicker Vitaly Pisetsky buried a 31-yard field goal in the first overtime game in school history. Head coach Barry Alvarez missed the game while awaiting knee surgery at the Mayo Clinic in Rochester, Minnesota.

"I felt like Barry was there every day this week in practice," said interim coach John Palermo, the team's defensive line coach. "I'd look over and expect to see him on the sideline in his golf cart. Inspirationally, he was there for us every day."

The triumph was part of a seven-game Big Ten winning streak, which culminated with a victory against Stanford in the 2000 Rose Bowl.

65 Watch the Fifth Quarter

One cannot underestimate how woeful Wisconsin's football program was when Michael Leckrone arrived on campus in the summer of 1969 to serve as director of the school's marching band. In 20 games over the previous two seasons, the Badgers' wins amounted to a grand total of zero. Given that on-campus protests over the war already meant few students wanted to wear a uniform and march military style, Leckrone faced a tall task in inspiring a fan base on game days.

Still, Leckrone, whose childhood fantasy was to lead a Big Ten band down the field, never wavered in his enthusiasm despite diminished band interest and bad football.

"I remember the band had really special cheers when we made a first down," Leckrone said. "We weren't worried about touchdowns. We were just delighted when we made first downs. The whole idea in those days was we're still proud of our school. Let's celebrate the fact that we're Wisconsin because we don't have much to celebrate on the field."

Initially, Leckrone followed a basic format that had been used since the early 1900s at universities across the country. After the game, the band would play a few school songs, such as "If You Want to Be a Badger," "Varsity," and "On, Wisconsin!" for about eight minutes. By that time, however, most of the fan base had already filed out of the stadium. Leckrone wanted to find a way to keep fans in their seats, even if the final score didn't finish in Wisconsin's favor—and it generally did not.

In 1978, the band began playing "You've Said It All," a spinoff of a beer commercial that changed the lyrics from "When you've said Budweiser, you've said it all," to "When you've said Wisconsin, you've said it all." It became a hit, and the stadium shook so much that Leckrone was forced to play it only as part of the postgame show—one of the main reasons fans began staying in their seats after games. About that time, sports writer Glenn Miller of the *Wisconsin State Journal* dubbed the band's show "The Fifth Quarter," and the name stuck.

"He made the comment in one of the newspaper clippings that it seemed like there were more people there for The Fifth Quarter than there were for the game, which may or may not have been true," Leckrone said. "I know there were students who told me they knew the game wasn't going to be too exciting, so they would just kind of sneak in—security was pretty lax in those days—and participate in The Fifth Quarter and then go about their business after having a little party."

Over the years, The Fifth Quarter evolved into a real spectacle despite continued mediocre football. Band members high-stepped,

The show isn't over once the game is over. Stay after Wisconsin football games to watch the Badgers band play in The Fifth Quarter.

strutted and played their hearts out, and crowds appreciated their versatility, spunk, and overall performance.

"At Wisconsin, 'The Fifth Quarter' is usually far more entertaining than the previous four, one reason hardly anyone heads for the parking lot until long after the game has ended," a *Washington Post* article noted in 1990. "That's when the marching band entertains the crowd with 45 minutes of sweet-tooting, foot-stomping, sing-along tunes. Even the security guards assigned to keep fans off the field tap their feet and occasionally join band members in impromptu do-si-dos on the sidelines."

Leckrone, who took over as director of the entire band in 1975, continued to find ways to entertain fans over the years. He once incorporated the "Chicken Dance" after the school's crew coach, Randy Jablonic, returned from a trip to Europe and suggested Leckrone play it at games. In the 1980s, several of his band members began mimicking Pee-wee Herman's "Tequila" dance, and the song quickly found its way into the postgame performance.

His band plays a cover of the Bruce Channel "Hey! Baby" song and "Swingtown" by the Steve Miller Band. He even made sure the band created its own instrumental rendition of the House of Pain song "Jump Around"—the track that is played after the third quarter of home football games and has pumped up fans since 1998.

"My biggest failure was a really pop culture thing," Leckrone said. "We tried to do the Macarena. We could do it. We tried to get the crowd to do it. By the time we got around to it, I think everybody was bored with it. The students booed, which was kind of fun. We were resurrecting a thing that they thought was very passé."

Now, the football program has given fans a reason to cheer before the postgame show, establishing itself as a Big Ten power. Leckrone's job, however, has remained the same.

"I'm still looking for anything that works," he said.

"On, Wisconsin!"

The school's fight song, "On, Wisconsin!" has an unusual backstory that provides another angle to the border battle with the Minnesota Gophers. William Purdy of Chicago wrote the tune and intended to enter it in a contest that offered a $100 prize for a new University of Minnesota football song. But his roommate, Carl Beck, wrote new words for the song and persuaded Purdy to submit it to the University of Wisconsin. Beck had attended Wisconsin in 1908 and left in February 1909.

On November 11, 1909, Purdy played the song at a pep rally at the armory on Wisconsin's campus, and it was an immediate hit. Two days later, the song made its game debut, ironically against Minnesota at Camp Randall Stadium. Famed band conductor John Philip Sousa called it "the best college melody I have ever heard," and the tune has become a popular fight song for thousands of schools across the country.

The lyrics:

On, Wisconsin! On, Wisconsin! Plunge right through that line!
Run the ball right down the field, a touchdown sure this time.

> On, Wisconsin! On, Wisconsin! Fight on for her fame,
> Fight! Fellows! Fight! Fight, fight, we'll win this game.
> On, Wisconsin! On, Wisconsin! Stand up, Badgers sing!
> 'Forward' is our driving spirit loyal voices ring.
> On, Wisconsin! On, Wisconsin! Raise her glowing flame!
> Stand, fellows, let us now salute her name!

66 Bud Foster

Walter Meanwell stood before the University of Wisconsin's athletics board during a lengthy Saturday afternoon meeting in July 1934 and laid out the reasons his former pupil should become his successor as Badgers basketball coach. Harold "Bud" Foster, Meanwell said, was ready for this opportunity despite having only one year of head coaching experience with the freshman team.

Meanwell, in recommending Foster, stressed the fact that he believed Foster would be able to handle the job particularly well because of his familiarity with the players and because of his ability. It was upon this recommendation, more than anything, that the 28-year-old Foster indeed succeeded Meanwell. He became the youngest coach in the Big Ten and received a one-year appointment that carried with it an assistant professorship and a salary of $2,500 a season.

The decision could not have worked out much better for either party. Over the next 25 years, Foster, a former Badgers All-American himself, coached Wisconsin's teams with pride. He finished with a record of 265–267, won three Big Ten titles in 1935, 1941, and 1947, and helped guide Wisconsin to the 1941 NCAA championship—Foster's greatest achievement as coach.

That 1941 team, behind the strength of consensus All-Americans Gene Englund and John Kotz, famously won its final

15 games, including three in the NCAA tournament, to win the title. Wisconsin defeated Dartmouth 51–50 and Pittsburgh 36–30 in games played at the UW Field House and then upset Washington State 39–34 in the title game in Kansas City, Missouri.

"According to the scribes, we were going down there for a train ride," Englund later said. "We didn't have a chance. That was the feeling among everybody but the team."

After winning the championship, Badgers players hoisted Foster on their shoulders and carried him off the court. Foster, like his players, was regarded as a hero.

"Among other things the title proved, as some of us have long claimed, that Bud Foster is a great coach, one who knows all the angles, and one who can get an awful lot out of the material at hand," wrote *Milwaukee Journal* sportswriter Stoney McGlynn after the team's 1941 championship.

"The manner in which he kept his club on the ground during the 15-game winning streak, the manner in which his club made the other teams play its game, speaks louder than words.... He showed the coaching genius and leadership and that he had the confidence and faith of his men."

Foster was a standout player from 1927 to '30 under Meanwell. During his three seasons with the team, the Badgers compiled a 43–8 record and were named Big Ten co-champions in 1929. He earned all-conference honors in 1929 and 1930 and served as captain of the 1930 team.

"Bud is no scoring giant in one game, or a flop the next, but plays steady ball against the good as well as the poor, both offensively and defensively," the *Milwaukee Sentinel* wrote in 1930.

Following a brief professional career with the Oshkosh All-Stars, he returned to his alma mater to coach. Foster's first team in 1935 went 15–5 in the Big Ten and won a share of the conference crown. During the season, Wisconsin won a memorable 37–27 game in overtime against Indiana at the UW Field House, holding the Hoosiers scoreless in overtime. For his efforts in winning a league title, Foster received a $500 raise. When he won the conference and national championship in 1941, his salary increased another $500 to $3,500.

In his final seasons, Wisconsin could not match the success it experienced early in his career. From 1955 to '59, the Badgers had a combined record of 22–66, including 3–19 his last season. He had been operating on a one-year reprieve from the previous season with the understanding that he produce a winner or face the consequences. Foster coached Wisconsin through the 1959 season, when he quit rather than deal with the possibility of being fired.

Foster, who died at age 90 in 1996, is a member of the Helms Basketball Hall of Fame, the Naismith Memorial Basketball Hall of Fame, the Wisconsin State Athletics Hall of Fame, and the University of Wisconsin Athletics Hall of Fame. His 265 victories at Wisconsin remained a record for 53 years after his last game, until Bo Ryan surpassed the mark in 2012.

67 A Short-Lived No. 1 Ranking

The rise to the top spot of the Associated Press college basketball poll was as methodical as a Bo Ryan swing offense possession. Wisconsin's 2006–07 team opened the season ranked ninth, climbed to seventh, and then fell to No. 12 after an unexpected November loss to Missouri State.

But the Badgers would win 22 of their next 23 games, taking down nationally ranked foes Marquette, Pittsburgh, and Ohio State along the way. With Alando Tucker, Kammron Taylor, and Brian Butch leading the charge, anything seemed possible. And finally, on Monday, February 19, 2007, Wisconsin ascended all the way to No. 1 for the first time in school history, 26–2 overall and 12–1 in Big Ten play. Two days earlier, top-ranked Florida's 17-game winning streak had been snapped in an 83–70 loss to Vanderbilt, and Wisconsin leaped over Ohio State from No. 3 to No. 1.

In typical Ryan fashion, he downplayed the accomplishment because Wisconsin faced its most difficult week of the Big Ten season. On Tuesday, Wisconsin would travel to Michigan State. On Sunday, a road contest against No. 2 Ohio State awaited in the first 1–2 AP poll matchup in league history. Before the season, Wisconsin's highest ranking in the poll had been sixth on December 4, 1962.

Ryan claimed he held his own 60-second celebration at home, with a large foam "We're No. 1" finger he took from his kids, a party favor, and a handful of paper torn into confetti.

"I ran around with the foam finger, blowing the horn and throwing the confetti for about a minute," Ryan told reporters. "Then I went back into my office and watched the DVD of a very good Iowa team losing by 30 to Michigan State....

"I'm really happy for the players and the university. It says something about the work that's been put in, not just this year but over the years. That's the reward. It does make a great statement for the program."

The elation lasted all of one day. Michigan State's Drew Neitzel scored 28 points in the Spartans' 64–55 victory against the Badgers. The sellout crowd at the Breslin Center began chanting "Overrated!" as the clock wound down, and students stormed the court at the final buzzer.

"If you start to chant "Overrated", I'm leaving," Ryan joked before addressing the media in his postgame comments.

Five days later, Ohio State upended Wisconsin 49–48 in Columbus. Buckeyes freshman Mike Conley Jr. buried a runner with four seconds remaining to give OSU the lead, and Taylor's last-second shot was blocked by Ron Lewis to seal the Badgers' fate. With the victory, Ohio State climbed to No. 1 in the next AP poll for the first time since 1962, while Wisconsin dropped to fourth. Late in the game, Butch severely dislocated his right elbow and was lost for the season, effectively ending Wisconsin's chance at being Ryan's first Final Four team with the Badgers.

Wisconsin earned a No. 2 seed in the NCAA tournament but lost 74–68 to UNLV in the second round, one of the most disappointing ends to a season in Ryan's tenure. UW finished the season 30–6, then a school record for victories in a single season.

"We got some things done and did a lot of things at Wisconsin," Ryan said afterward. "You never know if they're going to happen again, but it's going to be fun trying."

68 Controversy Follows a Soccer National Title

Jim Launder led Wisconsin on a magical ride through the 1995 NCAA men's soccer tournament that culminated with the Badgers winning their only championship and him capturing national coach of the year honors. A little more than one year later, he was out of a job, fired amid a swirl of controversy that shocked the soccer community.

Launder's 15-year tenure as coach will be remembered for both his incredible '95 team and the bizarre nature of his firing, when superiors sent him packing over poor evaluations by some student-athletes. It marked an ignominious end to an illustrious career—one Launder and many players struggled to comprehend.

That 1995 team stormed its way to a NCAA championship with a 20–4–1 record and set a national mark by not allowing a goal in five tournament games. In 25 games that season, Wisconsin surrendered just 11 goals and recorded 17 shutouts. And the Badgers played their absolute best down the stretch.

UW opened tournament play with a 2–0 victory against Bowling Green and then fended off William & Mary 1–0 in overtime. During the game, goalkeeper Todd Wilson dislocated an elbow and was lost for the season. Backup Jon Belskis stepped in and did not allow a goal in 321 minutes of tournament play. In the quarterfinal game against SMU, he recorded four saves as Wisconsin won 2–0.

UW then knocked off Portland 1-0 in the national semifinal and downed Duke 2–0 to win the championship. Former walk-on Lars Hansen, a senior from Drammen, Norway, scored off a rebound in the ninth minute after Travis Roy's shot caromed off a crowd. It marked his third goal in five NCAA tournament games. Teammate Chad Cole later scored in the 63rd minute to put away the title.

"We are the national champions," Badgers midfielder Mike Gentile said afterward. "I don't want to see it in the paper that it was a fluke. This was a great team, and I don't know what else we have to prove to anyone."

Launder, who had brought his team to the NCAA tournament for a third straight season, finally had his breakthrough moment as coach.

"In the Final Four, they played the best they have all year," Launder said. "In the beginning of the year we set goals for ourselves. We wanted to win the Big Ten and go to the Final Four. And then, almost as an afterthought, we said, 'While we're there, we might as well win it.'"

But the glow of a championship accomplishment soon faded. A month after the season ended, then-assistant athletics director Cheryl Marra sought to have Launder fired. He had been given poor evaluations by some of his players, and there also were indications of a personality conflict between Marra and Launder. After it was revealed Marra intended to recommend to the athletics board that Launder be terminated, negative publicity led the board to deny the recommendation, and Launder was retained.

In 1996, Launder's Wisconsin team went 11–5–5 but missed the NCAA tournament for the first time in four seasons. Launder was then fired in February 1997, only 14 months after winning the championship. His career record at Wisconsin was 183–76–30, and he never finished below .500 in any season.

Launder had been given a six-month probationary period, during which time his job performance received extra scrutiny. Then-athletics director Pat Richter said Launder did not improve relations with his players in three areas: respect, motivation, and communication.

"It just did not show up in the evaluation," Richter told the *Milwaukee Journal Sentinel*. "There was not significant improvement in those areas."

Launder was shocked by the decision.

"I think they made a very poor choice," Launder said. "How they came to it was beyond my comprehension. It doesn't make any logical sense.... I did everything you could ask for from an objective standpoint. But I got poor evaluations."

Although Richter said Launder's performance had been under review because some players complained about his coaching style, 17 players showed up to defend Launder after the athletics board invited team members to speak on his behalf. The firing led to a two-year review of the process used to retain or release coaches. A university committee ultimately determined the firing was flawed and should have been more thoroughly examined.

After leaving UW, Launder was hired as the coach at Dayton, where he guided a team that finished in last place the year before to the Atlantic-10 title and an NCAA tournament berth in his first year. Early in that season, six months after his firing at Wisconsin, he returned to Madison as Dayton's coach for a regular season game. Many of Launder's supporters were on hand, and the night before, they threw him a surprise banquet at the Ramada Inn.

He later returned to town and became coach of the Madison 56ers, an amateur regional soccer team. Launder was inducted into the Madison Area Soccer Hall of Fame in 2009 and the Wisconsin Soccer Hall of Fame in 2010.

69 Al Toon and the Bounce Pass Play

It was the type of trick play you might see at a Pop Warner game, when coaches make players feel inclusive by breaking with traditional standards and simply having fun. But in this setting? With a minute left in an important Big Ten game that could alter a team's postseason hopes?

Was Wisconsin football coach Dave McClain crazy? Or brilliant?

"Dave McClain had some experience with the play," former Badgers receiver Al Toon later told the *Wisconsin Radio Network*. "Apparently a few high school teams had run the play successfully in the previous season. So they said, 'Hey, we should try this.' So we worked on it for a couple, three weeks in practice and decided to use it in the game against Illinois."

Thus, the "Bounce Pass Play" was born—one of the most famous plays Wisconsin has ever run.

Wisconsin trailed Illinois 26–22 with time winding down on October 23, 1982. The Badgers had reached the Illini 40-yard line, but a field goal would not work. They needed a touchdown. So McClain called for some trickery with a play that involved quarterback Randy Wright throwing a lateral bounce pass to Toon, who would in turn float the ball over the top of the defense for a touchdown. Players felt they had perfected the play in practice, using the hard Astroturf surface to their advantage on the bounce.

"It was pretty successful," Toon recalled. "We had a lot of fun doing it, and we thought it would work."

On second-and-10 with 61 seconds remaining, McClain sent in the call. Wright pulled the ball from under center at the Illinois 40, dropped back three steps, looked left and nosedived a ball into the flat that bounced six yards behind the line of scrimmage. The pass landed in Toon's belly at the 47 and was so odd that it initially confused two Illinois defenders, who seemed to believe the play was dead as an incomplete pass. When a third defender then converged on Toon, he heaved a perfectly thrown pass down to the 10, where tight end Jeff Nault briefly stood alone. He caught the ball, outraced one defender, and scored a touchdown.

Wisconsin led 28–26 with 52 seconds remaining, and the Camp Randall Stadium fans were joyous.

"I didn't see him catch it," Toon said. "I got smashed by the defensive lineman as soon as I let it go. I kind of looked through a crack on the ground and then I heard the fans cheer. I assumed it was successful at that point...

"It was one of the plays of the year, I believe. Give kudos to the coaches for trying something a little off the map and allowing us to go out there and try it. It's been sticking in the memories of Badger fans forever."

Many fans and players, however, would like to forget the final 52 seconds. Wisconsin kicker Wendell Gladem's extra-point try hit the left upright and bounced back thanks, in part, to a bad snap, so the Badgers were left to protect their 28–26 lead.

"Extra points have been the biggest headaches I've had in my life," said McClain, whose team had converted only 10-of-15 tries that season. "That's my fault as a coach. We spent quite a bit of time on it."

Illinois quarterback Tony Eason quickly diced up Wisconsin's prevent defense, covering 51 yards in five plays. He found receiver Oliver Williams for 22 yards, giving Illinois a first down at its own 48. When he connected with tight end Tim Brewster over the middle for 23 yards with three seconds remaining, the Illini brought on their field goal team.

Despite Wisconsin's attempts to block the try, Illinois kicker Mike Bass drilled a 46-yard field goal as time expired. UW players sat on the artificial turf in stunned silence, mirroring the reaction of 78,406 fans.

Final score: Illinois 29, Wisconsin 28.

"I never felt worse in my life," Badgers free safety John Josten said. "That was the toughest loss I'd ever had to take."

Wisconsin, which had won four games in a row, closed the regular season 2–3 but rallied to win the Independence Bowl against Kansas State for the program's first-ever bowl victory.

Toon, of course, would accomplish plenty more catching passes during a stellar Badgers career. He was a back-to-back first-team All-Big Ten wide receiver and the school's first back-to-back team MVP since Alan Ameche. Toon established school records for career receptions (131), receiving yards (2,103), and receiving touchdowns (19). His 252-yard receiving performance against Purdue in 1983 set a Big Ten record and stood for 20 years until Wisconsin receiver Lee Evans broke the mark.

Toon also was an All-American in the indoor and outdoor triple jump and a three-time Big Ten triple jump champion. He went on to a successful career with the New York Jets from 1985 to '92. His son, Nick Toon, surpassed Al in career receptions (171) and receiving yards (2,447) and finished with 18 receiving touchdowns for the Badgers.

For all of Toon's achievements, the Bounce Pass Play remains one of the biggest topics of conversation when fans approach him—whether they choose to recall how the contest ended or not.

"It's pretty funny that most of the people that remember the bounce pass, at least the people that talk to me, think we won the game," Toon said. "They kind of forgot about the rest of the game. I guess the play was so exciting, they want to remember the good part."

70 Rufus "Roadrunner" Ferguson

Showmanship is an art. And few players in Wisconsin football history have better understood how to entertain fans quite like Rufus Ferguson, a one-of-a-kind dynamo who sent volts of excitement through the stands every Saturday.

He was a 5'6", 190-pound bowling ball of a man, radiating energy that teammates and Badgers supporters couldn't help but notice. When he arrived at Wisconsin from Miami, Florida, the football program had fallen on hard times. In the three years before he played, from 1967 to '69, the Badgers went 3–26–1, which included a 23-game winless streak. By the 1969 season, attendance had fallen to 48,898 people per game.

Enter Ferguson to the rescue. With a blend of personality, charm, and talent, Ferguson captivated the city. Wisconsin won more games his first season (four) than it had the previous three years combined. And by the time he left after the 1972 season, attendance jumped to 70,454, surpassing 70,000 for the very first time. It was no small coincidence.

"The spirit and the crowds are back at Wisconsin," wrote the *Chicago Tribune* in 1972, "and there is no question that the Pied Piper of Madison is Rufus (Roadrunner) Ferguson."

Ferguson said his nickname, "Roadrunner," began during his baseball-playing days in high school, after he stole 42 bases in

19 games and a writer from the *Miami Herald* coined the term that stuck. He was most associated, however, with his famous "Rufus Shuffle," a two-step dance he performed after scoring a touchdown in which he raised both hands over his head and flashed a victory sign with his fingers. The move caught on quickly and helped make him a national sensation.

"I don't think Rufus is a hot dog," Badgers coach John Jardine told the *Tribune*. "He's that way every minute of the day. His personality is just that way—he's always exuberant. Rufus thinks up a comment for every day."

The origin of his famous Rufus Shuffle stemmed from the team's September 18, 1971, road game against Syracuse, Ferguson said. All week, Ferguson heard how Syracuse was going to beat Wisconsin. But he scored two touchdowns in the game, which ended in an eventual 20–20 tie. And after one of those scores...

"I just let myself go," Ferguson told the *Milwaukee Journal*. "It was spontaneous, really, and it caught on. My offensive linemen liked it, and when they liked something, I wasn't going to argue. It seemed to beef up the enthusiasm of the whole team. I firmly believe that if you do anything without enthusiasm, you won't have success."

When Wisconsin returned home and Ferguson scored a touchdown, he performed his shuffle again. Fans went wild and began expecting it every time he scored. Ferguson, ever the master of ceremonies, obliged each time.

"I look at football as entertainment," Ferguson said. "People spend a lot of money to be entertained when they go to a game, so I tried to entertain them in addition to carrying out the fundamentals of football."

In 1971, Ferguson became the first running back in school history to rush for 1,000 yards in the regular season. And his popularity skyrocketed. The Wisconsin Publicity Department even produced a leaflet titled "The Many Faces of Rufus Ferguson," and the cover was filled with pictures of Ferguson—with a tray full of food in the lunch line, running outside, performing his shuffle in the end zone, and lining up at tailback. It contained a column full of coaches' comments about his ability as well as statistical information.

Though Ferguson took great pride in his football talents, he was equally proud of his accomplishments as a student—one of the biggest reasons he chose to attend Wisconsin.

"When I speak to kids, I tell them to go after the grades in high school, and to go after them in college," he said during his senior season. "That's the No. 1 priority, man, the No. 1. You need alternatives in life, you need to stand alone and make decisions and be ready for whatever happens. That's what I tell the kids. Black and white."

Ferguson rushed for 2,814 career yards, including 1,222 in 1971 and 1,004 in 1972. He left as Wisconsin's all-time scoring leader with 158 points, breaking the mark previously held by running back Alan Ameche. Ferguson was a first-team All-Big Ten selection in 1971 and 1972 and an academic All-American as a senior. The Atlanta Falcons selected him in the 16th round of the 1973 NFL draft, though his pro career was short-lived.

The day Ferguson surpassed Ameche's scoring mark in 1972, he carried 34 times for 197 yards and two touchdowns in a 21–14 victory against Northwestern. It was Parents' Day, and Rufus' father, Arlington, pleased the crowd by doing his version of the shuffle when introduced before the game.

Six years later, Rufus Ferguson returned for the team's 1978 homecoming game, the first time he had been back since he graduated in 1973 with a degree in economics. He was introduced on the field at halftime, and fans wildly cheered.

He was doing the Rufus Shuffle.

71 Jolene Anderson

She painted her basement steps red and white as a child, a Wisconsin Badgers basketball fan through and through. Jolene Anderson never had much doubt that, if she could play well enough to earn a scholarship on the UW women's basketball team, she would remain in state no matter how many other programs tried to lure her away. And when that scholarship offer finally arrived in the mail during a standout high school career, the deal was all but done.

"I always thought if I had a chance to represent my home state, nobody was going to come close," Anderson said. "I figured if I was lucky enough to go to Wisconsin, I was always going to take it."

Anderson, the pride of tiny Port Wing, Wisconsin (population 164), already had developed a legacy as the greatest high school scorer the state had ever seen, male or female. She averaged 21.9 points per game her freshman season at South Shore and helped the Cardinals reach their first state tournament appearance the next season. As a junior, she averaged 31.5 points per game and somehow one-upped herself as a senior, averaging 37.1 points and 15.1 rebounds. During that senior campaign in 2003–04, she set state scoring records for most points in a game (58), season (956), and career (2,881), and she was named the Associated Press prep state player of the year.

Yet for all those accomplishments, some wondered whether Anderson would pan out at a major Division I program. It was one thing to score at will against small-school prep competition and another thing entirely to do it against the Big Ten and the nation's best.

"There were always doubters," Anderson said. "Everybody telling my parents to move me to a bigger school so I can get better competition and people can see me more. But my parents always said if I was good enough that they'll find me wherever I am. So I'm happy that they kept me at South Shore, and it all turned out."

Did it ever. Not only did Anderson become a factor early at Wisconsin—she went after the scoring record books with the same fervor as she did in high school.

Anderson set a freshman record by averaging 17.8 points per game. She became the fastest UW player, male or female, to 1,000 points and the fastest female player to 1,500 points. With 2,312 points, she finished her career as UW's all-time leading scorer, surpassing the men's scoring record of 2,217 points set by Alando Tucker (134 games). Anderson needed only 118 games to achieve the new record. She also scored in double figures in 118 of 123 career games, breaking the previous school record of 105 in a career.

When Anderson's college career was over, she was named the 2008 Big Ten Player of the Year and the Frances Pomeroy Naismith National Player of the Year for players 5'8" and under.

Anderson credited her success to a work ethic that developed back in her hometown, nearly 350 miles and a 5½-hour drive from Madison. The closest YMCA to Port Wing was an hour away, she said, and playing on her AAU team required a 3½-hour drive to Menomonie, Wisconsin.

"I think maybe because where I came from, you had to work for everything you got," Anderson said. "We don't have a gym close by. Everything is like an hour away. You pretty much have to work by yourself. And then when I came to college, I just kind of had that same mindset that I worked so hard to get here and nothing was going to let me stop from what I was going to achieve."

Anderson was selected No. 23 overall in the second round of the 2008 WNBA draft by the Connecticut Sun. She later enjoyed a professional basketball career overseas, playing in France, Turkey, Poland, and Italy, where she continued to score in bunches. Her time and scoring accomplishments at Wisconsin, meanwhile, will remain near and dear to her heart.

"When you sit back and look at all the basketball players, even on the men's side who play professionally who came through Wisconsin, and to know that I'm on top of all of them, it's just an honor," she said. "When I go back, I'm kind of awestruck when people say I'm the all-time leader of both men and women."

Athlete Profile: Barb Franke

Two decades before Jolene Anderson established a new Badgers women's scoring mark, Barb Franke was a force unlike any Wisconsin had seen. The 6'2" post player, named Miss Iowa Basketball in high school, picked the Badgers over the Hawkeyes after Iowa saved its last scholarship offer for a point guard. Iowa's loss was Wisconsin's gain.

Franke helped lead Wisconsin to an unprecedented three 20-win seasons and three NCAA tournament bids. She was named Big Ten rookie of the year in 1992 when she averaged 11.3 points and 6.9 rebounds. After missing the 1992-93 season with a torn ACL, she returned to lead the Badgers in scoring, rebounding, and blocks in each of her last three years. She scored 1,994 points and started all 114 games of her career.

Franke was a two-time Associated Press All-America honorable mention pick who became Wisconsin's third professional women's basketball player. She was inducted into the UW Athletics Hall of Fame in 2005.

72 "Jump Around"

The history of "Jump Around" is relatively short, but it quickly has become one of the most recognizable traditions in college football and a quintessential part of the Camp Randall Stadium game day experience. What began on October 10, 1998, during Wisconsin's

One of the best traditions at Camp Randall? "Jump Around" at the end of the third quarter.

31–24 victory against a Drew Brees–led Purdue team at Camp Randall has continued—interrupted just once—ever since.

Kevin Kluender, an assistant marketing director at Wisconsin, was in charge of handling music over the public-address system that season. One of his tasks was finding a song to keep the crowd energized between the third and fourth quarters. Ryan Sondrup, an intern in the marketing department and a former Badgers football player, had provided Kluender with a list of suggested songs. And from that list, Kluender chose House of Pain's 1992 hit "Jump Around," forever changing the way Badgers fans experienced home games.

The stadium shook. The press box swayed. The crowd went berserk.

"I remember thinking maybe the students would get into it," Kluender said in the book *Tales from the Wisconsin Badgers*. "I initially turned my back to the field while the song was playing, but I saw people in the press box pointing out to the field. I turned back around and it looked like popcorn popping."

Popularity of the song only increased and was cemented as a staple at football games following a controversial decision in 2003. Then-athletics director Pat Richter asked the song not be played in the home opener against Akron because the stadium was under construction, and he feared the shaking could be dangerous. Students were enraged when the song did not play during the game, and it became a media story. When a study determined the building would remain structurally sound, Chancellor John D. Wiley announced "Jump Around" could be played the next week during a home game against UNLV.

For Badgers players, the reaction to the song is one they look forward to every home game.

"You hear the song start playing, you look over, and the fans are going crazy," Wisconsin center Dan Voltz said. "It's like, 'All right, we've got one more quarter, let's finish this thing out.' It's just a jolt of energy, and it's the coolest thing I've ever seen. To see it from the field and to have those fans doing it for you, it's an incredible feeling."

In 2012, "Jump Around" was voted the winner of SI.com's College Football Traditions Bracket. The voting process included 16 of the top college football traditions from across the country in a March Madness–style bracket. It beat out such well-known traditions as Ohio State's "Script Ohio," Tennessee fans singing "Rocky Top," and Texas A&M's "12th Man" tradition.

The song is so inspiring that, most games, the team can be found on the field jumping up and down along with the fans. Sometimes, so do the opponents.

"Obviously you know it's a good tradition if the other team starts joining in," said Badgers wide receiver Alex Erickson, a first-team all-Big Ten player in 2015. "It brings a lot more energy back into the stadium. Everybody is going to stay around for that, even if the game is out of hand. It's a pretty cool tradition, and it's something that everybody should experience once in their lives."

Other Game Day Traditions

The playing of "Jump Around" before the fourth quarter is just one of many traditions to occur at Camp Randall Stadium over the years. Here is a look at a few others:

Band Caps

After Wisconsin wins a football game, members of the band turn their hats around and wear them backward. The practice began in the 1920s to symbolize the band looking back at the victory as they marched toward the stadium exit.

Cane Toss

At the annual homecoming game, graduating law students throw canes over the crossbar of the goal post in a pre-game ceremony. If students catch their cane, legend claims they will win their first case. If the cane is dropped, they will lose the case. One report indicates the custom originated at Harvard and arrived at Wisconsin in 1910.

Sing "Varsity"

The traditional arm waving at the end of the song "Varsity" began in 1934 thanks to the brainstorming of band leader Ray Dvorak. He saw Pennsylvania students wave their caps after losing a game. Dvorak later instructed Wisconsin students to salute UW President Glenn Frank after each game. The song is still played at football games at the end of the band's halftime performance. The lyrics:

Var-sity! Var-sity! U-rah-rah! Wisconsin!
Praise to thee we sing
Praise to thee our Alma Mater
U-rah-rah, Wisconsin!

73 Bret Bielema's Stunning Departure

Their walks together around campus had become a weekly ritual, time to talk football and life, to bolster an already tight-knit relationship even tighter. They spoke every day. They ate dinners together several times a week. They had what Barry Alvarez described as "a father-son relationship."

And then on the morning of December 4, 2012, Alvarez's protégé, Bret Bielema, dropped a bombshell that would catch Alvarez completely by surprise and alter their bond. He walked into Alvarez's hotel room on a Tuesday in New York City, where the two men were attending a National Football Foundation awards dinner, and informed Alvarez he was about to become the next head football coach at Arkansas.

"I said, 'You're not telling me you're going to visit with the Arkansas people. You've already taken the job,'" Alvarez recounted to the *Wisconsin State Journal.* "The answer was yes."

Thus closed one of the most successful chapters of Wisconsin football, seven years after Alvarez chose Bielema as his handpicked successor to the Badgers' coaching throne. It also opened a rift between many Badgers fans who struggled to forgive Bielema's decision.

Bielema came to Wisconsin as a defensive coordinator in 2004 when Alvarez was still the team's head coach. Alvarez, a former defensive coordinator himself at Notre Dame, saw something special in Bielema and quickly took him under his wing. He announced that Bielema would succeed him as coach when he retired following the 2005 season. At age 34, Bielema had his first head coaching job.

For the next seven seasons, Bielema showed why Alvarez's choice was so wise. He compiled a 68–24 record (.739 winning percentage) with the same rugged rushing attack established by Alvarez, and he helped keep the Badgers a respected Big Ten power. He went 12–1 in his first season in 2006 and finished every season with a winning record. From 2009 to '11, Wisconsin tallied double-digit victories each year, marking the first time in program history the school achieved that feat. In his final act as coach, Wisconsin obliterated Nebraska 70–31 in the 2012 Big Ten championship game—the Badgers' third straight league title and trip to the Rose Bowl.

Three days later, however, Bielema was gone, off to take over an Arkansas team that had just finished 4–8 overall. The decision was stunning, though, in retrospect, some of Bielema's reasoning was understandable.

Bielema never seemed to be fully embraced by Wisconsin's fan base, partly because he came across as cocky at times, partly because he didn't win a Rose Bowl in his first two tries, and partly because he simply wasn't Alvarez—the most revered figure in modern Wisconsin athletics, whose success left a shadow over the program.

Bielema also wasn't happy he couldn't keep assistant coaches with what he believed was more competitive pay. He noted after the 2012 Rose Bowl that three of his assistants approached him about other coaching jobs. At Wisconsin, they made $225,000. Elsewhere, offers were reportedly flying in that exceeded $400,000. Not surprisingly, they left. Bielema said three more of his assistants were receiving interest from other programs after Wisconsin's Big Ten title demolition of Nebraska.

Still, it was the way in which Bielema left that most irked Alvarez, who said Arkansas athletics director Jeff Long never contacted him for permission to speak to Bielema. Alvarez was further upset by statements Bielema made during his introductory news conference at Arkansas that seemed to indicate winning a national title was more attainable with the Razorbacks. He also unwittingly revealed Alvarez would coach Wisconsin in the Rose Bowl before the decision had been officially announced back in Madison.

"I came here to chase a dream. I've never been to a place where I can give them something they've never had," Bielema told reporters at his news conference, explaining that winning the Big Ten championship at Wisconsin had been done even before he arrived.

"At Arkansas, it's never been done. We never won an SEC title. Been in the game three times. You don't have to be a rocket scientist to figure out you win the SEC title, you might be playing in the big one, especially after 2014. That is what a dream is all about."

Back in Madison, fans couldn't help but express frustration. On the surface, it made little sense to them that Bielema could leave a top-tier Big Ten program for a seemingly middle-of-the-road SEC school. Red T-shirts with Bielema's face inside an outline of Wisconsin popped up around town, with the mocking words, "We will never forget you, Bert."

At the time, Alvarez said he and Bielema were "too close" to rekindle their relationship but that he didn't feel betrayed by Bielema's decision.

"You know what? Life goes on," Alvarez said. "I have no animosity towards Bret. Bret did a good job for us here. Some things I disagree with in how they were handled, but everybody handles things their own way.... I don't sit there and hold a grudge on what happened—whether I agree with it or not."

Bielema's Arkansas teams reached a bowl game in two of his first three seasons there. Wisconsin, meanwhile, continued producing winning seasons, first with Gary Andersen and then with Paul Chryst. But the Alvarez-Bielema relationship remained fractured.

"There are so many things I miss about him and what we had," Bielema told *The Sporting News* in August 2015. "Dinner three or four times a week, the vacations, the jokes and laughs. We have mutual friends that have said we've got to get you guys together."

Bielema insisted his leaving had nothing to do with money—he would receive a $600,000 annual pay raise—or any type of previous rift between him and Alvarez. Still, the ending was one that left wounds for both men.

"The only burning thing in my gut, the one scar on my heart that's hard to deal with, is how my leaving was portrayed," Bielema said. "I know I hurt him. He hurt me a little bit."

Controversial Coach

Like him or not, the one thing Badgers fans must admit about Bret Bielema is that he provides no shortage of entertainment value. Bielema has demonstrated he is unafraid to speak his mind on any number of topics. At Wisconsin, he chided Ohio State coach Urban Meyer in 2012 for what he perceived to be "illegal" recruiting tactics. At Arkansas, he has feuded with Texas Tech coach Kliff Kingsbury, called taking a knee near the goal line of a bowl victory against Texas "borderline erotic," and even starred in his own online reality series, "Being Bret Bielema."

One of Bielema's first coaching tiffs came in 2010 when Wisconsin clobbered Minnesota 41–23 at Camp Randall Stadium to retain Paul Bunyan's Axe for a seventh consecutive game. With Wisconsin leading 41–16 and 6:39 remaining in the fourth quarter, Bielema decided to go for a two-point conversion. The attempt failed, and Gophers coach Tim Brewster chastised Bielema during the post-game handshake, calling the move "horse [expletive]."

"I told him I didn't agree with his decision and I thought it was a poor decision for a head football coach," Brewster said afterward. "He'll have to live with it. It was wrong. Everybody in here knows it, and everybody in college football knows it. It was wrong."

Bielema famously told reporters he was merely following the rules on what point margins warranted two-point conversion tries.

"I know Tim wasn't happy with it," Bielema said. "But you know what? If I'm down by 25 and it's the third or fourth quarter, I would call a play knowing that they're probably going to run a two-point conversion because that's what the card says."

74 Triple-OT Classic in the Field House

Embarrassment wasn't even a strong enough word to describe Wisconsin's worst basketball loss of the 1986–87 season. Yes, the Badgers showed up to Assembly Hall for their game against Big Ten power Indiana on January 15, 1987. Whether they were fully there, however, is open for debate.

That day, Indiana scored the game's first 12 points, cruised to a 22-point halftime lead, and crushed the hapless Badgers 103–65. It marked Wisconsin's sixth consecutive loss and dropped the Badgers below .500 for the first time in a season that would become much worse.

Where could Badgers coach Steve Yoder turn for inspiration when the Hoosiers made the return trip to the UW Field House less than five weeks later? To the VHS tape. Yoder and his staff scoured that film and prepared nothing but highlights of each Badgers player who participated in the first Indiana game. And for two days, that's all Wisconsin's team watched in the lead-up to the rematch.

Viewed in a vacuum, without knowledge of the second game's result, Yoder's decision would seem absurd. It would be akin to showing zoomed-in clips of a runner's 100-meter dash performance, then realizing at the finish line the runner had placed dead last, and everybody else already had cleared the track. But positive momentum came in small places for that Wisconsin team, and Yoder tried tapping into anything that might help.

The method nearly worked. On February 16, Wisconsin (the Big Ten's worst team) and Indiana (the league's best team) staged a game for the ages, one of the most memorable classics in Field House history. When it was over, Indiana had escaped with an 86–85 triple-overtime victory thanks to Dean Garrett's putback of a Joe Hillman airball with four seconds remaining. And 9,164 fans left with crushed spirits just seconds before it appeared they would storm the court to celebrate a monumental upset.

"Think what this would have done not only for the University of Wisconsin basketball program, but the state of Wisconsin at this point," Yoder said afterward.

Wisconsin had opened the season 7–2 and won five consecutive games, including a victory against a Cal team that finished third in the Pac-10 that year. Then, the entire campaign fell apart. The Badgers lost nine consecutive games and 14 of 15. They were in the midst of that free fall when second-ranked Indiana came to town. Wisconsin stood 11–14 overall and just 1–11 in Big Ten play. Indiana was 20–2, including 11–1 in the league.

For 55 minutes, however, one could never discern the disparity in a back-and-forth affair.

With 1:42 remaining in regulation and the Badgers ahead 60–58, Wisconsin's Tom Molaski was called for a pushoff while posting up on the block. Indiana then tied the score and grabbed the lead by two before Wisconsin forward Rod Ripley's baseline jumper with 45 seconds remaining sent the game to overtime.

"We should have won in regulation," Yoder said. "There's no consolation because we've come so close so many times. The game was a great credit to our ballplayers. Everybody thought we were going to quit."

Wisconsin fell behind by three points in each of the first two overtimes but managed to battle back. In the first extra session, Indiana took a 68–65 lead on Keith Smart's jumper from the lane. But Mike Heineman scored on a drive and was fouled, hitting the free throw to tie the score. In the second overtime, Ripley drilled a three-pointer with eight seconds remaining to forge another tie and send the game to a third overtime.

Indiana sharpshooter Steve Alford had several chances to end the game. Alford missed a 10-foot jumper just before the buzzer in regulation, misfired on a shot with seven seconds left in the first overtime, and clanked a 15-footer at the end of the second overtime. He finished the contest just 4-of-19 from the field, though he would become Indiana's all-time leading scorer, passing Don Schlundt, who played from 1952 to '55.

"It was like we were just hanging on with everything we had," Molaski said. "They always had the last shot, and you knew Alford was going to take it. So every time the buzzer went off, it was like we had a new life."

In the third overtime period, Trent Jackson, who scored 18 points for the Badgers, hit a jumper from the corner to give Wisconsin an 83–82 lead with 1:39 left. UW still led 85–84 when Wisconsin's Shelton Smith went to the free throw line for two shots with 26 seconds remaining.

He missed both attempts, setting up Garrett's game-winning shot.

"The first thing I'm going to remember it as is a loss," Smith said. "It was one of the greatest efforts you'll ever see this team give. It came down to somebody had to lose, and unfortunately it was us."

Afterward, Indiana coach Bob Knight even noted the Badgers "deserved to win the ballgame." His only tirade that night involved expressing his disdain for the late start time. The game was scheduled at 8:30 PM in Madison on a Monday so it could be shown live as part of ESPN's doubleheader.

"This Monday night television is just absolute bull," Knight said. "The people of this conference can't think enough of these kids to get them in a situation where they miss as little class as possible."

As for the state of the Badgers' program?

"The thing that Wisconsin has to understand is that you can't just get ready for teams like Indiana," Knight said. "You can't give it everything you've got just because Indiana is first in the league. That's why a team like Wisconsin hasn't won too many games."

Wisconsin, meanwhile, took no solace in the loss. UW finished the season 14–17 overall, 4–14 in the Big Ten. Yoder would coach five more seasons before being replaced by Stu Jackson, having never led the Badgers to the NCAA tournament in 10 seasons. Indiana finished the season 30–4, including 15–3 in the Big Ten and went on to win the national title, Knight's third and final NCAA championship.

"It was funny, in the locker room we were laughing," Heineman said. "It wasn't funny, but we couldn't believe we lost."

ESPN college basketball analyst Dick Vitale, who broadcast the game that night, would say months later that it was "the most exciting game of the year." For many heartbroken Badgers fans, it was a game that embodied the era of Wisconsin basketball—and one that they wouldn't soon forget.

"It had the excitement," Vitale said, "the intensity, the over-achievers playing way over their heads, the three-star players playing like five-star players."

75 Fun-Loving Badgers Take Nation by Storm

There are many ways to bask in the glow of an NCAA tournament victory, but the night of March 20, 2015, marked perhaps the first time in history a superstar college basketball trio spent it this way: chattering incessantly while standing behind the postgame stenographer, rapt and mesmerized at the methods she used for transcribing their quotes.

After No. 1 seed Wisconsin had dispatched No. 16 seed Coastal Carolina 86–72 in the opening round of the NCAA tournament, Badgers players Frank Kaminsky, Sam Dekker, and Nigel Hayes began walking back to their locker room following a brief postgame interview session on a podium adjacent to the court. That's when the three of them launched into a conversation about the woman in the front row, whose typing prowess had caught their attention inside the CenturyLink Center in Omaha, Nebraska.

What was that machine sitting in her lap? How did she type so fast? Could they go back and see it?

Badgers coach Bo Ryan, walking next to his players, said he wanted them off their feet and that a trip to the hotel was in order—Wisconsin would play Oregon, after all, less than 48 hours later in the Round of 32. But then Ryan relented and trailed them inside the interview room to watch how preposterously fascinated they were by a simple stenotype machine.

"I thought they would never come out," said Toni Christy, the stenographer who had worked for ASAP Sports since 2005. "When they asked me if I would show them what I did, I said sure. But in my mind, I'm thinking their coach isn't going to let them come out here and look at my machine. They're going to get back to the hotel and get to bed. So when they came bounding out of the curtains, it was pretty funny. And I could see they were genuinely interested in, 'How does that work?' Very curious."

What followed in the nearly deserted and dimly lit room was this exchange:

Dekker: "What if I press a button?"

Hayes: "Oh, that's S."

Dekker: "What if I go…"

Hayes: "Oh, you typed a word."

Dekker: "What if I do these three?"

Hayes: "How'd you do that?"

The sequence represented a brief snapshot that encapsulated every bit of what made the 2014–15 Badgers team one of the joys of the college basketball season. Wisconsin's players were outgoing, engaging, silly, and refreshingly loose. It was a rare combination, players contended, that also helped to make them one of the most talented teams in the country—a group that ultimately came within one game of capturing a national championship.

And just in case anybody thought other college basketball teams hung back after games to make similar inquiries about the transcription process, Christy offered an assurance that was not the case. She had covered six NCAA tournaments and hundreds of other news conferences in the past decade. What transpired that night?

"That's a first," she said. "And it was very cute."

Kaminsky, Dekker, and Hayes were the ringleaders of a group that only seemed to take themselves seriously when they were on the court. They created inside jokes that manifested with delirious laughter during press conferences at the NCAA tournament. They would purposely mispronounce easy words and try to find reporters in the audience who looked like other people they knew, giggling and pointing along the way.

Kaminsky, the national player of the year, returned for his senior season after eschewing the NBA and blogging that the pros sometimes looked "flat-out boring." He could be shy and self aware while also being ridiculous. When the Badgers won the Big Ten tournament, he tried, presumably at least half-jokingly, to eat confetti strands that fell into his mouth. He also wore a GoPro camera vest strapped around his chest during senior day introductions, as well as many other occasions before and after games. The inspiration behind his nickname, Frank "The Tank," came from the 2003 movie *Old School*, in which the hapless, fun-loving Frank "The Tank" Ricard (played by Will Ferrell) was best known for ripping a beer bong and running naked through the campus quad.

Dekker was Wisconsin's second-leading scorer and joined Kaminsky as a first-round NBA draft pick in 2015, opting to leave school a year early. Dekker often described himself as a "free spirit," and became one of the most quotable players on the team, unafraid to say whatever was on his mind, for better or worse.

Before his freshman season, Dekker—a die-hard Milwaukee Brewers baseball fan—stirred a small Twitter beef with Brewers relief pitcher John Axford after he blew a save, tweeting, "Seriously. I don't want Axford to ever have the ball in his hands ever again." To which Axford replied, "Personally I don't care what (a) freshman basketball player thinks!"

Dekker became a relied-upon vocal leader on the team and took it upon himself during a losing streak his sophomore season a year earlier to call out the Badgers in front of the media for being "soft," "unaggressive," and "lacking in all the categories that you need to win." That team promptly won 13 of its next 15 games and reached the Final Four.

Hayes' personality was such that it could sometimes be difficult to discern when he was being serious or facetious with his responses. He stole the show during the 2014 NCAA tournament as intrepid reporter "Nigel Burgandy," quizzing teammates on their favorite Justin Bieber songs, showcasing his dance moves in the locker room, and generally acting silly for a series of YouTube videos produced by the school's athletics department.

"I think it took one or two goofballs on the team to make everyone act goofy," Kaminsky said. "When you've got a guy like Nigel on the team not taking anything seriously, other than basketball itself, it kind of rubs off on other people and it kind of snowballs from there."

A day before Wisconsin's Round of 32 game against Oregon, Hayes returned to the podium for a news conference previewing the contest. He was asked the first question, about the growth he had made as a three-point shooter in his sophomore season. Instead, he looked toward the front row where Christy, the stenographer, was sitting, and began the day with a joke she could truly appreciate as she prepared to transcribe.

"Before I answer that question, I would like to say a few words: cattywampus, onomatopoeia, and antidisestablishmentarianism."

Cue laughter.

"Now, back to your question."

The blending of personalities that took place, perhaps not surprisingly, spawned an entire team filled with players willing to let loose, even as the pressure to win increased, prompting national reporters and TV personalities to gush over the Badgers' charisma and charm. Badgers assistant coach Greg Gard noted no one was immune to a few barbs landing his way, even Kaminsky—the best player in the country—who would "get as much crap from everybody else as he'll give out."

"I just think that's how we are," Dekker said. "We're not like trying to put on an act or anything. We're not trying to take it too serious. We're just trying to be us, and we do what we like to do. That's what you kind of have to do. I think some people sometimes take basketball too seriously. When we get on the court, it's obviously very serious. We want to win. We want to do well. But we also have lives other than just basketball."

Wisconsin and its crazy cast of characters nearly won a national title thanks to a remarkable blend of team camaraderie and talent, losing to Duke in the championship game. And the fact players had such trust in each other to show their true personalities off the court certainly didn't hurt their chances on the court. The entire package made for the most memorable Badgers basketball team in program history.

"You've got to stay loose," Dekker said. "The more fun you have with it, the better you'll be at it."

76 Matt Lepay: Voice of the Badgers

Matt Lepay thought his broadcasting career was finished before it ever really started. He was just a few years out of college, working a radio job at WPTW in Piqua, Ohio, calling high school football and basketball games in addition to American Legion baseball games. In his mind, he was chasing a dream but unsure whether he'd get there.

Lepay loved calling games. He grew up in Dayton, Ohio, about an hour north of Cincinnati, and vividly recalled listening to Reds broadcasters such as Al Michaels and Marty Brennaman. They were the first two announcers whose craft he studied to understand the intricacies of describing a game. He went off to college at Ohio State with visions of a similar career. But his radio job in Piqua was far less glamorous—a low-paying, long-hours position with minimal upward movement.

When he wasn't calling games, Lepay worked at the station, "playing the beautiful music of yesteryear," he said. "That was how they described it. Elevator music was really what we did. Radio bits. We gave the police report, whatever defined the newscast back then."

Finally, after nearly two years there, Lepay decided he'd had enough. He resigned with an aim on returning to school and finding a job in the public relations world. As fate would have it, however, he happened to see a job opening on the day he resigned in a publication called *Broadcasting Magazine*. The position: a sports anchor and play-by-play announcer covering Wisconsin basketball with WTSO radio in Madison. Lepay mailed an audition tape, interviewed, and was offered the job. He and his future wife, Linda, moved to Wisconsin in 1988 and have been there ever since.

Lepay will admit today he has been fortunate to become the voice of the Badgers. But Wisconsin fans should feel equally

WIBA's Matt Lepay is the "Voice of the Badgers."

fortunate to call one of the best broadcasters in the state their own. Lepay began calling Badgers men's basketball games in 1988 and has done both football and basketball games for WIBA since 1994. Over the next 20 years, he was named the winner of the Wisconsin Sportscaster of the Year Award on seven occasions.

Lepay described his move to Wisconsin as "a life-changer."

"I had set a goal in my mind," he said. "I had no idea where I came up with it, but I just thought within five years of graduating college it'd be great to be a broadcaster for a major college program. Through a lot of luck, I was able to do that. I was four years, I think, out of school when I was hired up here."

When Lepay arrived, Wisconsin's football and men's basketball programs were a mess. Neither team won much, the fan base was hardly inspired, and the athletics department faced a substantial debt. Now, both programs are generally fixtures in the national top-25 polls, and Lepay has been there to call nearly every significant game along the way.

"When I first got here, there were no thoughts of basketball being in the NCAA tournament so many years in a row and for the football team to play in bowl games and six Rose Bowls in the last couple of decades," Lepay said. "If you'd have told somebody that in the late '80s, they'd have probably looked at you like you had two heads. The fact that they built it and sustained it, to me, that's probably the best part."

Lepay has been on the microphone for Wisconsin's last five Rose Bowl appearances and has a long list of football and basketball games that rank among the most memorable in his career. Ben Brust's improbable half-court shot to tie No. 3 Michigan in 2013 at the regulation buzzer is one such game, in which Lepay triumphantly announced, "Let's play five more minutes in Madison!"

Wisconsin's back-to-back Final Four teams under coach Bo Ryan provided Lepay with two of his favorite games: the team's stirring national semifinal victory against previously undefeated Kentucky in 2015 and UW's thrilling overtime victory against Arizona in the 2014 Elite Eight. Lepay's call of the final moment of the Badgers' 64–63 overtime win against the Wildcats is a classic:

"And I CAN believe I'm gonna say it—Bo Ryan and the Wisconsin Badgers have punched their ticket to Texas. They're going to the Final Four!"

It was a reprisal of Lepay's famous 2000 call, after Wisconsin stunned the nation by beating Purdue to reach the Final Four as a No. 8 seed under coach Dick Bennett. "I can't believe I'm gonna say it, but here it comes—the Wisconsin Badgers are going to the Final Four!"

In football, Lepay listed Ron Dayne's 1999 regular season finale against Iowa, in which he broke the NCAA's all-time rushing record, among his favorite moments as a Wisconsin broadcaster. He also cited Wisconsin's 2010 victory against No. 1 Ohio State and UW's win against Michigan State in the inaugural Big Ten championship game in 2011. Wisconsin defeated Michigan State 42–39 and didn't take the final lead until 3:45 remained in the game, clinching a second straight Rose Bowl appearance.

"That game had everything," Lepay said. "Big plays. They had a great start. Then I was pretty convinced in my own mind that they were going to lose because Michigan State had rallied. They had the lead into the second half. If you didn't care, and you just wanted to sit back and watch a game, that was one you probably would not turn away from because it was just entertaining."

Entertainment that Lepay, no doubt, has significantly contributed to for numerous Badgers fans over the years.

77 The Shoe Box Scandal

Tom Mulhern assumed a light workload would make for a relaxing few months during his offseason in the summer of 2000. As the Badgers football beat reporter for the *Wisconsin State Journal*, he had recently finished covering a historic season in which running back Ron Dayne won the Heisman Trophy award and UW captured back-to-back Rose Bowls. A break, then, would represent a welcome reprieve.

But Mulhern was about to be inundated with a story that would rock the entire athletics department. Over the course of two months, his dogged reporting, along with *State Journal* investigative reporter Andy Hall, would ultimately reveal 157 Wisconsin student-athletes in 14 sports accepted at least $27,000 in discounts not available to other students, resulting in suspensions and university probation as well as administrative procedural changes. It was an incident known as The Shoe Box Scandal.

Mulhern first received a story tip from his boss that UW athletes were accepting unadvertised discounts at The Shoe Box, a shoe store located 25 miles from Madison in Black Earth, Wisconsin. He made the initial phone calls and found three current or former sales clerks at the store who verified, and were willing to talk on the record, about the large discounts being given to Badgers athletes—discounts that went above and beyond anything given to regular customers, thus breaking NCAA rules.

The package of stories ran on July 9, 2000. And most of the vitriol, Mulhern wrote in a 2010 column reflecting on the incident, was aimed at the newspaper rather than the UW athletics department. No other media outlet considered it a major story at the outset, while school officials also attempted to downplay its significance and the ensuing NCAA investigation. Just hours before Wisconsin's season-opening 19–7 victory against Western Michigan, however, the school—at the behest of the NCAA—suspended 26 football players, including eight starters, for one to three games.

Of the 26 football players, 11 would be suspended for three games apiece, while 15 were suspended for one game. In addition, three men's basketball players were suspended for eight games and one women's soccer player was suspended for two games. But the overall penalties on the university would prove to be far more severe and leave the athletics department with a veritable black eye.

NCAA rules prohibited university athletes from receiving discounts and credit arrangements unless the same benefits were generally available to the institution's students. The newspaper reported players received discounts of 25 to 40 percent and interest-free credit. Though the store's owner, a UW supporter, said he did not purposely commit any wrongdoing and routinely offered discounts to most of his customers without making any distinction between athletes and other customers, NCAA rules infractions were committed.

Many of the athletes noted the discounts came without their knowledge, but they were either suspended or required to perform community service. All of the athletes had to repay the amount of the benefits they received. The university then banned athletes, coaches, and athletics department administrators from shopping at The Shoe Box.

Wisconsin ultimately was placed on five years' probation and lost some football and basketball scholarships after the NCAA investigation, though the organization did not strip the school of any postseason awards, including its 2000 trip to the men's basketball Final Four. The university had disciplined itself the previous April. But the NCAA levied additional penalties because it was the school's third major rules violation since 1994, and the number of athletes involved was so substantial.

"This wasn't one or two athletes and someone bought them a Diet Coke," said Tom Yeager, a member of the NCAA Division I Infractions Committee. "This was hundreds of kids involving thousands of dollars. That's significant."

The university put itself on three years' probation, penalized itself $150,000, and stripped five scholarships over three years—four from football and one from men's basketball. The NCAA reduced the number of football scholarships the university could offer in the 2002–03 and 2003–04 school years from 25 to 20. It also ordered the school to cut a men's basketball scholarship in 2003–04.

Mulhern wrote that he was proud of the work the newspaper did on the story despite the tremendous blowback from fans. When he and his colleagues heard their names announced for winning an award on the project at a dinner in Dubuque, Iowa, some of the other journalists in the room booed, demonstrating to him the enormity and divisiveness of the work.

In the entire package of stories that ran the first day, Mulhern noted only one source, a UW football player who didn't have the athletics department's permission to speak, remained anonymous—something particularly difficult to do given such a controversial subject matter. Following a nine-month investigation, the university confirmed everything that had been written.

"Despite the reaction by a vocal segment of the fan base, I still believe most fans want a clean athletic department that follows the rules," Mulhern wrote. "I think most of them are of the opinion that you don't have to sacrifice success, or cut corners, to achieve that. In that context, maybe The Shoe Box was an important reminder, and a critical lesson, on the heels of two of the biggest sports accomplishments of the decade.

"Most fans would have loved to have the Rose Bowl and Final Four without The Shoe Box. But in terms of significance, the three moments certainly belong together."

78 Jordan Taylor

Before Jordan Taylor had even played a game in his senior season at Wisconsin, Badgers coach Bo Ryan was asked to assess the expectation levels his star player was about to face. His tongue-in-cheek answer reflected just how much pressure some felt Taylor would experience.

"I just hope he doesn't think he has to score 40 a game this year," Ryan said in October 2011.

No matter what Taylor did in his final year with the program, it would have been difficult to live up to the season he produced as a junior, when he earned second-team All-American honors. For that reason, some may consider his swan song to represent a slight step backward. But ask any Badgers fan to put together an all-time Wisconsin basketball team, and Taylor will rank right up there on the list.

Let's begin with this: few college basketball players in the country did a better job of taking care of the ball than Taylor. During his junior season, he led the nation with an incredible 3.83 assists-to-turnovers ratio and closed his career as the NCAA's all-time leader in that category (3.01), shattering the previous best of 2.70. In 71 career Big Ten games, Taylor turned the ball over a total of 79 times.

As a junior, Taylor put together one of the finest seasons in Wisconsin basketball history. He averaged 18.1 points, 4.7 assists, and 4.1 rebounds and developed a habit for making big plays in key situations. He scored 21 of his 27 points in the second half to fuel a spectacular comeback victory against No. 1 Ohio State. That season, he made 43 percent of his three-point tries after shooting just 19 percent and 33 percent during his freshman and sophomore years, respectively. With the help of senior Jon Leuer, the two formed one of the most formidable 1–2 punches in the Big Ten, if not the country.

But Leuer used up his eligibility following the 2010–11 season, and that left Taylor to run a relatively inexperienced team the next year while opponents game-planned specifically to stop him. He almost always had the ball in late-clock situations, which forced him into taking tough shots. Wisconsin also had the slowest pace of play in the country, thus decreasing the number of opportunities for Taylor to score. In addition, he played 36 minutes per game as a senior, which represented a school record for minutes played in a full season.

"I think people expected him to score 30 a game and dish out 15 assists," Badgers teammate Mike Bruesewitz said that season.

"It's tough for him. Every time out, he wants to go in with that assassin's mentality and take care of somebody and single-handedly take over the game. Sometimes that's not allowed with the caliber of teams we play."

Through it all, Taylor still led the Badgers in points (14.8) and assists per game (4.1) and helped Wisconsin to 26 wins, the third-highest single-season total in school history to that point. He was named a first-team All-Big Ten pick by the league's coaches and finished second in the Big Ten with an assists-to-turnovers ratio of 2.6. Wisconsin nearly knocked off No. 1 seed Syracuse in the Sweet 16 of the NCAA tournament before falling 64–63. In that game, Taylor scored 17 points and knocked down five three-pointers while playing all 40 minutes. His final shot, the potential game-winner, came up just short.

Taylor remained a steady leader the entire way. He finished his career second in school history with 464 assists and became the eighth player in Big Ten history with 1,500 points, 450 assists, and 400 rebounds.

"You've got to have confidence and you've got to believe in yourself," Taylor said. "You can achieve what you believe. It's kind of corny, but that's what people would tell me. If you think you're mediocre, then you're going to be mediocre."

Taylor was named as an Associated Press All-American honorable mention selection, one season after his second-team All-American nod. It marked just the second time a Wisconsin player had earned multiple All-American honors since the AP began selecting All-Americans in 1948. Taylor joined Michael Finley, who was a three-time honorable mention selection from 1993 to '95.

79 Formation of Women's Hockey

When the United States Olympic women's hockey team defeated Canada 3–1 for a gold medal on February 17, 1998, in Nagano, Japan, it represented an important moment for growth of the sport. Women's hockey at the collegiate level had not yet risen to NCAA Division I status, but momentum was growing. The Americans showed that day what was possible for the sport, which was making its first appearance in the Olympics.

Young players deserved more opportunities to showcase their talents, and the popularity of women's hockey had significantly increased. One month later, Wisconsin's athletics department took notice when the athletics board approved women's hockey as an NCAA sport for the 1999–2000 season.

"It's a great day for women's hockey," Badgers athletics director Pat Richter said then, channeling legendary Wisconsin men's hockey coach Bob Johnson. "The Olympics only provided a great impetus. There was greater exposure with the success they had."

Wisconsin then became a charter member of the Western Collegiate Hockey Association's women's league, which was voted into existence for the 1999–2000 season. The WCHA joined the Eastern College Athletic Conference as the second league in the nation to offer women's Division I competition. The league began with seven members, featuring Wisconsin, Minnesota, Minnesota–Duluth, Ohio State, Minnesota State–Mankato, Bemidji State, and St. Cloud State. And in 2004, North Dakota joined as an eighth team.

At the time of the decision, there were 13 other Division I schools that offered women's hockey, primarily on the East Coast. By the 2015 season, that number had grown to 35 Division I women's hockey teams. And the Badgers have since become a powerhouse under head coach Mark Johnson.

Johnson took over the program in 2002 as the third coach in four years, but he brought stability and an incredibly high hockey IQ. Johnson starred for the Badgers men's hockey team in the 1970s and was a key reason the U.S. won the 1980 Olympics, famously knocking off the Soviet Union in the semifinal game. He played professionally for 11 years and served as an assistant coach for Wisconsin's men's team from 1996 to 2002.

In 2006, the Wisconsin women became the first team from outside Minnesota to win the NCAA title in the six-year history of the championships. Over the next six seasons, the Badgers would win the title four times.

Wisconsin's success can be attributed to good coaching and the willingness of players from all over North America to venture to Madison. From 2007 to 2012, the Badgers had four Patty Kazmaier Award winners, given to the top female player in college hockey, and their backgrounds provided proof of the program's reach. The winners: Sara Bauer (from Ontario, Canada), Jessie Vetter (Cottage Grove, Wisconsin), Meghan Duggan (Danvers, Massachusetts), and Brianna Decker (Dousman, Wisconsin).

"You try to find the best players with a good academic background that can help continue the growth of your program," Johnson said. "There's no one particular spot. I think what we have seen, especially the last seven or eight years, the growth in women's and girls' hockey has been phenomenal. There's a lot more kids playing today than maybe eight or 10 years ago."

Badgers fans have taken to the women's hockey team, and their support has been evident over the years. On January 28, 2012, Wisconsin broke the NCAA women's hockey attendance record for a third straight year when 12,402 fans watched a game against Bemidji State at the Kohl Center as part of the program's "Fill the Bowl" campaign. On February 15, 2014, UW broke the attendance record again when 13,573 people watched top-ranked Minnesota shut out Wisconsin 4–0.

"It starts with challenging the people of Madison to get them to come out and look at it and see if they like it," Johnson said. "Come to a game. If they like it, they might come back for more. If they don't like it, then they don't have to come back. I think what we've found is as people come into our games, they like what they see. They see athletes that are very committed, very good at what they do."

In 2012, the women's team opened play in LaBahn Arena, which sits adjacent to the Kohl Center. The 2,273-seat facility became the second arena built specifically for women's college hockey, joining Minnesota's Ridder Arena. Nearly two decades after the program's formation, it remains as strong as ever.

"It's a commitment from our department that they want women's hockey to do well, not only within our community but throughout the country," Johnson said. "It's been a great relationship."

Athlete Profile: Hilary Knight

The most prolific scorer in Badgers women's hockey history never won a Patty Kazmaier Award, though she was a top-10 finalist three times. Hilary Knight was surrounded by talented teammates, three of whom won the honor for nation's best player during her time at Wisconsin. Knight's statistics, however, stack up better than anyone to put on the uniform.

Knight finished her Wisconsin career in 2012 as the school's all-time leader in goals (143), shots (986), points (262), game-winning goals (30), and power play goals (37), among other marks. She also was tied for third in career assists (119). Knight helped Wisconsin win two NCAA championships while making four title game appearances. She led the nation in goals twice and was a three-time American Hockey Coaches Association Division I All-American.

As a senior, she sacrificed individual numbers for the good of the team and played center, when she could have scored more goals as a winger. Knight ranked first on the team in blocked shots and still ledthe nation in game-winning goals. Teammate Brianna Decker, meanwhile, won the Patty Kazmaier Award that season.

Knight's artistry on the ice was on display in international competition as well. She was the youngest member of the U.S. Olympic women's hockey team in 2010 and tallied one goal with seven assists to help Team USA capture a silver medal. The Americans earned another silver medal in 2014 with Knight leading the charge, scoring three goals with three assists.

80 Greg Gard

On a cold January morning in 2014, Greg Gard sat at a small table in his Kohl Center office and talked about pig manure. And if that sounds far removed from the world of big-time college athletics, well, it is. Except Gard had a story to tell. And when it was finished, his rise to becoming one of the top assistant coaches in college basketball started to make a little more sense.

Gard grew up on a small hog farm in Cobb, Wisconsin (population roughly 400). It was there where Greg, along with brothers Garry and Jeff, first learned the value of responsibility. When their father, Glen, worked Saturdays for a local farm credit loan company, they were assigned chores to complete before he returned home.

Sometimes, that meant scraping out hog manure from the stalls. It wasn't glamorous. But the job needed doing for the good of farm and family. If they missed a spot, they'd be sure to hear about it and be tasked with walking back to the stalls to do it again.

"It goes back to pride, discipline, work ethic," Greg Gard said. "Doing things right and taking some personal ownership. When my dad or my grandfather walked into that hog house, if it was as clean as it could be, you could take some pride in that."

Attention to detail, Gard learned quickly, mattered more than simply fulfilling the assignment. That's how the three Gard brothers won multiple showmanship awards at the Iowa County Fair for hog showing. They didn't just appear with a pig. They spent months feeding it properly, cleaning it, training it. And with the right amount of preparation and detail, they could achieve something special. Otherwise, why bother showing up?

"It was emphasized to us even at a young age that you can't take shortcuts in life and try to get ahead," Jeff Gard said. "It's always going to catch up to you. You've got to put the time in and be willing to do things the right way."

Greg Gard carried those same principles into coaching, scouting, and recruiting. When he found something he truly loved, he went after it with everything he had. That is how a onetime agricultural business major with no college basketball playing experience filled a void in his life and became the right-hand man to Bo Ryan, one of the most successful coaches in the sport, building an unwavering trust level on his way to being a longtime assistant at Wisconsin.

Do the best you can. Get out what you put in. Make the most of each day, and the reward will follow. But never overlook the small steps necessary to achieve those goals.

"He just knows what I'm looking for," Ryan said in 2014. "He knows why we do drills the way we do them. Why we do things in a game the way we do them. He understands the personalities and the interactions of the players.

"Greg's a guy that knows the teams in the league, works extremely hard at scheduling, which is a very difficult job. Scouting reports. He just does it all."

If Gard had followed through on the career path he initially chose while a student at the University of Wisconsin–Platteville, he said he'd probably be out selling tractors somewhere, making good on his background in agriculture. But the turning point in his life came as a college sophomore, when he was cut from the baseball team and had no outlet to fuel his competitive drive.

That's when he found a small wanted ad in the local shopping news for an eighth grade boys' basketball coach at a school 15 miles south of Platteville. Gard interviewed, got the job, and was soon imparting the knowledge he learned as a three-sport athlete at Iowa-Grant High School. He made $800 for the entire season, but he connected with players, understood the game, and enjoyed being close to the sport.

Ryan was the basketball coach at UW–Platteville at the time, and he would see Gard working his summer camps as a volunteer throughout college. Ryan approached Gard about helping as a student coach, and he quickly became an invaluable asset—a hard worker who wanted to please, even if it meant performing mundane tasks like scouting and charting practice.

Gard switched to an education major so he could teach and coach, never considering the prospect of becoming a Division I assistant. If he wound up coaching at nearby Fennimore High School, he said that would've been enough for him.

"It started with this is something I really like to do," Gard said. "I wanted to be able to help young kids. You just tried to do a good job and make sure you didn't screw it up."

Gard took a leap of faith in Ryan, who convinced him to stay at Platteville after he earned his undergraduate degree despite opportunities to serve as an assistant coach at other programs. And in their second season together, in 1994–95, he was rewarded when Platteville finished 31–0 and won the Division III national championship—the first of three titles Gard would win coaching alongside Ryan, who had also won a championship in 1990–91.

It proved to be the start of a long climb up the coaching ladder, with Gard following Ryan to his first Division I coaching opportunity at UW–Milwaukee and then on to Wisconsin in 2001. Gard was entrusted to handle opposing team scouting reports, schedule games, and offer informed pointers to players. Ryan, meanwhile, became the winningest coach in Badgers program history, reaching consecutive Final Fours in 2014 and 2015.

Gard was there every step of the way, a behind-the-scenes force that kept the team in order and was a loyal coach on whom Ryan could lean. His faith in Ryan for so many years was rewarded after Ryan abruptly retired just 12 games into the season on December 15, 2015, and handed the coaching reins to Gard on an interim basis. He had earned the opportunity to show he deserved to be the permanent coach, and there was no stronger supporter of his talents than Ryan.

Over the next three months, Gard engineered a remarkable turnaround that convinced athletics director Barry Alvarez he was the right man for the full-time job. By focusing on the small tasks, the bigger goals fell into place. He re-implemented Ryan's patented swing offense to create more floor space and extended the minutes of his bench players.

Wisconsin stood 9–9 overall and just 1–4 in the Big Ten on January 12, 2016, following a road loss against Northwestern. But the Badgers then reeled off victories in 11 of 12 games and tied for third place in the Big Ten with a 12–6 record, extending the program's streak of top-four finishes in league play to 15 seasons. Wisconsin qualified for the NCAA tournament and advanced all the way to the Sweet 16.

Gard was named the next head coach on March 7, 2016, and was officially introduced one day later—the fulfillment of a dream for a man whose hard work over 23 years in college coaching was evident.

"It's just special for the state of Wisconsin from the standpoint of being one of their own that's been able to trek through their career at various stops around the state," Gard said. "To ultimately be in this position to be able to lead your home state institution's flagship school into the future, it's something that I am extremely proud of."

Postseason Success

When Badgers coach Greg Gard led his team on a stirring midseason turnaround to reach the 2016 NCAA tournament, it continued one of the more remarkable streaks in major college sports.

For the 14th consecutive season, Wisconsin's football team played in a bowl game in the same school year that the men's basketball team advanced to the NCAA tournament. That achievement continued the longest such streak in NCAA history. The previous best mark of 12 years belonged to Texas, which reached a football bowl game and the NCAA men's basketball tournament every season from 1998–99 to 2009–10.

81 Running Back U

There is something to be said for being a model of consistency to a throwback era despite playing at a time in which spread offenses and gadget plays proliferate college football. You want tricks? Go to a magic show. You want a ruthlessly efficient offensive attack, when opponents know exactly what is coming and still can't stop it? Wisconsin is the place.

Watch a Badgers football game, and chances are you'll find them grinding away in the trenches, force-feeding a running back until the opposition finally cracks. It's not exactly the old "three yards and a cloud of dust" mantra of yesteryear, but it's a tried-and-true method that has come to define everything about Wisconsin football.

Toughness. Work ethic. Focus. And a history of really, really good running backs and offensive linemen. All of which makes Wisconsin the perfect candidate to be known as "Running Back U."

"Our approach is there's been a standard set," said Wisconsin running backs coach John Settle, who has held the position on two separate occasions. "And the past, I think it's been to try to live up to that standard and the tradition of those that have played running back here at the University of Wisconsin.

"I try to play on that. From Alan Ameche to you name it, we try to point it out to the guys in the room of the history of the position and that we've had a lot of success. And the standard is the standard. We want guys that have a desire to be the best."

The formula is one former coach Barry Alvarez is credited with helping to start. Alvarez realized recruiting big offensive linemen from the state of Wisconsin and finding punishing tailbacks willing to work hard and carry a big load would provide the Badgers with the greatest chance of sustained success. And in 1993, Wisconsin running back Brent Moss rushed for 1,637 yards and became the first 1,000-yard rusher for the Badgers in eight years. A year later, tailback Terrell Fletcher gained 1,476 yards to solidify Alvarez's game plan.

"We were tailor made for running the football," Fletcher said. "It's the philosophy of Coach Alvarez and the philosophy that came out of Lou Holtz and the Notre Dame concept. Strong running backs, beastly offensive line, and a downright antagonistic defense. That was who we were."

Before the '93 season, a Wisconsin running back surpassed the 1,000-yard mark only seven times in the history of the program. It happened 22 times from 1993 to 2014. UW also finished in the top 15 nationally in rushing in seven consecutive seasons (2008–14) after Alvarez stepped down as coach. In 2010, the Badgers nearly became the first school in Division I history to have three tailbacks rush for 1,000 yards. John Clay and James White achieved the feat, while Montee Ball missed the mark by four yards.

During Wisconsin's recent string of rushing success, three different tailbacks went on to be Heisman Trophy finalists, and all three won the Doak Walker Award as the best running back in college football: Ron Dayne (1999), Ball (2012), and Melvin Gordon (2014). Dayne also became the second Badgers player to win the Heisman, joining Ameche, who claimed the honor in 1954.

Here is the list of 1,000-yard rushers at Wisconsin from 1993 to 2014 (*denotes Heisman Trophy finalist):

- Brent Moss (1,637 yards), 1993
- Terrell Fletcher (1,476 yards), 1994

- Carl McCullough (1,038 yards), 1995
- Ron Dayne (2,109 yards), 1996
- Ron Dayne (1,457 yards), 1997
- Ron Dayne (1,525 yards), 1998
- Ron Dayne (2,034 yards), 1999*
- Michael Bennett (1,681 yards), 2000
- Anthony Davis (1,466 yards), 2001
- Anthony Davis (1,555 yards), 2002
- Brian Calhoun (1,636 yards), 2005
- P.J. Hill (1,569 yards), 2006
- P.J. Hill (1,236 yards), 2007
- P.J. Hill (1,161 yards), 2008
- John Clay (1,517 yards), 2009
- James White (1,052 yards), 2010
- John Clay (1,012 yards), 2010
- Montee Ball (1,923 yards), 2011*
- Montee Ball (1,830 yards), 2012
- Melvin Gordon (1,609 yards), 2013
- James White (1,444 yards), 2013
- Melvin Gordon (2,587 yards), 2014*

Reaching 1,000 yards is considered no small feat at Wisconsin. The running back room includes plaques of every 1,000-yard rushing season in school history. That display represents a reminder of the hard work that has come before and the expectations placed on current and future players.

Wisconsin has attained such a high level of rushing success that the best running backs in the country put the Badgers squarely on their recruitment radar. Just ask Wisconsin running back Corey Clement, a New Jersey native who picked UW after watching Wisconsin dismantle Nebraska 70–31 in the 2012 Big Ten championship game when three different running backs—Gordon, Ball, and White—each surpassed 100 yards rushing and combined for an astounding eight rushing touchdowns.

"It's about the legacies [that have] been left in previous years," Clement said. "Everybody drives off of the previous year and wants to be better than the next. You don't want to go out as being under anybody. The bar is set pretty high, and that's what makes us Running Back University."

82 The Water Bottle Game

Longtime men's hockey rivals Wisconsin and North Dakota have played more than 160 games against each other since the two teams first met in the 1967–68 season. Given that both programs own a combined 14 national championships, the teams have had their share of heated affairs on the biggest stage, including the 1982 national title game.

Still, nothing is ever likely to top the rivalry's signature moment, which took place two months earlier on January 30, 1982, in an event known, quite simply, as the Water Bottle Game.

Wisconsin led North Dakota 3–0 in the series finale at the Dane County Coliseum, and tempers briefly flared between Wisconsin's Bruce Driver and North Dakota's Gord Sherven, both of whom yelled at each other near the blue line. Sherven's teammate, Cary Eades, skated over and shoved Driver before officials separated the players.

Badgers center John Newberry watched the events unfold, and when Eades skated by Wisconsin's bench during a line change, he squirted him with a water bottle. Eades stopped, and Newberry squirted him once more.

"Their door was open, so I went in to have a talk with him," Eades told the *Grand Forks Herald* in commemoration of the 30-year anniversary of the game in 2012.

According to the *Herald*, Eades put his stick near Newberry's throat, which prompted Badgers defenseman Pat Ethier to run down the bench and land a punch on Eades' head. North Dakota's entire bench emptied, and a massive brawl ensued inside Wisconsin's bench. It spilled out down the hall into the beer garden area, where North Dakota's all-time penalty leader, Jim Archibald, began fighting with fans.

The escalation of a seemingly innocuous on-ice dispute has been preserved on video via YouTube and watched thousands of times. Here is how Badgers hockey announcers Paul Braun and Bill Howard described the unfolding of events.

> **Braun:** And now we've got Driver and Eades.
>
> **Howard:** And just a little pushing and shoving. Friendly conversation once again at the Dane County Coliseum. And they're going to talk a little more. Eades isn't done yet, and Driver's not done yet. But their talk's going to get them nowhere. The official's in there pushing them farther and farther apart, so they can't communicate. Now Eades is over and he went into the Wisconsin bench after a player! And here we go! Eades went right into the Wisconsin bench after the players. North Dakota has emptied their bench. They have emptied their bench.
>
> **Braun:** They're fighting out in the aisles and every place else!
>
> **Howard:** And Eades went right into the Badger bench. He initiated it. They're down through the aisles! They're fighting with the police! They're fighting with the fans! And North Dakota has done it again! And there's no question about who started that. Eades walked right into the door of the Wisconsin

bench and started swinging his stick.... They're beating up on Badgers 2-on-1 now in the runway. And here they go again.

Braun: Oh boy.

Howard: And you tell me why it's North Dakota that has every single one of these, Paul. You tell me why it is. And they're not done yet.... Oh, what a horrible display for college hockey. What a horrible, horrible display. They did it with Minnesota. They did it with Denver. Now they've done it here in Madison.

What the announcers failed to realize in the moment, of course, was how exactly the fight had begun—with those water bottle squirts from a Badgers player that set off the explosive brawl. Just as the fight began to ease, Archibald returned to the beer garden area and punched a Badgers player, igniting even more fighting among the teams.

North Dakota defenseman Craig Ludwig skated over to Eades to inform him that Ethier had punched him when the fight began, prompting Eades to grab Ethier and wrestle him to the ground. There, Eades recalled hearing a police officer yell, "One more punch, and you're going to jail!" When the brawl was nearly over, Wisconsin's Todd Lecy and a few teammates began throwing North Dakota's equipment into the stands.

"I suppose the North Dakota players aren't supposed to get upset about that," North Dakota's play-by-play announcer said on the school's broadcast. "Wisconsin players are throwing stuff into the stands like gloves and sticks. Of course, this is a big lift for the fans here. They love this stuff."

Eades, Archibald, and Dan Brennan received game disqualifications for North Dakota. Newberry, Ethier, and Steve McKenzie of Wisconsin also were ejected. Later, the Western Collegiate Hockey Association suspended Newberry and Eades for two games and Archibald for five games. And the Water Bottle Game, after all these years, continues to live in infamy.

83 Barry Un-Retires, Part I

Barry Alvarez's cell phone buzzed endlessly on December 4, 2012, with calls from colleagues inquiring about his finding the next football coach at Wisconsin. Alvarez, the Wisconsin athletics director, was understandably too busy to answer most calls. He was simply trying to formulate a plan for who would coach the Badgers in the Rose Bowl the following month.

At the time, he had no inkling it would be him.

But when Alvarez reached for his phone to check his messages, he saw there were two from a Green Bay area code he did not recognize. They belonged to Badgers senior linebacker Mike Taylor, a co-captain, who had poured his emotions into the phone.

The captains had decided they wanted Alvarez to coach Wisconsin in the Rose Bowl, Taylor told him. Alvarez's prior coaching success and significance to the program made him the perfect man for the job.

"I just thought that would be the right thing to do," Taylor would say. "Kids like me come up in Wisconsin watching him coach on the sideline. That's just something you always dreamed of, playing for a coach like that. That's what really was the driving force behind it."

The messages were poignant enough to lure Alvarez, a College Football Hall of Fame coach, out of retirement for one game only. Although he had not coached a game in seven years, Alvarez had no reservations about returning Taylor's call and accepting the offer.

"I told him I would be honored to coach them, and I wanted them to understand, if I were going to coach, we weren't going to screw around," Alvarez said two days later during a news conference. "We were going to go out there to win."

The decision capped a stunning three-day period inside the football program. Wisconsin destroyed Nebraska 70–31 in the Big Ten championship game to reach its third straight Rose Bowl, lost head coach Bret Bielema to the same position at Arkansas, and then gained a local icon to lead Wisconsin against sixth-ranked Stanford on January 1, 2013, in Pasadena.

A spot in the Rose Bowl was nothing new to Alvarez, who had already compiled a 118–73–4 record in 16 seasons at Wisconsin and helped guide the program from a Big Ten doormat into a perennial contender. During his tenure, the Badgers played in three Rose Bowls and won each time. Wisconsin defeated UCLA in 1994 and 1999 and beat Stanford in 2000.

"It doesn't get a bit old to me," Alvarez said. "I will enjoy every second of it."

Wisconsin lost both of its Rose Bowl appearances under Bielema the previous two seasons, falling to TCU and Oregon. If nothing else, Alvarez, then 65 years old, brought hope when he told reporters, 13 camera crews, team captains, and assistant coaches that he would end his retirement to coach in the game. Hope left the podium that day and spread through practices, infusing a university and an entire state with visions of grandeur. After all, how could Wisconsin lose with the most iconic coach in program history roaming the sideline?

But nearly four weeks after Alvarez announced his return, hope slowly evaporated as Wisconsin lost 20–14 to Stanford. This time, Alvarez couldn't recapture the magic he had experienced so many years earlier.

"Every game we had out here was very competitive," Alvarez said afterward. "The only thing that's different than the other teams that I coached was somehow we found a way to win. And we weren't fortunate enough to get a win today."

Many assumed Alvarez's mere presence would lead to a reversal of fortunes from the past two years under Bielema. Alvarez carried with him a quiet confidence, exuding cool in practices. He watched from afar and let the assistant coaches handle the game plan, making them promise to stay through the Rose Bowl even though six had accepted jobs elsewhere.

But Wisconsin looked quite similar to the teams that showed up for its five losses during the season by a total of 19 points—close, but not good enough.

A game plan that called for 45 running plays and 17 passes didn't work. UW failed to convert on a fourth-and-goal from inside the 1-yard line during the first half. And quarterback Curt Phillips passed for just 83 total yards.

Somehow, Wisconsin did find itself in position to win the game in the final minutes. But Phillips threw an interception with 2:03 remaining in the fourth quarter after he guided the Badgers' offense to the Stanford 49-yard line.

Wisconsin never saw the ball again.

"You're at midfield or close to midfield with a chance to win the Rose Bowl," Alvarez said. "I just felt like maybe we were a team of destiny."

Wisconsin, the first unranked Rose Bowl participant since 1984, would close the season 8–6. Despite the defeat, the entire month became a story more about Alvarez serving as a unifying force than him finally losing a Rose Bowl as coach. His trek out of retirement had shown just how important he was to the team and the fan base. And, little did anyone know, it wouldn't be his last foray into coaching.

"To have Coach Alvarez come back, having our seniors and captains ask and he agree, I think it calmed guys' nerves," former Badgers linebacker Chris Borland said. "It brought everybody together and excited everybody."

84 Freddie Owens Saves the Day

Freddie Owens wasn't sure just how effective he could be on one good ankle. But in the NCAA tournament, where seasons are defined and heroes born, nothing was going to keep him from finding out.

Owens, a Wisconsin guard, had sprained his right ankle in the 2003 NCAA tournament opener against Weber State, and his status was unclear for a second-round matchup against Tulsa. He laced up a brace under his shoe anyway and fought through the pain.

"I didn't care how bad it was feeling," Owens would say afterward. "I was going to give it my all."

He and the rest of the Badgers sure are glad he did.

Owens buried a three-pointer from the left wing with one second remaining to cap the greatest comeback in school history and give Wisconsin a heart-stopping 61–60 victory against Tulsa, earning the Badgers a berth in the Sweet 16. It was an improbable moment for a player and a team, which trailed 58–45 with less than four minutes remaining in the game.

No. 13 Tulsa—the lowest-seeded team to advance past the opening round—had taken a 32–25 halftime lead on No. 5 seed Wisconsin and fended off every potential threat. When Golden Hurricane forward Kevin Johnson buried a three-pointer to give Tulsa a 13-point lead with 4:08 left, the Badgers' season seemed all but over.

"We were saying, 'What can we do?'" Wisconsin forward Mike Wilkinson said.

Badgers coach Bo Ryan provided a swift answer, offering one last-gasp bit of encouragement.

"In the huddle with about three or four minutes to go, I told those guys, 'This is going to be one that they'll talk about for a long time,'" Ryan said.

He was right. Wisconsin unleashed an 11–0 run, which featured baskets from Devin Harris, Alando Tucker, and Wilkinson, to pull within two at 58–56. Tulsa led 60–58 when Jason Parker missed the rim on a runner, causing a shot clock violation and giving the ball back to the Badgers with 12.1 seconds remaining.

Harris took the inbounds pass and dribbled to the right of the key, crossed over back toward the middle, and drew a swarm of Tulsa defenders, who refused to let him win the game. Less than three weeks earlier, Harris made a game-winning free throw against Illinois with 0.4 seconds remaining to give Wisconsin its first outright Big Ten regular season title since 1947.

Wide open, in the corner, stood Owens. He squared up, caught Harris' pass, and let fly for the win. Swish. After Tulsa's Jarius Glenn stepped over the baseline in an attempt to inbound the ball, Wisconsin's unbelievable comeback victory was sealed.

Wisconsin fans chanted, "Freddie, Freddie," as Owens conducted a courtside radio interview. Owens, who had made only 4 of 16 shots in the tournament to that point, was a March Madness hero.

"It was a great feeling," Owens said afterward. "I work on shots like that every day, and this is where it pays off. This was one to tell your kids and grandkids about."

Bronson Koenig's Buzzer Beater

Wisconsin guard Bronson Koenig wasn't the first option, but he told teammate Ethan Happ he wanted the ball anyway. Then, in the closing seconds of a second-round 2016 NCAA tournament game, Koenig got his wish and buried a game-winning shot for the ages.

No. 7 seed Wisconsin and No. 2 seed Xavier were tied at 63 when Badgers coach Greg Gard called a timeout with two seconds remaining. Wisconsin had possession on the sideline, and Gard drew up a play designed first for forward Nigel Hayes to catch the ball near the post. Hayes was double-teamed, however, and Koenig caught the pass from Happ while curling toward the right corner. He dribbled once and fired a step-back jumper over the outstretched arm of Xavier guard Remy Abell while falling back into the Wisconsin bench as the buzzer sounded.

The three-point shot swished through the net, sending Wisconsin to the Sweet 16 and setting off a wild celebration in front of the Badgers' bench. It marked the program's fifth Sweet 16 trip in a six-season stretch.

"I like to have the ball in my hands in those kinds of situations because I believe in myself," Koenig said afterward. "I wust let it fly and knew it was going in. I can't really explain the feeling. It was my first real game winner like that. It was a lot of excitement."

The final minutes represented a microcosm of Wisconsin's rollercoaster season. When longtime Badgers coach Bo Ryan abruptly retired on December 15, 2015, Wisconsin stood just 7–5. Gard was named interim coach, but his long-term status appeared in jeopardy when Wisconsin fell to 9–9 overall and 1–4 in Big Ten play following a surprising loss at Northwestern.

A players-only meeting back in Madison meant to reestablish goals helped the season begin to turn. Wisconsin would win 11 of 14 games to easily earn an 18th consecutive trip to the NCAA tournament. Badgers athletics director Barry Alvarez removed the interim tag and named Gard head coach on March 7. Still, reaching the second weekend of the big dance seemed highly improbable, even late in the game against Xavier.

Wisconsin trailed Xavier 58–49 with 6:19 remaining before staging a late-game comeback. Koenig's long three-pointer with 11.7 seconds left tied the score at 63. On the ensuing possession, Badgers guard Zak Showalter drew a charge on Xavier guard Edmond Sumner with 4.3 seconds remaining to give the ball back to Wisconsin. Koenig then dribbled across half court, where Gard called timeout to set up the final, game-winning shot.

"He made a Bronson Koenig move," Showalter said. "I've seen him make a lot of big shots, but none bigger than that one. That kid has a flair for the dramatic."

85 Barry Un-Retires, Part II

The words that rocked Wisconsin's football program yet again had settled in the air, and what remained was stunned silence from players. An impromptu team meeting inside the McClain Athletic Facility on December 10, 2014, had resulted in head coach Gary Andersen informing his group that he was leaving to take over Oregon State's program.

Andersen thanked players for their two years together. Athletics director Barry Alvarez assured them he would find a great coach to lead the program into the future. And, once more, players were left to try and make sense of a move they later insisted they never saw coming. Practice had been canceled for the day, and the reality of the moment began to set in.

Gary Andersen is gone. We have no head coach. We're supposed to play in a bowl game soon.

"You could tell everyone was kind of like, 'What do we do now?'" Badgers right tackle Rob Havenstein said. "'What happens here?'"

What followed was a plan that ultimately would help to save a season that ended with a New Year's Day Outback Bowl appearance against Auburn in Tampa, Florida. And it all came together in a matter of minutes.

Havenstein and fellow fifth-year senior Marcus Trotter asked the entire senior group to remain in the team meeting room, while underclassmen and assistant coaches filed out. They voiced their frustrations about the unfortunate series of events and considered the immediate future. They needed someone to serve as a temporary head coach. And the obvious choice was right down the hall.

"We'd done it before," Badgers tight end Sam Arneson said. "We had a lot of Wisconsin seniors, guys who grew up in this state.

It's pretty special we thought to have Coach Alvarez coach us in our final game. So we kind of all looked at each other and said, 'You think if we ask him, he'll coach us again?'"

Two years earlier, the senior class had asked Alvarez to coach the Rose Bowl after Bret Bielema left to take over the program at Arkansas. Alvarez, touched and flattered at the gesture, obliged for the sake of the players. His mission as athletics director, he often said, was to make sure the seniors squeezed the best experience out of their time at Wisconsin. UW went on to lose the Rose Bowl against Stanford 20–14, but Alvarez's brief period out of retirement had helped the team and the program tremendously between coaches.

Alvarez, flattered again, told the group he would sleep on the decision. With the news of Andersen's departure now forcing him to search for a head coach, he needed time to gather his thoughts. But the next day, he informed the team that, yes, he would emerge from retirement once more to coach the bowl game. Players needed him, and he was glad to be there for them.

The reaction from Wisconsin's senior class was a mixture of joy and relief. Paul Chryst would be hired six days later as the next coach. But for three weeks in December, Alvarez was in charge again.

This time, Alvarez insisted things would be different. He would insert himself more into the game plan as the interim coach. He would take charge during critical moments of the game. He would lead in the way he had when he won eight bowl games during his Hall of Fame career—something he did not feel he accomplished when he unretired two years earlier, remaining too passive in leaving in-game decisions up to others.

Alvarez followed through on his word and became a more vocal leader, having a hand in all of the team's fourth-down decisions. He bypassed a potential game-tying 50-yard field goal on fourth-and-5 in the final minutes, and quarterback Joel Stave connected with Arneson for a first down. Kicker Rafael Gaglianone ultimately buried a 29-yard field goal with seven seconds remaining in regulation to send the game to overtime.

"I'll tell you the difference that I noticed in preparation was that we were so much more confident because Coach Alvarez is a winner, he doesn't take any nonsense, and he makes the right calls," Badgers linebacker Derek Landisch said afterward. "He makes the gutsy calls, too."

Wisconsin would win the game 34–31 in overtime after Auburn kicker Daniel Carlson's 45-yard field goal attempt to force a second extra session bounced off the right upright and fell harmlessly to the grass. The moment sent players spilling onto the field for hugs and high fives with members of the student band and marked Wisconsin's first bowl win in five tries, since 2009.

When Alvarez conducted a television interview on the field, Havenstein and fellow offensive lineman Dallas Lewallen crept behind and dumped a jug of blue Gatorade on him, a smile creasing Alvarez's face as the remains clung to his skin. Dozens of players then hoisted Alvarez in the air, with Alvarez lifting his right arm and pumping his fist while the team chanted, "U-DUB! U-DUB! U-DUB!"

"I've had a couple of those, and I like them," Alvarez said. "It's a little uncomfortable afterward, but I like them. And it's special for those seniors. It meant a lot to them. They've won a lot of games here. They haven't won a lot of bowl games. They've put a lot into it. They bought into it. They gave us strong leadership when it was needed, and now they can enjoy it."

Alvarez's work on the sideline, one last time, was done.

86 Billy Marek

Injuries to his toe, hip, knee, and wrist had kept Billy Marek out of two full games and part of a third during his junior season in 1974. With three games remaining, Wisconsin's standout running back had rushed for only 475 yards, and repeating as a first-team All-Big Ten performer seemed almost impossible.

Marek, however, had other plans. He was finally healthy and ready to run. And no Big Ten team was going to stop him from another 1,000-yard season. Over his final three games, he put together a streak for the ages, gaining 740 yards with 12 touchdowns to not only blow past 1,000 yards but also earn first-team all-league honors for a second straight season.

The burst began when Marek rushed 34 times for 206 yards and four touchdowns in a 28–15 victory against Iowa. He carried 29 times for 230 yards and three touchdowns in a 52–7 win against Northwestern the following week. He then closed the season with a truly epic performance, carrying 43 times for 304 yards with five touchdowns—all school records at the time—in a 49–14 victory against Minnesota.

For his achievement, Marek was named the Associated Press national college football back of the week for the second time in three weeks. In the process, he tied 1973 Heisman Trophy winner John Cappelletti's NCAA record for consecutive 200-yard rushing games. But Cappelletti totaled 626 yards in his three-game burst at Penn State, 114 yards fewer than Marek.

During the Minnesota game, 55,869 fans at Camp Randall Stadium serenaded the tailback with chants of "We want Marek," and he received several standing ovations, particularly as he approached the 300-yard plateau—something that had never been done in school history.

"I heard over the loudspeaker that I had 297 or something, but that's about all," Marek said. "I heard the fans. How can I not say it felt great to hear them cheering like that? It's great for any player."

Marek's 19 touchdowns and 114 points represented a school record and propelled the Badgers to a 7–4 finish, their best since 1962 when they won the Big Ten title and played in the Rose Bowl. He also won the Big Ten scoring title and the rushing crown that season, finishing with 1,215 yards—just seven short of Rufus Ferguson's school mark of 1,222 set in 1971.

One of Marek's other signature moments that season came when he scored a touchdown in Wisconsin's historic 21–20 victory over No. 4–ranked Nebraska. The Cornhuskers had crushed Oregon 61–7 the previous week and appeared to be an unstoppable force.

Like any running back, Marek's success would not have been possible without a stellar offensive line, which he credited whenever he had the chance. He noted Wisconsin guard Terry Stieve told him a couple games before the end of the season that the line would do whatever it could to help him reach 1,000 yards.

"I think he picked up the whole offensive line by doing that," Marek told the *Milwaukee Sentinel.* "It got 'em united on a goal, and they seemed to enjoy the game more themselves. It's a good feeling knowing you have guys like these blocking for you. You won't find a better offensive line in the country this year than ours."

Marek's rise was surprising considering his background. He wasn't recruited to play high school football because he had Osgood-Schlatter disease, a knee ailment that affects teenagers, and he also didn't play seventh and eighth grade football. In his freshman season at Wisconsin, he carried the ball just once. But when he earned his opportunity, he was difficult to stop, his offensive lineman explained.

"Even when somebody tackles Billy, that doesn't mean he's going to go down," Stieve said. "He keeps those legs churning all the time."

Before Marek's senior season, he was at the center of an April Fool's Day joke played by *Wisconsin State Journal* columnist Tom Butler in 1975. Butler claimed Marek was being moved from running back to free safety because Badgers coach John Jardine was looking for a backup to safety Steve Wagner, who underwent offseason knee surgery.

The column ended with the phrase, "April Fools!" Unfortunately, wire service reporters did not make it to the last line, and called Jardine's house for confirmation. The Associated Press moved the story on its national wire for nearly 30 minutes before the hoax was discovered. Thankfully, Marek remained at tailback for his senior season.

"If he stays healthy, there's no way they can keep him under 1,200 or 1,300 yards," Stieve vowed.

Stieve was spot on. Marek rushed for 1,281 yards as a senior to earn first-team All-Big Ten at running back for a third consecutive season. He left as the school's leading rusher with 3,709 yards and was inducted into the Wisconsin Athletics Hall of Fame in 1994.

87 Volleyball Returns to Title Match

Inside a locker room in the Key Arena bowels, Kelly Sheffield stood in front of his players to offer one final pep talk. Wisconsin's volleyball team, seeded 12th in the NCAA tournament, was about to take on top-seeded Texas, the defending national champion, at the Final Four in Seattle, Washington.

If there were volleyball odds, they certainly were not in Wisconsin's favor the night of December 19, 2013. Texas had won 23 consecutive matches, and no team seeded as low as the Badgers had ever reached the championship match. But Sheffield maintained that, if his players believed they could win, they could achieve something special. He preached playing with the same fearless execution behind the serving line they had all season while converting points off digs.

"One last thing," he told his players. "It's going down."

It was a moment of levity for the underdog Badgers, a reference to a team-wide favorite song "Timber" by Pitbull and Ke$ha. Players cheered wildly, converged in a huddle in the middle of the locker room, then took the floor with a level of freedom and talent even the mighty Longhorns couldn't handle.

Four sets later, after Deme Morales pounded her 14th and final kill, Wisconsin had upset Texas 3–1 to advance to its first national championship appearance since 2000. Players dropped to their knees, pumping their fists and screaming, while Sheffield hugged his assistant coaches.

Back in the locker room after the match, Badgers players hummed the tune to "Timber" while Sheffield danced, crouching and clapping in the middle of a team circle.

"We believed that we could win this match," Sheffield said afterward. "And I think that's a big part of it any time you go into anything. This has been a team that no matter who we played, we believed, the players have believed that there's a way to win."

Two days later, Wisconsin would lose 3–1 to powerhouse Penn State, which captured its fifth national title in seven seasons. But the defeat could not diminish Wisconsin's accomplishments in Sheffield's first season, which continued the program success previously built under head coach Pete Waite. The team finished 28–10, marking the program's highest win total since the 2000 national runner-up team coached by Waite.

Waite helped establish Wisconsin as a major player in the Big Ten. In 14 seasons, his teams reached nine NCAA tournaments, including the 2000 title match, and won the Big Ten championship in 2000 and 2001. He finished with a record of 305–146 at Wisconsin and 170–108 in Big Ten matches. From 1999 to 2007, his Badgers finished no lower than fourth in the Big Ten and qualified for the NCAA tournament in each season. UW could not replicate that success over his final five seasons, going 77–80, and he resigned on November 26, 2012.

Despite Waite's resignation, he was largely responsible for recruiting many of the players who helped Sheffield reach the national championship, including top-rated high school recruit Lauren Carlini. Sheffield, in turn, was often quick to credit Waite for the program's success, even after he was gone.

"One of the things I'm really proud of is that even in our down years I was able to get some great players to come in here," Waite told the *Wisconsin State Journal* in 2013. "My vision was that we'd get back to that high level when they all came together with this last class. I think my vision came true, it's just that I thought I might be part of that vision."

Waite and Sheffield shared a similar career arc in their paths to Wisconsin and developed a great appreciation for each other despite the difficult coaching transition. Both coaches graduated from Ball State and found success at mid-major programs. Waite went 266–102 in 11 seasons at Northern Illinois, while Sheffield excelled for 12 years at Albany and Dayton, reaching a combined eight NCAA tournaments in his final nine seasons at both schools.

When Sheffield was hired at Wisconsin, the Badgers' program had hit a snag. But he was undaunted by the task ahead and even occasionally picked Waite's brain later about coaching strategies.

"There's no magic into doing it," Sheffield said about revitalizing the program. "We're not talking a lot about the past. We're just talking about 'What's our goal out in front of us? And let's just keep our head down and move forward.' It's kind of really, really boring. It's all I know how to do."

He also knew how to win. In Sheffield's second season at Wisconsin in 2014, the Badgers reached the Elite Eight of the NCAA tournament before losing to Penn State. UW closed the season 31–3, the second-most wins in program history and the school's best winning percentage ever in a single season. In Year 3, he followed up that act with another Sweet 16 berth. Without question, Badgers volleyball was back on firm ground, mirroring the success Waite had found so many years earlier.

Athlete Profile: Sherisa Livingston

When Sherisa Livingston's volleyball career began as a high school freshman in Simi Valley, California, she was about as far from being an All-American as any player could be. She was tall but not yet coordinated, a 14-year-old still trying to grasp the rules of the sport. But when her athleticism and knowledge began to sprout, Livingston became a talent few could stop.

During Livingston's Wisconsin career from 1998 to 2001, she helped the Badgers win two Big Ten titles and make four appearances in the NCAA tournament. Her leaping ability was second to none. She could touch 10'9" inches on her approach—well above the height of a basketball hoop, which helped her set the school record for career kills (1,912) and hitting percentage. In 2000, she became the first Badgers volleyball player to earn first-team All-American honors. A year later, she became the program's first two-time first-team All-American.

Livingston helped lead Wisconsin to the national championship in 2000. Nebraska defeated Wisconsin 3–2 to capture the title, and it would take the Badgers another 13 years to make a return trip to the final. She was inducted into the UW Athletics Hall of Fame in 2007.

"Sherisa's become a legend in Madison," Badgers coach Pete Waite said the week of the 2000 title match. "When introductions take place and she's the last one mentioned, it's like being in the United Center when Michael Jordan is introduced—you can't hear a thing. The Wisconsin fans show her how much they appreciate what she's done."

88 The Kangaroo Kicker

He was dubbed the "greatest drop kicker and placement kicker the world ever knew." And then he dropped off the face of the earth for 15 years, creating one of the great mysteries ever to involve a Wisconsin football player.

Pat O'Dea arrived in Madison much as he disappeared—seemingly out of the blue. By the time his trials at Wisconsin were finished, he'd become one of the first great Badgers athletes to be known on a national stage. The native of Melbourne, Australia, surprised his brother, Andy, then a UW crew team coach, with a visit in the spring of 1896. The following fall, O'Dea enrolled at Wisconsin, and his exploits as the team's standout kicker grew.

He punted the ball 85 yards in his first college game against Lake Forest. He smashed a 75-yard punt against the Carlisle Indians in a December 1897 game at the original Chicago Coliseum. He was such a unique talent during a time when offenses relied on running the football a few yards at a time that his head coach, Phil King, was said to have built the team's fortunes around O'Dea's ability as a punter, drop kicker, and place kicker.

In an 1898 game against Northwestern, he kicked a 62-yard field goal on a drop kick during a heavy blizzard—an American football record that stood for the next 17 years. O'Dea also recorded an 87-yard punt in the contest. According to legend, he once kicked a football from goal line to goal line against Yale. O'Dea was so good because he had learned to play his native Australian Rules football, where all punting and drop-kicking occurred on the run.

In his book, *University of Wisconsin Football*, Dave Anderson wrote, "The Kicking Kangaroo went on to astonish players and spectators in football contests all over the Midwest. In Milwaukee's Western League Baseball Park, on November 11, 1899, versus Illinois, he kicked a 60-yard field goal that the Wisconsin Athletic Review said 'would have scored had the distance been 75 yards, for it cleared the bleachers, the high fence behind them and landed in the street, outside the ball park! It must have traveled at least 80 yards in the air.'"

O'Dea became a football coach after his playing days and spent time at Notre Dame and Missouri. But he soon tired of the fame he had achieved, and he moved to San Francisco to practice law. Then, in 1919, he disappeared and eventually newspapers presumed him dead, the victim of some unknown battle while fighting for the Australian army. All the while, O'Dea continued living a low-key life in San Francisco, where he could be known for his post-football accomplishments.

Not until sportswriter Bill Leiser wrote an article in the *San Francisco Chronicle Sporting Green* on September 19, 1934, one day after having dinner with O'Dea, did the world finally come to know the truth. O'Dea had changed his name to Charles J. Mitchell of the Red River Lumber Company of Westwood.

"It was his fame that drove him out of sight," Leiser wrote. "Always he had to talk football. He didn't like living in what were to him 'mere student days of the past.' With the war, his income from the homeland was knocked down to nothing. He had an opportunity to start in a new field, off where no one knew him—off where he could be just himself and not the man who kicked footballs for Wisconsin."

O'Dea, who was inducted into the College Football Hall of Fame in 1962, made his triumphant return to Madison after word of his story had spread. On November 16, 1934, he ventured to UW during homecoming festivities in front of an expected 30,000 spectators. He was described in the *Chicago Tribune* that week as "the Rip Van Winkle of collegiate football."

The story noted O'Dea's mere presence could be enough for Wisconsin to defeat Illinois on homecoming.

"The old grads will go home and be assured that the story, about how the phantom Pat O'Dea in 1934 came from out of the land of the missing, shuffled into Camp Randall field and inspired a hapless lot of Wisconsin players to a point where they whipped the prospective champions, will be passed on down from one generation to another.

"With Pat O'Dea on hand, there isn't anything impossible, Wisconsin alumni believe."

Perhaps they were right. Wisconsin would go on to beat undefeated Illinois 7–3.

89 Tim Krumrie

NFL personnel were trying to evaluate Tim Krumrie's talent before the 1983 draft when a rather incomplete one-paragraph computer printout emerged. The analysis on Krumrie, Wisconsin's standout nose guard, was unflattering, to say the least. It read:

"**TIM KRUMRIE:** Slow (5.0 in 40); short (6-2); poor pass rusher; strong against the run; superior strength (heavyweight wrestler); senior season nowhere near as good as previous season; has dropped from pick in first three rounds to anywhere from fifth on up."

Ultimately, Krumrie was not selected until the 10th round of the draft by the Cincinnati Bengals—at No. 276 overall. All he did in a Bengals uniform was lead the team in tackles in five of his 12 seasons, make the Pro Bowl in 1988 and 1989, register 1,017 career tackles with 34.5 sacks, and play the fourth-most games in Bengals history with 188.

What computer printouts overlooked were traits that Badgers fans witnessed from Krumrie every Saturday for four years.

"It's tough to measure heart in a computer," Krumrie would tell the *Milwaukee Sentinel.* "It's tough to measure desire. They just came up a bit short on that part."

Krumrie brought with him a tenaciousness and ferocity that was unparalleled. Before the Badgers opened the 1979 season against Purdue, starting nose guard Dan Yourg was injured, and coaches asked Krumrie to step in. For the next four seasons, Krumrie started all 46 games in which Wisconsin played.

By the time he finished his career in 1982, he had set the school record for solo tackles (276) and total tackles by a defensive lineman (444). His solo tackle record still holds, and his total tackle mark ranks third overall in school history, behind only Gary Casper's 447 (1989–92) and Pete Monty's 451 (1993–96).

"He's tough, and he understands leverage," then-Badgers coach Dave McClain said. "But his biggest asset is his never-say-die attitude. Anybody can be blocked. But he doesn't stay blocked. He hustles to the football. He plays the run very well."

Krumrie was a big-time football player whose work ethic helped him rise from the small town of Mondovi, Wisconsin (population of roughly 2,700), about 20 miles south of Eau Claire. He came to Wisconsin on a football scholarship, but he also was a state high school wrestling champion at Mondovi. Krumrie said one of the main reasons he picked Wisconsin was that McClain provided him with assurances that he could participate in wrestling. He finished fifth at the Big Ten championships as a sophomore in the heavyweight division.

"I just like competition," Krumrie said. "I'm a competitive person all around. Wrestling is one-on-one, just like me going one-on-one with the center in football."

Football would prove to be the sport that won out. He was named to three first-team All-Big Ten teams and was twice named an All-American. He also developed a knack for playing his best in the biggest games. When Wisconsin stunned No. 1 Michigan 21–14 to open the 1981 season, Krumrie recorded 13 tackles and was named the nation's defensive player of the week by the Associated Press. Krumrie earned MVP honors during Wisconsin's 14–3 Independence Bowl victory against Kansas State in 1982, when he again finished with 13 tackles and helped hold the Wildcats below 200 yards of total offense. He was elected to the UW–Madison Athletics Hall of Fame in 1999 and the College Football Hall of Fame in 2016.

Krumrie developed a reputation in the pros as the fiercest competitor around—someone who would pace the sidelines and instigate training camp fights with teammates, often playing with a bloody nose.

Cincinnati Bengals coach Dave Shula recalled seeing an agitated Krumrie telling the team's equipment manager not to adjust his helmet to sit higher on his head. Krumrie said he wanted the helmet to smack the bridge of his nose when he tackled somebody, so it would leave a mark on the nose and he would feel like he had put in a day's work on the field.

Just how tough was Krumrie? He broke his left leg during the first quarter of Cincinnati's January 1989 Super Bowl loss to the San Francisco 49ers. He had a 15-inch steel rod inserted in the leg and continued his NFL career without missing a game the following season.

Krumrie retired from professional football at age 34. He said he had achieved all his goals, including playing in the Super Bowl and the Pro Bowl, surpassing 1,000 career tackles, and not missing a game since the seventh grade. He certainly left his mark well before then as one of the toughest Badgers in quite some time.

"In football, you better have a guy who is consistent from week to week," McClain told the *Sentinel* in October 1983, one season after Krumrie's college departure. "Tim never was up and down. Attitude, that's the key. He worked in the offseason to get ready for camp. He simply worked his tail off. He lifted. He ran like mad. He's a peach. I wish I still had him."

90 Otto Puls, Official Scorekeeper

Before the biggest game of their college basketball lives, members of Wisconsin's starting lineup stepped onto the Lucas Oil Stadium court in Indianapolis, walked to the scorer's table, and stopped to rub the crew-cut head of an 82-year-old man for good luck. As the team's official scorekeeper, Otto Puls had seen every game of their Badgers careers—and nearly five decades worth of games on top of that.

But this night would prove to be the most special game Puls had ever witnessed. On that night, April 4, 2015, Wisconsin would take down undefeated Kentucky in the Final Four to reach the program's first national championship game since 1941. "No. 1 on my list, as far as I'm concerned," Puls recalled of his most memorable moment.

In the postgame locker room, amid the festive scene, Badgers coach Bo Ryan gave Puls the final words before they departed.

Ryan: "Everybody up, and Otto, you're on."

Puls: "Hey, guys. Way to gooooooooo!"

He punched his right fist in the air with unbridled joy, and the team surrounded him, clapping the night away. Puls was all too happy to play a small role in the celebration.

Badgers fans likely know the stories of the program's most well-known players and coaches. But Puls, a retired Lieutenant Colonel in the United States Army Reserves, had been as much a part of the program as anybody over the years, serving a vital role while becoming something of a grandfather figure to the team. In 1964, then-Badgers coach John Erickson approached Puls and three others about being an official scorekeeper for the team. He fulfilled those duties admirably for the next five decades.

"All four of us were game officials," Puls said in 2015. "We worked at state universities, we worked high school games, state tournament games. That was the start of it. But I'm the last one now."

Puls, a Madison native, graduated from Wisconsin in 1955. He was talented enough to letter on the Badgers' baseball team from 1952 to '54 and batted .293 during his final season, led the team in stolen bases, and earned a tryout with the Baltimore Orioles. But a professional baseball career did not materialize, and he used his pharmaceutical degree from Wisconsin to become a pharmacist in nearby Middleton. To earn money on the side, he began officiating football and basketball games in high school and college. He first honed those skills when the university hired him to officiate intramural sports.

"It put three of my kids through college with the everyday things I made— $15 here, $17 here," Puls said. "It put some shoes on the kids also."

Puls spent the next 17 years working high school and small-college football games as an official. In 1972, he was added to the Big Ten football staff, and over 20 seasons, he worked 238 Big Ten games—including two Rose Bowls (1977 and 1982), an Orange Bowl (1981), a Gator Bowl (1985), and a Citrus Bowl (1989). He retired from the Big Ten in 1991 and was approached by the university about helping as an assistant equipment manager for the men's basketball team.

Puls continued to hold a whistle in his mouth during the team's practices into his eighties, hovering under the basket while maintaining a watchful eye on the proceedings.

"Otto's the man. I look up to Otto," national player of the year Frank Kaminsky said during the 2015 Final Four. "He's still out there refereeing all of our practices. He doesn't ever make the right call, but he's still there."

Over his more than 50 years as the team's official scorekeeper— and through 10 different head coaches—Puls certainly saw just about everything. He recalled that his most famous—or infamous— moment occurred on March 5, 2000, in Wisconsin's regular season home finale at the Kohl Center against Indiana, which would prove to be coach Bob Knight's final trip to Madison with the Hoosiers.

Puls was sitting next to an Indiana University media relations worker who, by Puls' recollection, "got obnoxious and started to get really upset about the officiating" as Indiana's lead slipped away in the second half. Indiana blew a 12-point lead in the last nine minutes, and Wisconsin squeaked out a controversial 56–53 victory. Indiana's Dane Fife missed a three-pointer with three seconds left, and television replays showed the ball bounced off a Wisconsin player and landed out of bounds with at least one second remaining. But the clock ran out, the officials declared the game over, and students stormed the court.

Amid the celebration, the IU media relations worker, furious about the game's outcome, stood to leave and pushed Puls back into his seat, knocking his glasses off. A police officer and Wisconsin athletics director Pat Richter later approached Puls and asked if he wanted to press charges.

"I said, 'Nah, just let it go,'" Puls said. "That next day, Pat Richter called the Indiana athletic director, and theoretically the guy never did apologize to me, but he apologized to Pat and said he was sorry."

The incident reminded Puls, still a referee at heart, about the importance of remaining neutral while performing his game-day job responsibilities—even though he developed a strong bond with every Badgers basketball team that came through the program. And before every game, fans have been able to see that bond on display at the scorer's table.

"I never, ever say anything to those kids and say you have to shake my hand and go by and touch my head or whatever," Puls said. "It's automatic now. The player that started that was Mike Kelley back when he was playing with Dick Bennett. He did it, and as time went on, different players started to touch my head. Brian Butch did it. Alando Tucker did it. Sam Dekker did it all the time.

"They feel I guess maybe it's a good luck charm or whatever it is. They've continued it now the last 20-some years, and it's been pretty good to us."

91 Chris Solinsky

On the eve of the NCAA men's indoor track championship in 2007, Wisconsin coach Ed Nuttycombe saw a fire burning inside star runner Chris Solinsky that could not be extinguished. The

Badgers had a very real opportunity to become the first Big Ten program to ever win an indoor team title. But the only way for it to happen was for Solinsky to make a selfless move that would cost him a piece of individual glory.

Solinsky had won the 3,000-meter national championship in each of the previous two years. In 2007, however, he insisted on running the 5,000-meter race the day before, knowing full well he likely wouldn't have enough gas left in the tank to win the 3,000 only 24 hours later. What the Badgers needed if they were to win was points, and he could secure nearly twice the amount if he ran both events.

"He was willing to kind of give up the opportunity to perhaps be the only NCAA athlete to win three of them in order to help the team," Nuttycombe said. "He was not going to allow us to hold him out of the 5,000 in order to enhance his opportunity to try to win the 3,000 because he knew we had a chance to win."

On Friday, Solinsky excelled to win his first 5,000-meter individual championship. The next day, he almost pulled off a stunning double title before finishing second to Northern Arizona's Lopez Lomong, nearly two seconds behind. Still, Solinsky's decision provided Wisconsin with the points necessary to outpace Florida State 40–35 for the national championship, finally putting a Big Ten team on top.

Solinsky summed up the mindset he carried with him during his entire college career: "Individual stuff is great," he said. "But to be able to share with the team, you can't beat that."

As competitors go, there were few as driven as Solinsky, who grew up in Stevens Point, Wisconsin, and dominated the high school scene by winning eight state titles as a middle-distance runner. During his time with the Badgers, he became the most decorated men's track and field and cross country athlete. He earned All-American honors 11 times in track and was a three-time All-American in cross country.

Solinsky also shined when it mattered most. He was a five-time NCAA champion, winning each of his last three years indoors (the 3,000-meter race in 2005 and 2006, as well as the 5,000-meter race in 2007). Additionally, he won his last two outdoor titles in the 5,000 in 2006 and 2007. Solinsky won four individual Big Ten titles and helped Wisconsin sweep the Big Ten team championships all four years. He is the only Badgers runner to win individual national championships in two sports.

Nuttycombe said two things separated Solinksy and "made him exceptional as opposed to very good." One was his ability to remain healthy despite the physical toll endurance running takes on the body. Nuttycombe could not remember Solinsky missing a single meet of significance because of injury. He also said Solinsky's drive to excel was impressive.

"He had a willingness to do anything and everything necessary to be the best athlete he could be," Nuttycombe said. "He was a relentless trainer, dedicated to all the details that are necessary to get to that level."

There was no better example of that than at the 2007 men's indoor championship. Solinsky said he knew history was not on Wisconsin's side. Teams from the Southeastern Conference had won 22 of the past 23 national titles, and Florida State of the Atlantic Coast Conference was a formidable foe as well.

Solinsky said he met with Nuttycombe and fellow coach Jerry Schumacher and asked what he could do to help the team bring home a title.

"They laid down the plan," Solinsky said. "I worked really hard over the winter and early indoor season, planted the seed in all my teammates' minds that this is possible. We can do this. Week after week, excitement was getting generated. Luckily for us, performances started falling into place."

At the national meet, Solinsky's teammates also delivered. Senior Demi Omole finished second in the 60-meter dash, while the distance medley relay team of Craig Miller, James Groce, Joe Pierre, and Jack Bolas placed third. Senior Joe Detmer took fifth in the heptathlon, senior Tim Nelson finished fifth in the 5,000 meters, and sophomore Stu Eagon placed 13th. In total, the Badgers earned 10 All-American honors.

"It was pretty amazing," Solinsky said. "We didn't take it lightly that no Big Ten team had ever won an NCAA title. We were hearing about that, and we knew about that."

Solinsky moved to Portland, Oregon, where he trained as a professional runner for Nike and the Oregon Track Club under Schumacher. He was a member of Team USA at the 2009 World Outdoor Championships, finishing 12th in the 5,000 meters, and he was the runner-up in the event at the 2009 U.S. Championships. In 2010, he broke the American record in the 10,000-meter race by more than 14 seconds to become the first man not born in Africa to ever break 27 minutes in the event. He also ranked second all-time in U.S. history in the 5,000 and 10,000. He announced his retirement from professional running in April 2016.

Solinsky turned his attention to coaching, working as an assistant coach with distance and middle-distance runners at William & Mary. He previously spent one year as a student assistant while finishing his degree at Wisconsin and two years as a volunteer coach at the University of Portland. He credited Badgers coaches, including Nuttycombe, Schumacher, Mark Napier, and Mark Guthrie, for instilling values he carried with him into coaching. And he hoped to give back in a similar way to future runners.

"Those guys really had a huge influence on not only the athlete I became but just the person and the man that I became," Solinsky said. "I'm kind of following in their footsteps in terms of getting into the coaching industry. Maybe someday, fingers crossed, I can come back and do the same thing they did for the Badgers."

Matzdorf's World Record

Before Pat Matzdorf entered the World All-Star Meet representing the United States against the Soviet Union on July 3, 1971, he was a little-known high jumper whose athletic feats evoked minimal response in the sporting world. His personal best was an indoor jump of 7'3"—a height exceeded by 12 other active jumpers.

But that all-star showcase in Berkeley, California, forever etched Matzdorf into history. Matzdorf, an NCAA high jump champion for the Badgers and a future UW Athletics Hall of Famer, tied Dick Fosbury's American record of 7'4½". As he celebrated, one question came to mind: What should he try next?

"You might as well go for it—7'6"," American teammate Tim Heikkila told Matzdorf, according to *Sports Illustrated*. The world record beginning the day was 7'5¾"—or 2.28 meters—a mark that belonged to the Soviet Union's Valeriy Brumel and had stood for eight years.

The bar was then set at 2.29 meters, which equaled 7'6¼". Using a bent-knee straddle approach over the more conventional straight-leg method, Matzdorf cleared the bar on his third attempt, creating a frenzied atmosphere on the track. The native of Sheboygan, Wisconsin, was now a world record holder—something he would lay claim to until it was bested two years later.

"It didn't surprise me," teammate Reynaldo Brown told *Sports Illustrated*. "Pat psyches himself like no one else. I told him he'd have his day sooner or later."

92 An Incredible Olympics Rowing Streak

The seeds of an Olympics berth began with a generic postcard mailed to the home of Grant and Ross James, offering the pursuit of a new athletic adventure in college. The twin brothers had no idea just how much that postcard would change their lives.

It came from the University of Wisconsin rowing team, which had sent hundreds of identical recruiting cards to high schoolers across Minnesota, Wisconsin, and Illinois with a simple message: if you're taller than 6'2" and want something new, try rowing.

The message resonated with the James brothers. At 6'5" and 190 pounds, the twins had the perfect build for the sport. They just didn't know it until arriving on campus. Seven years later, on May 22, 2012, they would continue one of the most remarkable streaks in Badgers athletics. That day, the two helped the United States earn the eighth and final spot at the Olympic Qualification Regatta in Lucerne, Switzerland, meaning the brothers would represent their country in the 2012 London Olympics.

Wisconsin's rowing program was now responsible for sending at least one rower to a 12th consecutive Summer Olympics, dating all the way back to 1968 in Mexico City. Yes, Madison is a city surrounded by four lakes. But how could such a streak be explained?

"They have a great tradition," said United States national rowing team coach Mike Teti, a three-time Olympic rower. "I think that's where it starts. They've always had great coaches and they have a great facility. I know they have a harsh winter. I think that sort of makes them more resilient. They work really, really hard through the winter when a lot of the other programs are in the water. They have a great work ethic. I think that carries through."

It is not uncommon for American rowers to have never rowed before college. Wisconsin puts an emphasis on finding students with athletic builds who have plenty of successful experiences in other sports and are willing to work in a team environment.

"We get football and basketball players from Wisconsin and Minnesota," said Badgers rowing coach Chris Clark, who took over the program in 1996. "We stick with what's close. We send out thousands of letters. We'll accept anybody. Ideally you want super tall guys. People may not realize how hard it is to be an Olympian. It takes 10,000 contacts with recruits to create one Olympian.

"But if you're going to be good, you get good fast. We're looking for guys who were born rowers who don't know it yet. Most kids have tried football, basketball, and all sorts of things. They've never tried rowing. They have no idea they can be great at it. That's what we're counting on."

The James brothers represented yet another such example. They already were outdoorsy types growing up in DeKalb, Illinois, and preferred rock climbing, whitewater rafting, and rifle shooting to baseball and football. In 2006, they won the High Power Rifle Marksmanship championship as part of the Illinois State Rifle Association. The brothers attended Wisconsin from 2005 to '09 and both walked on to the rowing team. They would later be a part of the Badgers' 2008 national championship varsity eight boat—the ninth national title for the program and first since 1990.

Wisconsin's women's rowing teams also have experienced tremendous success. The women's rowing team won national titles in 1975 and 1986, and several have gone on to compete in the Olympics as well. The Badgers' lightweight women's rowing team won five national championships in a six-year span from 2004 to '09. Since 2005, the men's and women's teams have trained at Porter Boathouse, a 50,000-square-foot complex on Lake Mendota.

UW's magnificent Olympics streak stood in jeopardy in 2011, when the United States was not among the top seven countries to qualify at the world championships. It forced the Americans into the Final Olympic Qualification race in Switzerland, when only a first-place finish would lead to the Olympics.

Grant and Ross James won that Olympic qualifying race and a month later helped the U.S. edge New Zealand and France for the eighth and final Olympic spot, a result that saved the Americans considerable embarrassment. Never before in the modern era of the Olympics had the U.S. failed to qualify at the previous world championships.

Despite a difficult road, the James brothers had made history—for their country and for Wisconsin. And, like many before them, they had the Badgers' program to thank for their success.

"They cast a wide net," Ross James said. "They end up pulling in a lot of raw material. Guys that are athletic and have the build and mental capacity it takes to do well at something like that. I think Coach Clark has established an exceptional system that allows athletes like that to go from never having touched a boat or an oar to the Olympics in six, seven years."

Olympic Qualifiers

Wisconsin's men's rowers qualified for 12 consecutive Olympic Games through the 2012 London Olympics. Here is a list of each qualifier:

2012 London: Grant James, Ross James

2008 Beijing: Beau Hoopman, Micah Boyd

2004 Athens: Beau Hoopman, Matt Smith

2000 Sydney: Eric Mueller, Kurt Borcherding (alternate)

1996 Atlanta: Eric Mueller

1992 Barcelona: Mark Berkner

1988 Seoul: Robert Espeseth Jr., Dave Krmpotich

1984 Los Angeles: Robert Espeseth Jr.

1980 Moscow: Robert Espeseth Jr. (U.S. boycotted the Olympics)

1976 Montreal: Neil Halleen, Robert Espeseth Jr.

1972 Munich: Stewart MacDonald, Tim Mickelson

1968 Mexico City: Stewart MacDonald

93 Jamar Fletcher vs. Freddie Mitchell

Jaw jacking between UCLA's Freddie Mitchell and Wisconsin's Jamar Fletcher had reached a crescendo in the build-up to kickoff of the 2000 Sun Bowl. And then, it somehow elevated even higher when the game began, creating one of the more memorable back-and-forth battles between competitors in recent Badgers history.

Mitchell regarded himself as the top wide receiver in the country during the 2000 season and insisted Fletcher could not stop him. Fletcher, meanwhile, already had won the Jim Thorpe Award as the nation's best defensive back, having intercepted six passes, and argued he could not be beaten. It would be—to borrow a timeworn football phrase—"good on good" when the two squared off against each other on December 29 in El Paso, Texas.

"It's going to be a mighty good show," Fletcher promised.

During game week, Mitchell, a 5'11" junior from Lakeland, Florida, expressed shock that he had lost out on the Fred Biletnikoff Award, presented to the nation's best wide receiver, to Pittsburgh's Antonio Bryant.

"That is why I say that the Biletnikoff Award is no longer a prestigious award," Mitchell said. "As a receiver, don't even think about the Biletnikoff. Get that out of your mind. Maybe in a couple of years, I'll have a Freddie Mitchell Award for the true best receiver in the nation."

Fletcher, a 5'10" junior from St. Louis, Missouri, never was one to shy away from sharing his true feelings, either, which only ratcheted up the drama. As a freshman during the 1999 Rose Bowl, Fletcher secured what proved to be the game-winning score when he picked off UCLA quarterback Cade McNown and returned the interception 46 yards for a touchdown in the fourth quarter of a

38-31 victory. Afterward, he called UCLA's entire team "soft" and said the Bruins lacked the toughness to play Big Ten football.

"This wasn't as hard as I thought it was going to be," Fletcher bragged. "We just beat them up. You could see it in their eyes."

UCLA's players hadn't forgotten his words two seasons later, and Fletcher was involved in a pregame scuffle that cost the Bruins a 15-yard penalty at kickoff—although Fletcher admitted he was the culprit. "I was doing the pushing," he said. "They got the penalty."

When the game began, Mitchell and Fletcher staged an epic duel in which Fletcher would leave humbled—only slightly. During the first quarter, Mitchell caught a 64-yard touchdown pass from quarterback Cory Paus to tie the score at 7–7, and then drew a 15-yard penalty for taunting Fletcher. It was the first touchdown Fletcher had allowed in man coverage in his college career, though the Badgers claimed it was zone coverage, and Wisconsin coach Barry Alvarez blamed himself for the mistake.

"I told him, 'You can't stop me! Bye-bye!'" Mitchell recounted after the game.

Later, Mitchell drew another taunting penalty, though he would not be ejected, after using his forearm and hitting Fletcher in the head. The penalty caused the Bruins to have a first-and-goal on the 23-yard line instead of the 8. Mitchell would catch nine passes for a Sun Bowl record 180 yards and earn MVP honors. Fletcher, however, would have the final word.

With UCLA driving toward midfield for the potential game-winning score and only a minute remaining in the contest, Fletcher stepped in front of UCLA receiver Brian Poli-Dixon to intercept quarterback Scott McEwan's pass and preserve a 21–20 Wisconsin victory. It marked Fletcher's seventh interception on the season and the 21st of his career, which is tied for first in program history.

The interception helped soothe Fletcher, who had been burned by Mitchell and required postgame X-rays after injuring his left shoulder in the first half.

"He's a great cornerback," Mitchell said. "But everybody saw today that he couldn't stop me."

Retorted Fletcher, "We got the win, whether he thinks he got the best of me or not."

Fletcher, who had been a key piece to Wisconsin's previous two Rose Bowl–winning teams, finished his career as a two-time All-American, including a consensus first-teamer in 2000 as the Big Ten's defensive player of the year. He also earned three straight first-team all-conference selections. He was inducted into the Wisconsin Athletics Hall of Fame in 2013.

Both he and Mitchell declared one year early for the NFL draft, making the Sun Bowl their final college game—though Mitchell had plenty more to say about Fletcher's performance.

"After the game he had today," Mitchell said, "he'd better stay."

The Philadelphia Eagles selected Mitchell at No. 25 overall in the first round of the 2001 NFL draft. Fletcher went one pick later, 26th overall, to the Miami Dolphins.

94 Paul Chryst Era Begins

He remembered the bicycle route that brought him as a young boy to the corner of Monroe and Regent streets on the west side of Wisconsin's campus, where he routinely delivered six fresh newspapers to the football stadium offices.

He reminisced about the days when he would sneak inside Camp Randall Stadium just to throw footballs and dream big, pretending to make play calls as the Badgers' quarterback. He recalled all those Sunday mornings in the fall, how the ritualistic nature of serving on a cleanup crew with family members inside the stadium after games stirred an inexplicable level of excitement to be part of something bigger.

Over the years, football came to define Paul Chryst. But more specifically, University of Wisconsin football came to define Paul Chryst. And the memories of what shaped him into the man he became were not lost on him.

A piece of him never left Madison. And on December 17, 2014, he returned in grand fashion.

Chryst was introduced as the 30ᵗʰ head football coach in Wisconsin's program history inside the Nicholas–Johnson Pavilion at the Kohl Center in front of boosters, fans, old friends, and family. His wife, Robin, and three children, Katy, JoJo, and Danny, sat in the front row, periodically turning to hug familiar faces from days gone by.

"To be able to do this and come back home to Wisconsin, it truly is special," Chryst said. "There was a spirit that is undeniable here."

It was, without question, a day not only for Chryst and his family to celebrate, but it also was one that caused Badgers fans to rejoice. Because few hires during the offseason college football coaching carousel involved a man who understood his new program better than Chryst.

"I had a lot of choices, and I've always said fit is very important," Wisconsin athletics director Barry Alvarez said at Chryst's introductory news conference. "And I don't know where you can find a better fit and qualified person than Paul and his family."

Chryst's story was one with which many locals were familiar. He was born in Madison in 1965. He returned to letter three times as a Badgers quarterback after winning a high school state championship in Platteville. And after following his father's footsteps into coaching, he served two stints as an assistant coach at Wisconsin.

In 2002, Chryst worked as the Badgers' tight ends coach. He spent seven more years as the team's offensive coordinator from 2005 to '11 and helped the program set school records for points per game (44.1) and total offense (469.9) in his final year. Chryst left only to pursue his first head coaching job at the University of Pittsburgh—a difficult decision he felt was necessary to advance his career.

At the time, Bret Bielema was entrenched in his sixth season as Wisconsin's head coach, consistently won games, and showed no sign he was unhappy there. When Bielema left for Arkansas in 2012, Alvarez made the honorable decision not to pursue Chryst. He had, after all, recommended Chryst for the Pitt job only one year earlier and did not feel comfortable putting the Panthers in such a tough spot by plucking him right back.

That brought Utah State's Gary Andersen to Madison as the next head coach. And though he tried to say the right things, Andersen had spent his entire career on the West Coast and ultimately left the program in stunning fashion to take the head coaching job at Oregon State. In two years, Wisconsin had lost two head coaches, leaving some to wonder whether Wisconsin—despite all its football success—was considered a so-called destination job.

Chryst's intention was to change that by following the path of Alvarez, who arrived as Wisconsin's football coach in 1990 and took over as athletics director in 2004. He stopped short of calling Wisconsin a dream job for him and his family, but Chryst's heartfelt words and emotions indicated as much. He noted that within 15 minutes of arriving at a hotel the day before his introductory news conference, all three of his kids had scattered to reunite with friends.

"When you talk about destination job, I think you've got to earn the right to stay that long," Chryst said. "There's two great examples: Coach Alvarez, and I think what Bo [Ryan] is doing right now in hoops. They've earned the right to make it that destination job, and I sure hope to work to try to make it that. But you've got to earn it, I believe."

What the 49-year-old Chryst provided was a man who understood the challenges that were unique to Wisconsin. He recognized the importance of maintaining in-state recruits—an area Alvarez acknowledged had perhaps slipped in two years under Andersen. He also was someone who accepted the academic challenges that came with coaching the Badgers, which was an issue that clearly irked Andersen on his way out the door.

"I think one of the things that gives Wisconsin an edge is the quality of guys that you get to do it with," Chryst said. "When you go out and recruit, you're offering an education. When you can go into that person's home and tell them, and you know it to be true, that you're offering a world class education and they also get an opportunity to play, like Coach Alvarez said, this is a tremendous program football-wise. When those two match up, you've got a lot to offer, and I think recruiting is about finding the fit."

There were bound to be questions about schemes, recruiting, and expectations in the coming months. Chryst's wife even admitted after the introductory news conference that, despite the homecoming feeling surreal, she knew her husband needed to win games in order for the family to stay in Madison. In Chryst's first season at Wisconsin, the team finished 10–3 with a Holiday Bowl victory against USC, and his future with the program appeared bright.

"It makes for a very good story," Badgers quarterback Joel Stave said. "It's cool how for him it's all worked out."

95 Kathy Butler

The day Kathy Butler caught the racing bug, she was 10 years old and in the fifth grade at a school in England. It was then when she participated in her first informal race against classmates, as young children tend to do on the school playground, boys and girls lumped into one big group.

"I beat everyone," Butler recalled, "including all the boys."

Speed and endurance came naturally to Butler, who quickly found herself entering a series of local races featuring the fastest kids in her school. She never finished worse than third. Running—and more specifically middle-distance running—became a part of her identity and would lead her to great heights as a Badger.

Butler and her parents moved to Canada, where she transformed into a sensation. She was a four-time provincial cross country champion in high school at the Ontario Federation of School Athletic Associations meet, winning in 1987, 1989, 1990, and 1991. She won two Canadian cross country championships and was a three-time member of Canada's junior national team. She attended college in Canada at the University of Guelph, where she set a 1,000-meter school record that stood for nearly 20 years.

As her career was about to skyrocket, Butler was diagnosed in 1994 with Graves Disease, an immune system disorder that results in the overproduction of thyroid hormones. She feared she would not be able to compete again, but her condition improved after a few months on medication and went into remission, and she was able to return to racing.

"It was definitely pretty scary," she said. "And in some ways it makes you realize how much you love running and how much it means to you when potentially it's going to be taken away from you forever."

When it came time to transfer to a major American Division I college, Butler's finalists were Oregon, Washington, and Wisconsin. On her visit to Madison, she developed a rapport with Badgers women's cross country and track coach Peter Tegan and was sold.

"He didn't just have the attitude of we have you for this amount of time, and I want to get as much as possible out of you," Butler said. "We could succeed in the long term with my running. He had that attitude about people in general where running is important but there's more to life than just how fast you go in two laps, four laps, 25 laps, or whatever.

"It just seemed like the right fit for me. It came down to a few places. Wisconsin had everything I wanted."

At Wisconsin, Butler became a five-time NCAA champion and one of the most decorated runners in Badgers history. She won the women's 3,000-meter run three straight years at the NCAA track and field meet, from 1995 to '97. Her team won a title in the 1997 indoor distance medley relay, and she also won the 1995 cross country NCAA championship. She was a 13-time All-American, a 17-time Big Ten champion, and a two-time Wisconsin female athlete of the year.

Butler represented Canada in the 1996 Atlanta Olympics and ran for England at the 2004 Athens Olympics. In 1999, she finished fourth in cross country in the world championships. She competed professionally for 12 years before retiring and instructing coaches and track athletes in Colorado.

Butler said her proudest moment at Wisconsin was winning the cross country national championship because every runner in the country participated in the same event, rather than a specific distance, as in track. And she remembers her time in Madison and everything athletics represented quite fondly.

"Having not grown up with the whole university being almost bigger than anything in the state other than the Packers, it probably made an even bigger impression on me because it does have such a backing and support from the community and the state as a whole," Butler said.

"You just really felt like you were part of something, especially as an athlete. Even in a sport that got less exposure than the big sports, people would know how you did and follow the sports. To have that much backing was a pretty special feeling for sure."

96 Ben Brust's Half-Court Heave

When fans reflect on Ben Brust's career as a Wisconsin basketball player, they will undoubtedly remember both his fearlessness and willingness to take shots from a distance that would make most coaches cringe. What were the boundaries of his range? Try anywhere inside half court.

For further proof, take the afternoon of February 9, 2013, when Brust stretched the parameters of reason with a miraculous running 40-foot swish at the buzzer to send a game against No. 3 Michigan into overtime. His heave helped the Badgers beat the Wolverines 65–62 in the extra session at the Kohl Center and sent students rushing onto the court in celebration. It was perhaps the most improbable shot in the building's history—and one more example of the preposterous shooting range Brust possessed.

"I've got to shoot within reason," Brust said after the game. "I'm not going to cross half court and jack it up now that I hit this one. Although that would be fun."

It certainly would've been fun to watch him try.

The play that etched Brust's name into Badgers folklore began with Wisconsin trailing Michigan 60–57 and only 2.4 seconds remaining in regulation. Badgers forward Mike Bruesewitz took the ball out of bounds under the Michigan basket and surveyed his options out of a set Badgers coach Bo Ryan had run several times. Brust curled around and caught Bruesewitz's pass inside the red motion W logo before half-court. He dribbled once and released a bomb near the right sideline over the outstretched arm of Michigan defender Caris LeVert that dropped through the net.

"Coach Ryan actually put his arms up," Bruesewitz said. "He showed some emotion, which was odd. I've never really seen him do that. Every once in a while, he'll bring it out."

Michigan coach John Beilein tried to instruct LeVert to foul Brust before he went into the act of shooting. But Brust caught the ball with a step on LeVert, putting him out of position to foul, lest he risk surrendering three free throws.

"He was not a guy you want to give that type of room to," Beilein admitted.

The origins of Brust's shooting range stemmed from a slanted driveway of his home in the Chicago suburb of Hawthorn Woods, Illinois. A sidewalk extended from the driveway, winding beside the grass in his front yard, and it became a safe haven from older brothers Jonathan and Stephen, who would beat up on Ben if he dared enter their territory near the basket. So he began making any number of ridiculous, long, looping shots.

"I couldn't get by my big, older brothers," Brust said. "So I had to learn to shoot back where they couldn't get me. I credit that to learning how to shoot from deep. The sidewalk rule. The one square of relief rule is what I call it."

Over his college career, Brust developed into a player who was much more than a threat to win a game of H-O-R-S-E. He learned to play defense, to cut hard, and to make little plays to be a valuable asset on the court. He recorded five double-doubles because he put himself in position to snag rebounds even though he stood just 6'1". But it was his three-point shooting that truly set him apart.

Brust finished his career as the most prolific long-range shooter in program history. He buried a school-record 235 three-pointers and broke his own single-season mark by knocking down 96 threes as a senior. The previous career record of 227 belonged to Tim Locum, who played at Wisconsin from 1988 to '91.

Always one with a flair for the dramatic, Brust would break Locum's record with a three-pointer to give Wisconsin a 77–75 lead against Oregon with 1:07 remaining in a thrilling 85–77 Badgers victory during the 2014 NCAA tournament. UW would ride the win all the way to its first of two consecutive Final Four appearances.

That game against Michigan, by the way, was far from over after Brust's half-court shot. But what would a good story be without more Brust heroics? With 43 seconds remaining in overtime, Brust drilled a 25-foot three-pointer over LeVert to give Wisconsin the lead for good at 65–62. Soon, fans mobbed the team, storming the court for the first time since Wisconsin defeated No. 1 Ohio State at home two years earlier.

"People were putting hats on me," Brust said. "I was like, 'Where did this come from?' It was awesome. Something I'll remember forever, and I'm sure a lot of people will."

97 Run Elver Park Hill

On the right September or October weekday afternoon, casual observers near Madison's west side may stumble upon a team enduring perhaps the least comfortable workout routine across the college basketball landscape. In what has become an annual tradition in camaraderie and endurance building, Wisconsin's men's hoops program takes to a patch of land known simply as "The Hill" for a preseason conditioning experience unlike any other.

Take the contrast in layout—lush green grass that stretches toward a bright blue sky, nestled near rows of trees, a disc golf course, three tennis courts, and a city swimming pool at Elver Park. In the middle of it all is a hill that makes most grown men weak at the knees, 125 ominous yards upward, with an incline not intended for the faint of heart.

"Depending on what kind of shape you're in and what else you've been doing, obviously the hill is different," Wisconsin basketball coach Bo Ryan explained. "The quick rise in the pulse causes people a lot of discomfort. That's a nice way to put it."

Ryan, who coached the Badgers from 2001 to '15, was the man responsible for instituting the preseason custom. As the story goes, when Ryan was an assistant coach at Wisconsin in the 1970s, he watched Badgers basketball players train by running up and down steep concrete steps inside the football stadium as part of preseason conditioning. What struck him most were the complaints he heard from players about sore joints when the season ended.

One of the school's track coaches noted some countries' track and field teams prepared for international competitions by running hills instead as a newer method of training. Ryan filed that conversation away, and when he accepted his first college head coaching job about 70 miles southwest of Madison at the University of Wisconsin–Platteville in 1984, he made sure to find a suitably menacing hill for players. He continued the tradition at UW–Milwaukee in 1999 for two seasons and then brought it back to Madison in 2001.

In Ryan's early years at Wisconsin, players conditioned at the hill twice a week. Later, he scaled back to once each week, with the team beginning at 10 laps and increasing by two until the final run of 20 just before official practices commenced in October. Student managers laid out orange cones to pave a path up the hill for the team, which broke into four groups based on position: point guards, shooting guards, forwards, and centers. The fastest group typically took roughly 25 seconds, while the slowest needed about 29 seconds. The only rest between sets was the lengthy walk back down the hill after reaching the top.

Achieving timing goals were important to Ryan, but the most significant aspect to the training centered on team bonding.

"Some days are better than others," said Ryan, who rated Madison's hill as the second-most difficult of his three stops behind Platteville. "It's really neat the way the guys pick each other up, though. For the bigger guys, it's a little tougher."

The hill has a way of instructing the mind to quit. About two-thirds of the way up, it substantially steepens and makes participants' legs wobble and stiffen. Over the years, Ryan saw many newcomers struggle on their first days. The ritual even prompted past players, like all-conference forward Jon Leuer, to remark that running his last hill at Wisconsin was better than Christmas. And for those curious about just how difficult a task it is, let it be known those in less than ideal physical condition are likely to suffer the consequences—something I learned the hard way while running alongside the team for a preseason story.

On an afternoon in which the Badgers were required to run 12 hills, I managed only four before collapsing in the grass at the bottom due to lightheadedness while upheaving the contents of my lunch. The hill was so steep and so ornery that lower back soreness remained for more than a week. My pride, however, was wounded for far longer. When Ryan saw me a month later, his first question was whether I had any Pepto-Bismol on me, a humorous derision aimed at a most embarrassing moment of stomach weakness.

The lesson was clear—don't mess with the hill.

98 Sing the Bud Song

Beer, cheese, brats, and football will remain atop the list of Wisconsinites' favorite sources of entertainment until the end of time. But if another item could be added to the list, it would be polka. Wisconsin even lays claim to a Polka Hall of Fame in Appleton—a lifetime membership costs only $100 and will get you a free Wisconsin Polka Hall of Fame CD (Volumes 1 and 2), among other privileges.

With that information in mind, it's easier to understand how an early 1970s Budweiser commercial jingle has become a staple at Wisconsin sporting events, beloved among band members and fans for decades. It began, as Wisconsin band director Michael Leckrone recalled, during a 1973 Badgers hockey game at the Dane County Coliseum. The Beer Barrel Polka already was a staple in the UW band's arsenal, and fans simply could not get enough polka at the game, hollering at the band with demands for more.

At that time, the band was rotating through a series of commercial jingles, including those from Coca-Cola, Dr. Pepper, and Budweiser. The Budweiser tune, "Here Comes the King," was released in 1971 with a style imitative of a typical German band. It also happened to sound a lot like a polka song, Leckrone realized.

"I told the drummers to play this beat instead of what you would normally play and it'll sound like a polka and they'll shut up," Leckrone said. "That's almost the exact words I said to him. We played it, and the students danced. It seemed to satisfy them."

It became a ritual of sorts at hockey games for the jingle to be played. Students initially yelled the original lyrics, "When you say Budweiser, you've said it all"—something Leckrone thought was a bad idea because people might think students had been drinking. As a result, Leckrone instructed band members to yell "Wisconsin" instead of "Budweiser," and a battle was waged between students and band members as to which version would be loudest. Ultimately, the band's hollering won out, and Wisconsin replaced Budweiser. It was a hit at the 1973 NCAA men's hockey championships in Boston, when the band traveled to play during Wisconsin's national title run.

But the song did not truly gain the type of traction it has now until a famous 1978 home football game against Oregon. Wisconsin trailed 13–0 in the fourth quarter, when Leckrone instructed the band to play the tune.

"The crowd was kind of lackadaisical," Leckrone said. "I thought, *We need to do something*. On, Wisconsin! wasn't working."

The Badgers promptly scored their first touchdown of the game. After Oregon took a 19–7 lead with seven minutes remaining, the outcome seemed bleak for the Badgers. Leckrone had the band play the song again, and Wisconsin scored to cut the deficit to 19–14. Wisconsin recovered an onside kick and won the game 22–19 in the final two minutes.

The song became such a hit that the upper deck of Camp Randall Stadium swayed when it was played, prompting then-athletics director Elroy Hirsch to tell Leckrone not to play the song during games. Instead, Leckrone had the public address speaker make an announcement that it would not be played until five minutes after the game had completed, a tongue-in-cheek way of "giving people who were faint of heart an opportunity to get out of the upper deck," he said. But the announcement did little to persuade fans to leave.

Leckrone continued to honor Hirsch's request not to play the song during the game. Instead, it is incorporated into the rest of the band's Fifth Quarter postgame show.

"It gave real momentum to the mystique of The Fifth Quarter," Leckrone said.

99 Claude Gregory

An innate level of nastiness is required to own the battle of the boards 40 minutes a night against the best college basketball players in the country. That was Claude Gregory. Opponents thought he was downright mean because of his maniacal competitive spirit. And during his sophomore season at Wisconsin in 1978, he famously remarked, "There's no reason to smile in basketball."

In his excellent four-year career for the Badgers from 1977 to '81, Gregory had plenty of reason to smile. He left Madison with 11 school records—more than any player in UW history. The list included career records as the school's leader in field goals, field goal attempts, free throws, free throw attempts, minutes played, and games played. His 1,745 career points rank fourth on the all-time list. To this day, he still holds the Badgers' career rebounding record (904). Joe Franklin, who last played in 1968, is the next closest, 46 rebounds behind Gregory.

Gregory came to Wisconsin from Coolidge High School in Washington, D.C., to follow his brother, James "Stretch" Gregory. For that reason, Claude developed the nickname "Little Stretch," though there was nothing little about him. He stood a chiseled 6'8" and 205 pounds and became a starter in the Badgers' final six games of his freshman season, when he averaged 17.3 points. He won the most improved player award and the freshman achievement award.

In his sophomore season, Gregory developed into a star. After St. Louis lost to Wisconsin in the title game of the Wisconsin Invitational Tournament, Billikens coach Ron Ekker called Gregory "as good a forward as we've ever played against. He's so physically strong underneath that it's going to be a real battle for anybody to stop him."

Claude's brother, James, could not play basketball for the Badgers in 1979. He pleaded guilty to a shoplifting charge, was ruled academically ineligible for the second semester the previous season, and wound up returning home to Washington, D.C. The turn of events were tough on Claude, but he didn't let it affect him on the court.

"No matter what happens, I'll think of myself as his little brother," Gregory said then. "I grew up with the title 'Little Stretch' and I don't look at it as being either bad or good. It's just the way things are. You have to accept it."

Gregory honed his skills as a player who scored as close to the basket as possible. He became so valuable that Badgers basketball coach Bill Cofield once pronounced Wisconsin had little chance to win unless Gregory scored at least 17 points per game. This came after a December loss to Davidson in the 1980–81 season in which Gregory scored only four points.

"I know when I have a bad game—especially when I don't score in double figures—it's going to show," Gregory said during his senior season in 1981. "Especially when we lose, I know I'm gonna get chewed on."

Gregory was a third-team All-Big Ten pick as a junior and a second-team all-league selection as a senior. He was voted team MVP in 1981 after finishing third in the Big Ten with 20.4 points and 9.2 rebounds per game. His final game was a memorable one. Against rival Marquette in the UW Field House, Gregory poured in 29 points and 17 rebounds. As was too often the case during that era, however, Wisconsin lost 64-53 and the Badgers finished the season 11–16, ninth in the Big Ten.

Gregory was selected in the second round of the 1981 NBA draft by his hometown Washington Bullets. His professional career spanned nine seasons and took him to the CBA, Spain, and Italy. During his time in the CBA, Gregory appeared in four all-star games and owned career averages of 23.3 points and 10.3 rebounds per game. In 1998, he was named to the CBA's 50th anniversary all-time team.

100 Take In the Beauty of the Terrace

One of the most iconic scenes in Madison can be found on campus behind the 800 block of Langdon Street, where the Memorial Union Terrace offers the opportunity to relax, sip a brew, and stare out at the stunning beauty of Lake Mendota—all while sitting in some equally iconic chairs. In many ways, the entire experience has gone unchanged over the years, providing students, faculty, and members of the community with a unique gathering place.

"The terrace is the campus' great equalizer," said Memorial Union Director Mark Guthier, who has held the position since 2001. "It is a place that everybody feels like it's their space. You're not surprised to see anybody there because everybody is welcome. It's a great place for people at all levels to feel like they're all on the same level."

The Memorial Union first opened in 1928 to serve as "a unifying force in the life of the college," said Porter Butts, the first Union director from 1926 to '68. And the exceptionally distinct views have made many students fall in love with the campus.

As Butts once wrote, "Where, other than at Wisconsin, may one step from university soil into a canoe, see the crews sweeping by, watch a glowing marine sunset while music plays from nearby student houses or the Union Terrace?"

The famous terrace chairs go hand in hand with the history of the terrace. It is unclear when they first appeared, but they can be seen in photographs taken before 1938. The style of chair is now known as the Sunburst and is produced in three colors—John Deere Green, Allis Chalmers orange, and yellow—to pay tribute to Wisconsin's farming tradition. Additionally, they represent the primary colors of spring and fall, when students generally use the terrace most. Guthier said anticipation rises every year as the time to put out the chairs approaches.

"We try to hit as close to April 15 as we can, but it's really weather dependent," Guthier said. "We're geared up to bring them out by the middle of April every year. But if we hit a cold spell and it's only 30 or 40 degrees out or it's raining for three or four days in a row, we might miss that. Our goal is always to have the terrace back open three or four weeks before commencement."

Beer, of course, is a big part of the union experience as well. On March 23, 1933, the board of regents approved the sale of 3.2 percent alcoholic beer on campus, making Wisconsin the first student union to serve beer at a public university. On April 25, 1933, Wisconsin became the second state to ratify the 21st Amendment to repeal Prohibition, only 10 days after Michigan. And the beer choices have only grown over the years.

In 2015, a student competition was held, with the winning team gaining the opportunity to sell its beer at the terrace that spring. The only specifications were to create a red lager with less than 5.5 percent alcohol by volume. The winning team comprised of Andrew Lefeber, Sean Hinds, and Elizabeth Wolff created "Inaugural Red," which went into full-scale production at the Wisconsin Brewing Company.

Activities on the terrace, Guthier said, are entirely student run. In the last decade, the union has begun to sponsor a series of festivals on the terrace, including the Madison World Music Festival and a jazz festival. In addition, Terrace After Dark presents live music from Wednesdays to Saturdays in May through August, while Lakeside Cinema operates a "Movies on Mondays" every Monday, also between May and August.

The new Union South opened on April 15, 2011, and is located across the street from Camp Randall Stadium. On football game days, the school band participates in "Badger Bash," the longest-running public tailgating party at UW–Madison. In 2016, it celebrated its 44th year hosting the entire UW marching band, as well as throngs of Badgers football fans. The band entertains the crowd two and a half hours before every home football game and marches to the stadium.

"Coming down here, participating in that, keeps you young," Guthier said. "And I think it's also a reason why the terrace speaks to alumni because it felt like their place when they were here. When alumni come back here for Badger athletic events, of course they're going to think about, 'Can I get to the terrace?' Because they have in their mind it was for them when they were here, and it was. And it still is."

Tasty Madison Restaurants

The Memorial Union Terrace is only one stop on the must-do list of eating and drinking establishments around town. Any catalog is subject to debate, as there are almost too many good ones to name. But here are some that would surely come up on many lists:

Ian's Pizza: The first shop opened on October 31, 2001, in Madison at 319 N. Frances Street, just a short walk from the Kohl Center. The second location opened on State Street in July 2006 and moved across the street into a bigger space in 2012. Ian's isn't afraid to try some off-the-wall slices, from the favorite mac n' cheese to penne Alfredo to chipotle sweet potato. The number of offerings should provide a taste anybody can appreciate.

State Street Brats: Seymour "Shorty" Kayes opened the Brathaus on 603 State Street in 1953 with business partner Warren "Lammy" Lamm. Now known as State Street Brats, this iconic establishment offers all sorts of reasons to stop by. Tuesday is "Flip Night," which provides customers with a chance to earn 75 percent off their drink orders if they win a coin toss. And who could forget the beer stock exchange, where beer prices go up or down depending on how often they are purchased. While there, try a famous red brat, which Klement's makes specifically for the restaurant.

Essen Haus: A restaurant that serves beer from a glass boot? Yes, please. Located at 514 E. Wilson Street, Essen Haus is an authentic German restaurant that boasts 16 German beers on tap, 200 import bottles, and a live polka band. Order "das boot" if you plan to arrive with a group, and follow the six rules of the game as you pass it around the table.

Mickie's Dairy Bar: This quaint restaurant has operated continuously at 1511 Monroe Street since 1947 and is located across the street from Camp Randall Stadium. The diner is known for its giant breakfast portions, and it typically closes by 2:30 PM. Make sure to get there early on weekends—the line for entrance can snake out the door.

The Old Fashioned: Established in 2005, this restaurant on the capitol square at 23 N. Pinckney Street notes that it highlights meats, cheeses, produce, and local specialties from small Wisconsin producers. From the Friday fish fry to Saturday prime rib to great fried cheese curds, you can't go wrong. Order a classic, hand-muddled Old Fashioned—voted best cocktail by *Madison Magazine* in 2015.

Nitty Gritty: The original Nitty Gritty was established on October 3, 1968, by Madison TV personality Marsh Shapiro at 223 N. Frances Street. The restaurant once featured live music gigs by the likes of Muddy Watters, B.B. King, Buddy Guy, Cheap Trick, and Jefferson Airplane. In 1985, it re-formatted to be Madison's official birthday place. A patron celebrating a birthday receives all-you-can-drink free beer, a memento mug, and a birthday balloon.

Other eateries and bars to try: **Dotty Dumpling's Dowry** for burgers, **Babcock Hall Dairy Store** for ice cream, **Graze** for capitol square ambiance and locally sourced food, **Bassett Street Brunch Club** for brunch, **Wando's** for Tuesday free bacon night and fishbowl drinks, **food carts** downtown, and any number of vendors from the **Saturday Dane County Farmers' Market on the Square**.

Acknowledgments

It's funny how a series of events years earlier can alter the course of your life down the road when least expected. But, without a great deal of fortune and good timing, I never would've had the opportunity to live in Madison and gain the appreciation of Badgers sports history to write this book at all.

I had been working for nearly two years at a newspaper in Muncie, Indiana, as the lead high school sports reporter, when I received an out-of-the-blue email from Scott Reinardy, a former journalism professor of mine at the University of Kansas. Contained in the email was a one-paragraph job description to cover the Green Bay Packers for a relatively new regional website venture called FOX Sports Wisconsin.

Frankly, I wasn't sure what to think. I had never covered the NFL and had never even been to Wisconsin. But this was the Packers, it seemed worth looking into, and in late summer of 2011, I exchanged a series of emails with the editor, Dan Graf.

Over the course of phone interviews, I soon learned the website did not have its Wisconsin Badgers beat writer, either. It had been a dream of mine for several years to cover the football and men's basketball teams of a major Division I program, and few had been as consistently successful as Wisconsin. There is a certain charm associated with following the lives of college athletes over four- and five-year careers, building their trust, telling their stories—sometimes for the first time—and watching them leave as different people.

To make a long story short, Madison and the Badgers proved a perfect match for me. I arrived in early October 2011, just after Russell Wilson and Montee Ball helped Wisconsin obliterate Nebraska 48–17 in a nationally televised game at Camp Randall

Stadium with ESPN's *College GameDay* crew on hand. I was thrust into a whirlwind—one that would culminate with a trip to Pasadena, California, and the Rose Bowl less than three months later in the highest-scoring game in Rose Bowl history.

To say I was exceptionally fortunate would be a vast understatement. Over the next four seasons, I chronicled both the football and basketball programs, as Wisconsin went to two Rose Bowls and made two Final Four trips, including a national championship appearance in 2015—a team that is arguably the best the program has ever seen. That fall, I became a college football reporter with ESPN.com, covering both Wisconsin and the Big Ten while remaining based in Madison.

Sometimes, things have a way of working out. I couldn't have known Madison would be my next destination back in 2011, but it will now always hold a special place in my heart. It is a beautiful city, with good beer, better food, and great sports programs that provided me with wonderful storytelling opportunities, including many that appear in this book. It is also the place where my wife and I moved into our first house.

This was my first book project, and it felt especially daunting when I began with a blank canvas. Over the course of months, however, I found the challenge of compiling and tweaking each chapter to be quite enjoyable. It is my hope you will also find reading *100 Things Wisconsin Fans Should Know & Do Before They Die* to be equally enjoyable and entertaining.

Thank you to the people who took the time to share their stories with me for this book. Thanks to Jim Polzin and Andy Baggot, whose input on chapter selections proved invaluable. Thank you to Wisconsin sports information directors Patrick Herb, Brian Mason, and Brian Lucas for providing me with the access to talk to players and being so fantastic to work with over the years. Thanks to the folks at Triumph Books for allowing me the opportunity to write this book and to Barry Alvarez for his thoughtful foreword.

A big thank you to my family: my dad, Scott, and mom, Rachel, for being so supportive of my dreams, my sister-in-law, Melissa, and my brother, David, for showing me what ambition and perseverance looks like. To Bill, Trudy, Matt, and Dave, thanks for taking me in as one of your own.

Finally, thank you to my wife, Jamie. You have been with me on this journey from the very start, and your love and unwavering support means everything. Thank you for offering so much encouragement and taking a genuine interest in my work with this project and beyond. I love you, always.

Sources

The author gratefully acknowledges the following sources used in researching and writing this book. Some of the quotations found throughout were gathered from personal interviews with players, coaches, university employees, and administrators specifically for this book. Others were selected from previous articles written by the author while covering the teams. Such material provided courtesy of FOXSportsWisconsin.com.

A special thank you to the fine writers through the years at the *Wisconsin State Journal, Milwaukee Sentinel, Milwaukee Journal,* and the *Milwaukee Journal Sentinel* for all their coverage of Badgers athletics.

Books

Anderson, Dave. *University of Wisconsin Football.* Chicago: Arcadia Publishing, 2005.

Butler, Tom. *Field House Echoes.* Middleton: Badger Books Inc., 2003.

Doherty, Justin. *Tales from the Wisconsin Badgers.* Champaign: Sports Publishing, 2005.

Doherty, Justin, and Brian Lucas. *Tales from the Wisconsin Badgers Sideline: A Collection of the Greatest Badgers Stories Ever Told.* Champaign: Sports Publishing, 2012.

Frei, Terry. *Third Down and a War to Go: The All-American 1942 Wisconsin Badgers.* Madison: Wisconsin Historical Society Press, 2005.

Hugunin, Marc, and Stew Thornley. *Minnesota Hoops: Basketball in the North Star State,* pp. 37–38. St. Paul: Minnesota Historical Society Press, 2006.

Knight, Bob, and Bob Hammel. *Knight: My Story*, pp. 88–89. New York: St. Martin's Griffin, 2003.

Kopriva, Don, and Jim Mott. *On Wisconsin! The History of Badger Athletics*. Champaign: Sports Publishing, 2001.

Lepay, Matt. *Why Not Wisconsin? From Barry to Bo: Broadcasting the Badgers from the Best Seat in the House*. Chicago: Triumph Books, 2012.

Manoyan, Dan. *Alan Ameche: The Story of "The Horse."* Madison: University of Wisconsin Press, 2012.

Moe, Doug. *Lords of the Ring: The Triumph and Tragedy of College Boxing's Greatest Team*. Madison: University of Wisconsin Press, 2004.

Ryan, Bo, and Mike Lucas. *Another Hill to Climb*. Stevens Point: KCI Sports Publishing, 2008.

Sweeney, Vince. *Always a Badger: The Pat Richter Story*. Boulder: Trails Books, 2005.

Wallenfeldt, E.C. *The Six-Minute Fraternity: The Rise and Fall of NCAA Tournament Boxing, 1932-60*. Westport: Greenwood Publishing Group, 1994.

Personal Interviews

Alex Erickson, August 10, 2015
Corey Clement, August 10, 2015
John Settle, August 10, 2015
Dan Voltz, August 10, 2015
Jolene Anderson, August 12, 2015
Matt Lepay, August 17, 2015
Michael Leckrone, August 19, 2015
Otto Puls, August 20, 2015
Mark Guthier, August 21, 2015
Pat Richter, August 26, 2015
Kathy Butler, September 1, 2015

Mark Johnson, September 17, 2015
Chris Solinsky, September 28, 2015
Ed Nuttycombe, October 14, 2015
Steve Underwood, December 7, 2015

Websites

AnnArborChronicle.com (John U. Bacon)
Cals.wisc.edu (Caroline Schneider)
Chron.com (Tania Ganguli)
ESPN.com (Dana O'Neal, Wayne Drehs)
FoxSportsWisconsin.com (Jesse Temple)
GrandForksHerald.com (Brad E. Schlossman)
Huskers.com
Library.wisc.edu
MLB.com (Rhett Bollinger)
News.wisc.edu (Karl Knutson)
SI.com (Jerry Barca)
SportingNews.com (Matt Hayes)
SportsOnEarth.com (David B. Zarley)
ThePostGame.com
UWAlumni.com (Chelsea Schlect)
UWBadgers.com (Mike Lucas, Paul Braun)
Union.wisc.edu
WRN.com (Amy Winder)

Newspapers

Chicago Tribune (French Lane, Charles Bartlett, Bo Logan, Skip Myslenski, Robert Markus, Mike Kiley, Reid Hanley, Terry Bannon, Gary Reinmuth, Roy Damer, Wilfrid Smith, Jody Homer, Ed Sherman)

Daily Cardinal (Zach Rastall)

Eugene Register-Guard (Bob Rodman)

Los Angeles Times (Earl Gustkey, Bernie Lincicome, Scott Howard-Cooper, Helene Elliott, Bill Plaschke, Robyn Norwood, Mike Bresnahan)

Madison Capital Times (Mike Ivey)

Michigan Daily (Mark Mihanovic, Frank Longo)

Milwaukee Journal (Oliver Kuechle, Terry Shepard, Bob Wolf, Jim Cohen, Gary Van Sickle, Bill Letwin, Steve Weller, Chuck Salituro, Nolan Zavoral, Tracy Dodds, Dennis Chaptman, Evans Kirkby, Perry A. Farrell, Tom Flaherty, Roger Jaynes)

Milwaukee Journal Sentinel (Dennis McCann, Bob Wolfley, Dan Manoyan, Don Walker, Jeff Potrykus, Mark Stewart, Gary D'Amato, Michael Hunt, Meg Jones, Pete Ehrmann)

Milwaukee Sentinel (Michael Hunt, Bud Lea, Lloyd Larson, Pat Stiegman, Tom Silverstein, Harry Golden, George Sauerberg, Vic Feuerherd, Ken Bunch, Mike Christopulos, Stoney McGlynn, Don Kausler, Jim Lefebvre, Neil H. Shively)

New York Daily News (Eric Barrow)

New York Times (Pete Thamel, Bill Finley, Greg Bishop, Ken Gurnick, Alex Yannis)

Omaha World-Herald (Conde Sargent, Tom Ash)

Pittsburgh Post-Gazette (Phil Axelrod, Bob Smizik)

Rockford Register Star (Matt Trowbridge)

Runner's World (Megan Hetzel)

Toledo Blade (John Gugger)

Washington Post (Leonard Shapiro)

Waterloo Region Record (Mark Bryson)

Wisconsin State Journal (Mike Lucas, Dan Simmons, Jim Polzin, Tom Mulhern, Andy Baggot, Tom Oates, Bob Hooker, Doug Moe, Rob Schultz, George Hesselberg, Dennis Punzel, Glenn Miller, Melanie Conklin)

Magazines

American Golfer Magazine (W.D. Richardson)
Inside Wisconsin Sports (Mike Beacom)
Sporting News (Dave Kindred)
Sports Illustrated (Booton Herndon, Grant Wahl, Jim Kaplan)
Varsity Magazine (Patrick Herb)

News Services

Associated Press (Bob Baum, Harold Claasen, Greg Beacham, Ralph D. Russo, Rusty Miller, Tim Korte, John Nolan, Arnie Stapleton, Rob Gloster, John Zenor, Ron Dzwonkowski)
Knight News Service (Bob Ford)
Knight-Ridder Newspapers (Bruce Bennett)
McClatchy-Tribune News Service (Michael K. Bohn)
United Press International (Fred Lindecke, Tommy Devine, Milton Richman, Rob Zaleski)

Videos

ESPN Depth Chart, Russell Wilson
YouTube.com